THE PENGUIN POETS

D33

FRENCH VERSE

3: THE NINETEENTH CENTURY

D1320564

THE PENGUIN BOOK OF

FRENCH VERSE

3

THE NINETEENTH CENTURY

*

INTRODUCED AND EDITED BY

ANTHONY HARTLEY

*

WITH PLAIN PROSE TRANSLATIONS
OF EACH POEM

PENGUIN BOOKS

Penguin Books Ltd, Harmondsworth, Middlesex
U.S.A.: Penguin Books Inc., 3300 Clipper Mill Road, Baltimore 11, Md
AUSTRALIA: Penguin Books Pty Ltd, 762 Whitehorse Road,
Mitcham, Victoria

—

First published 1957
Reprinted with revisions 1958

Made and printed in Great Britain
by Richard Clay & Company, Ltd,
Bungay, Suffolk

TABLE OF CONTENTS

*

Introduction   xiii

JEAN-PIERRE DE BÉRANGER (1780–1857) wrote many
political songs and poems of social significance. Imprisoned
under the Restoration, his works helped to spread the Napoleon cult that brought about the advent of the Second Empire.

Le Vieux Vagabond   1
Les Souvenirs du peuple   3

MARCELINE DESBORDES-VALMORE (1786–1859)
passed a life chiefly notable for a passionate and unhappy love
affair, of which the poem given here is one of the results. She
also worked as an actress.

La Promenade d'automne   7

ALPHONSE DE LAMARTINE (1790–1869) had a career
spent in diplomacy and politics, first in the service of the re-
stored Bourbon monarchy and later on the Liberal side. His
best volume of poetry, *Méditations* (1820), owed something
of its inspiration to the death of Mme Charles, the Elvira
of *Le Lac*. In his later poetry the religious theme became
dominant, and the epic fragments *Jocelyn* and *La Chute d'un
ange* can hardly be called a success.

Le Lac   10
Tristesse   14
Élégie   16

ALFRED DE VIGNY (1797–1863) was from the start of his
literary career one of the pillars of Romanticism, writing a
novel in the manner of Scott (*Cinq Mars*, 1826) and trans-
lating Shakespeare. The best of his poetry is to be found in
Les Destinées (published 1864), and his *Journal d'un poète*
contains a series of *pensées* on life and literature, which are
among the best of their kind.

Le Cor   18
La Colère de Samson   23
La Bouteille à la mer   30
Le Mont des Oliviers   41
L'Esprit pur   49

TABLE OF CONTENTS

VICTOR HUGO (1802–1885) in the course of a long life produced an immense quantity of work, including novels, plays, and poetry. At first he placed himself at the head of the Romantic movement, but his later verse goes far beyond this, and his achievement is to be seen at its greatest in such works as *La Légende des siècles*, *La Fin de Satan*, and *Dieu*, as well as in the two late collections of verse, *Toute la lyre* and *Les Quatre Vents de l'esprit*. *Les Contemplations* strikes a more elegiac note than these, largely inspired, as it was, by the deaths of his daughter and son-in-law, who were drowned near Villequier in Normandy. In *Les Châtiments* he produced a collection of political verse directed against the government of Napoleon the Third, whose arrival in power had been the cause of his exile in the Channel Islands. He returned to France after the overthrow of the Second Empire in 1870.

Puisque j'ai mis ma lèvre	53
Nuits de Juin	54
L'Expiation	55
Demain dès l'aube	59
A Villequier	60
Booz endormi	69
La Trompette du Jugement	74
A Théophile Gautier	84
Ave, Dea; moriturus te salutat	88

ALOYSIUS BERTRAND (1807–1841) did only one thing of note, which was to write the strange prose poems collected under the title of *Gaspard de la nuit*. These were published posthumously in 1842 owing to the efforts of Sainte-Beuve.

Le Maçon	89
Le Nain	91
Le Deuxième Homme	93

GÉRARD DE NERVAL (1808–1855) (his real name was Labrunie) wrote a number of excellent short tales, of which *Sylvie* is perhaps the best known. He also translated Goethe's *Faust*, and produced a good deal of journalism. The main events in his life were journeys to Italy, Germany, Austria, the Low Countries, and the Levant. Unfortunately, he suffered from outbreaks of madness, which eventually culminated in his suicide.

Une Allée du Luxembourg ... 95
El Desdichado ... 96
Myrtho ... 97
Horus ... 98
Antéros ... 99
Delfica ... 100
Artémis ... 101
Le Christ aux oliviers ... 102
Vers dorés ... 107
Chanson Gothique ... 108

ALFRED DE MUSSET (1810–1857) had a life only distinguished by a catastrophic affair with George Sand. In addition
to his verse, he wrote many plays, the most famous of which is
probably *Lorenzaccio*. *Les Confessions d'un enfant du siècle*
is a romanticized autobiography in the most typical vein of
the time and, like most of his best work, was written in the
1830s.

A Julie ... 109
Chanson: à Saint-Blaise, à la Zuecca ... 111
Lettre à M. de Lamartine ... 112
Chanson de Barberine ... 126
Une Soirée perdue ... 127
Sur une morte ... 131

THÉOPHILE GAUTIER (1811–1872) abandoned quickly
enough the famous red waistcoat he had flaunted on the opening night of *Hernani* and led a peaceful life with his cats and
sisters. The best of his volumes of verse is *Émaux et Camées*
(1852). In the preface to *Mlle de Maupin*, a novel he published in 1836, he put forward the formula of Art for Art's sake.
He was also a perceptive critic of literature and art.

A une robe rose ... 132
La Mansarde ... 134
L'Art ... 137

LECONTE DE LISLE (1818–1894) was born in the West Indies
and came to France to study law, a pursuit he soon abandoned for journalism and poetry, becoming the acknowledged
leader of the Parnassian school of poets. His best volumes are
Poèmes antiques and *Poèmes barbares* (1852 and 1862).

Midi   139

Les Taureaux   141

Le Rêve du Jaguar   142

Le Cœur de Hialmar   144

CHARLES BAUDELAIRE (1821–1867) made a voyage to
Mauritius in 1841, which may have supplied some of the
imagery of his poetry, but this was the first and last great
event in a life harassed by debt, editors, illness, and his step-
father. In 1857 he published *Les Fleurs du mal*, which was
the subject of a prosecution by the Imperial Government,
taken with one of its periodical fits of morality, and this may
be considered as the major work of his life, though the prose
poems of *Le Spleen de Paris* (published in 1869 after his
death) are noteworthy and his criticism, literary and artistic,
is among the most revealing of the period (see *L'Art romantique* and *Curiosités Ésthétiques*).

A une Dame créole   146

La Crépuscule du soir   147

L'Albatros   149

Harmonie du soir   150

Sed non satiata   151

Je t'adore à l'égal de la voûte nocturne   152

La Chevelure   153

Correspondances   155

Un Voyage à Cythère   156

Moesta et errabunda   159

Spleen   161

Les Bijoux   162

Les Sept Vieillards   164

Le Voyage   167

La Chambre double   175

Enivrez-vous   180

JOSÉ-MARIA DE HÉRÉDIA (1842–1905) was born in Cuba
and educated in France. He studied at the *École des Chartes*, and
the archaeological training he received there affected his
poetry profoundly, as may be seen from the sonnet sequence
Les Trophées (1893), which is his main work. He was also
much under the influence of Leconte de Lisle and can be said
to be the best of the Parnassians.

L'Oubli	181
Villula	182
La Trebbia	183
Antoine et Cléopâtre	184
Floridum Mare	185
La Mort de l'aigle	186

STÉPHANE MALLARMÉ (1842–1898) worked throughout his life as a teacher of English in a lycée, and his struggle to write poetry in conditions of discomfort and poverty provides an illustrious example of devotion and sacrifice for art. Teaching first at Tournon, then at Avignon, he was eventually appointed to a post in Paris, where his Tuesday *salon* in the Rue de Rome became a rendezvous for young writers during the last fifteen years of his life. His main works were *L'Après-midi d'un faune* (1876), *Les Poésies* (1887), and *Divagations* (1897).

Le Pitre châtié	187
Brise Marine	188
Don du poème	189
L'Après-midi d'un faune	190
Quand l'ombre menaça de la fatale loi	196
Le Vierge, le vivace et le bel aujourd'hui	197
Prose pour des Esseintes	198
Feuillet d'album	201
Le Tombeau de Charles Baudelaire	202
Toute l'âme résumée	203
Tombeau	204
Plainte d'Automne	205
La Pipe	207

CHARLES CROS (1842–1888) was an inventor as well as a poet. His poetry is to be found in two collections, *Le Coffret de santal* (1873) and *Le Collier de griffes* (1908). The example given here is typical.

Scherzo	209

PAUL VERLAINE (1844–1896) varied Bohemian debauchery with religious nostalgia throughout a life marked by a tragic decline. His famous affair with Rimbaud culminated in his wounding him with a revolver shot in Brussels and, conse-

quently, being sent to prison. After repenting and back-
sliding for some twenty years more, he died in a public in-
firmary. His best volumes of verse are *Fêtes galantes* (1869)
and *Romances sans paroles* (1874).

Nuit du Walpurgis classique   211
Nevermore   214
Clair de lune   215
Colloque sentimental   215
Il pleure dans mon cœur   217
Dans l'interminable   218
Bruxelles   219
A Poor Young Shepherd   221
Sagesse d'un Louis Racine, je t'envie!   222
Non. Il fut gallican, ce siècle, et janséniste!   223
Art poétique   224
Parsifal   226

TRISTAN CORBIÈRE (1845–1875) found many of the in-
gredients of his poetry in his native Brittany, its sea-coast and
sailors. He died young, but not before he published his
Amours jaunes (1873), a book of verse, which was to set the
tone for a type of irony increasingly to be found in modern
French and English poetry.

Matelots   227
Vénerie   234
Cantique du pardon de Sainte-Anne   235
Paria   239

ISIDORE DUCASSE, COMTE DE LAUTRÉAMONT
(1846–1870), had a career that is entirely obscure. Almost all
that is known of him is that he wrote the compilation of
prose poems called *Les Chants de Maldoror*, which was published after his death. He also wrote some more prose poems
called *Poésies, préface à un livre futur*. His title was of his own
adoption.

Debout sur le rocher   243

ARTHUR RIMBAUD (1854–1891) gave up writing at the age
of nineteen or twenty, after producing *Les Illuminations*,
and *Une Saison en Enfer* (1872–1873). His short, fiercely
productive literary life was marked by his liaison with Verlaine, and the rest of his life was spent in Africa and the East,
where he carried on a series of trading operations.

Le Cœur volé 247
Les Premières Communions 249
Les Chercheuses de poux 257
Qu'est-ce pour nous, mon cœur, que les nappes de sang 259
Chanson de la plus haute tour 260
Aube 262
Being Beauteous 263
Mauvais Sang 264
Matin 276
Adieu 277

ÉMILE VERHAEREN (1855–1916) brought to his poetry the vision and the realism of his native Flanders. His Christian Socialism led him to paint sombre pictures of the growth of the modern city and the breakdown of traditional ways. His best volumes are *Les Villes tentaculaires* (1895) and *Les Forces tumultueuses* (1902).

Les Paysans 280
Le Moulin 281
La Bêche 283
Vers le futur 285

JULES LAFORGUE (1860–1887) died young, but not before having published a number of volumes of poetry. Originator of the apparently inconsequent poem written in *vers libres*, and guided by a free association of ideas and images, he was to enjoy considerable popularity abroad, where his irony was imitated by English and American poets. His main volumes of verse were *Complaintes* (1885), *Imitation de Nôtre-Dame la Lune* (1886), and the posthumous *Derniers vers* (1890).

Locution de Pierrot 288
Esthétique 289
La Mélancolie de Pierrot 290
L'Hiver qui vient 291
Dimanches 296

RAYMOND DE LA TAILHÈDE (1867–1938) was one of the members of the *École Romane*, a group of poets gathered around the Greek, Jean Moréas. He collected a number of his

poems in a volume called *De la Métamorphose des fontaines* (1895).

Ombres   299

EMMANUEL SIGNORET (1872–1900) published a number of volumes of poetry, of which the best are perhaps *La Souffrance des eaux* (1899) and *Le Premier Livre des élégies* (1900). His talent was for a sparkling, Mediterranean kind of poetry, though many critics find his style too emphatic.

Les Alcyons   301
Les Oliviers   303
La Souffrance des eaux: Élégie 2   304
Le Vaisseau   305

Index of First Lines   309

INTRODUCTION

AN English reader encountering French poetry for the first time is bound to feel an overwhelming impression of strangeness. Poetry is notoriously the most difficult part of any literature for a foreigner to appreciate, and when the two languages concerned are as different in their traditions as French and English, the difficulty becomes acute. Of course these traditions were not always far apart: a reader of Chaucer can appreciate Guillaume de Machaut or Eustace Deschamps (if he has a sufficient knowledge of medieval French) without feeling that any fresh approach is required from him. Ronsard is near enough to Sidney for an English-speaking reader to be at home with him, and the same is true of most of the French sixteenth-century poets. It was the process of purification and abstraction of language that went on in France in the seventeenth century that changed matters. This winnowing had no parallel in English, and one of its effects was to make French poetry more rigid and classical in its structure than that of any other European language. The divorce between it and common speech was completed by the time of Racine, and there took shape at this moment those general characteristics which are likely to cause trouble to the foreign reader.

I

The most mechanical of these is metre. As opposed to the English verse line, which is governed by stress, French verse has a syllabic basis. The Alexandrine, for instance, which is one of the most commonly used lines, has twelve syllables with a caesura (the main pause) after the sixth. But the variation in importance of the elements of the line is given by the pitch of the vowels, and, even in classical verse, there are other pauses to provide variety. In a line like this famous one from *Phèdre*:

> *Le jour n'est pas plus pur que le fond de mon cœur.*

> The day is not more pure than the depth of my heart.

jour, *plus*, and *pur* seem to benefit from what might be called an accent of pitch, and consequently have rather more prominence

than the other words. The main pause comes after *pur* with a minor one after *jour*. But, in spite of variations, classical French verse had a comparatively rigid rhythmical structure, and throughout the nineteenth century attempts were to be made to break up the line. Victor Hugo moved the caesura in the Alexandrine and introduced *enjambement* (the carrying-on of a sentence from one line to another; the classical alexandrine has a stop at the end of each), but little was done to revolutionize the rhythms of poetry until the end of the century and the introduction of *vers libres* (poems with lines of all lengths, much repetition and a free use of rhyme and assonance) and the prose poem. Rhyme, indeed, was disputed in the second half of the century:

> Ô qui dira les torts de la Rime?
> Quel enfant sourd ou quel nègre fou
> Nous a forgé ce bijou d'un sou
> Qui sonne creux et faux sous la lime?

O who will tell of the wrongs done by Rhyme? What deaf child or mad Negro made us this halfpenny jewel that sounds hollow and false under the file?

Significantly enough, Verlaine's sweeping judgement is, itself, not merely rhymed, but rhymed with the classical alternation of masculine and feminine endings (endings without and with *e mute*). Rhyme has persisted in French poetry, and its latest apologist is M. Louis Aragon, Surrealist and Communist. By and large, attempts to revolutionize the metrical structure of French poetry have failed – except, of course, in recent literary movements (like *Dada* or the *Lettristes*), where the single word has become the only poetic unit. For the English reader these rhythms of French poetry are less emphatic than those he is used to, and he may fail to catch the delicate variations within the line. It is necessary to develop an ear for French verse, and this can only be done by reading a good deal of it or, better still, by listening to French people reading it.

Another inheritance from classical French poetry is rhetoric. The greatest French poet, Racine, was not only a dramatist, but a dramatist writing a type of play which did not give much scope for anything other than the set speech. There are no songs, for

instance, as in Shakespeare (the choruses from *Esther* are hardly comparable). Right up to and beyond Baudelaire poets tended to write as if they were addressing someone. Even a light piece like Musset's *Une Soirée perdue* is a sustained argument-cum-narration. Only in a song, like the same poet's *Chanson de Barberine*, was there what might be called gratuitous poetry, and this neglect of what the English reader usually regards as the purer poetic elements presents an obstacle which has often led foreign critics to deny French poetry the place in European culture that it deserves. Moreover, we have become unaccustomed to the theatrical side of rhetoric.

> *Ô drapeaux de Wagram! Ô pays de Voltaire!*
>
> O banners of Wagram! O country of Voltaire!

sounds uncomfortably like *O Sophonisba, Sophonisba O!* We can far more easily put up with ten low words creeping in one dull line than we can with this exclamatory inflation. However, the dangers of the declamatory style were quickly realized. When Baudelaire praised Hugo for expressing 'avec l'*obscurité indispensable*, ce qui est obscur et confusément révélé',* he was expressing his own revolt against rhetorical inflation and a falsely logical order of development. One of the aims of the innovations attempted by Baudelaire and the poets who followed him was to strip French poetry of its rhetorical coverings. They tried to write a type of poetry that could be received more directly by the reader. 'Prends l'éloquence et tords-lui son cou',† wrote Verlaine, and Mallarmé's attempt to destroy logic went as far as the destruction of syntax itself.

The poets of the latter half of the nineteenth century therefore largely escape the dangers of declamation and its accompanying bathos. However, they do present another difficulty for the foreigner – a difficulty that has to do with the way in which what is called poetic emotion is communicated through the medium of words. One of the results of the formation of classi-

* With the indispensable obscurity, what is obscure and confusedly revealed.

† Take eloquence and wring its neck!

cal French in the seventeenth century was an increased precision in use and abstraction in meaning of words. And, of course, precision in the application of words does necessarily carry with it a considerable degree of generalization. A *house* can only always be exactly a house, if it refers more to the idea of a house than to the individual building on the horizon. But, in referring to the idea, it will have lost some of its power of affective communication. It will be a *house*, but it will not strike anyone as particularly the house in which they live. This process is part of the normal development of civilized languages, but it has been carried further in France than elsewhere, since the opposition to new words and slang managed for a long time to prevent the normal renewal of affective language from those sources. A poet like Baudelaire, who wanted to write more directly affective poetry, was therefore faced with a problem. He could not restore its primitive solidity to his vocabulary, though he could, and did, add new words to it. Continuing to use a language far more intellectualized than that of an English poet, he achieves his effects by a sort of lucid intensity, which had always been the mark of French poetry, but which the Romantics had abandoned in favour of the declamatory side of the classical inheritance. Lines like those in *Les Bijoux*:

> *Quand il jette en dansant son bruit vif et moqueur,*
> *Ce monde rayonnant de métal et de pierre*
> *Me ravit en extase, et j'aime à la fureur*
> *Les choses où le son se mêle à la lumière.*

When dancing it throws off its bright, mocking noise, this shining world of metal and stone transports me into ecstasy, and I love to distraction things where sound is mingled with light.

are sensuous indeed, but their sensuality is of a kind that does not exist in English. One has the impression of looking through sheet after sheet of glass, until the idea presented dies away in the shimmering of multiple refracted images. The eye is not on the object, but on the idea of the object. The description is sensuous, but not tactile, and the English reader, accustomed as he is to a more concrete imagery, may find this difference of level of abstraction one of the greatest obstacles to his appreciation of French poetry.

Difference of consciousness, too. French poets almost invariably give the impression of being well aware of what they are doing. Their creations are constructed with a theory behind them (that the final result may be very different from what was originally intended does not matter; the important thing is the conscious effort to create according to certain formulas). Hence the predominance of the school and the manifesto, hence the highly Byzantine discussions on poetry which went on throughout the second half of the nineteenth century. Of course, many of the consequences of this consciousness of a literary position are repugnant, and among them are the showing off, brawling, and shady behaviour, which were the by-products of the Parisian literary underworld and have been widely adopted since as the correct bardic insignia. Yet, much of the more eccentric practice and theory of French poets of this period must be accepted as proceeding from ideas, which, however wrong in themselves, nonetheless provided myths on which poetry could conveniently and legitimately be based.

*

I have dealt rather fully with the difficulties that an English reader might find on a first encounter with French nineteenth-century poetry, because such a reader will not find a great deal of help in either English or French critics of these works. There is a tendency among foreign critics to lose themselves in an *O altitudo* (supposing they are not hostile to French poetry in the first place), and this is all the more comprehensible in that French academic criticism is largely still at the stage of the demonstration of *beauties*. At its worst, this *Ô que c'est beau* * can involve an assent to entirely mediocre poems. At its best it does not go much beyond saying that lines are good because they are good. French poetry (and literature in general) could do with the same sort of academic revaluation to which F. R. Leavis has subjected English literature, but it has not received it. There are, indeed, brilliant French critics, but they are not always a help to anyone tackling a new literature. What is wanted is a central guide, and

* O how beautiful it is!

the nearest thing to this is Marcel Raymond's *De Baudelaire au Surréalisme* – a work that gives a convincing account of the development of French poetry from Baudelaire onwards and which, for want of competition, is the starting-point for all discussion of the subject. Suggestive ideas about nineteenth-century literature in general will be found in Sartre's essay *Qu'est-ce que la littérature?* (*Situations 2*) and in *Le Degré Zéro de l'écriture* by Roland Barthes, a young critic who is not as well known as he should be in this country. But, until a proper reappraisal is completed, there will be no generally accepted academic tradition of the development of French poetry, which is both just and critically respectable.

I do not propose to give here a detailed history of French poetry during the nineteenth century, but a few facts and dates would seem to be inevitable. Three dates in particular are important: 1830, 1857, and 1866. The first marks the apogee of the Romantic movement in France. The second is the date of the first (unbowdlerized) version of Baudelaire's *Fleurs du mal*. The last is the date of publication of the anthology *Le Parnasse contemporain*, in which Mallarmé and Verlaine appeared side by side and which marks conveniently the appearance of a generation of poets who had been influenced by Baudelaire. The history of French nineteenth-century poetry, then, is that of two revolutions – one effected by the Romantics and the other by Baudelaire and his successors. Before we look at these transformation scenes, however, we should glance at the situation in 1815, just after Waterloo.

II

To say that the greatest poet of the French eighteenth century was thought at the time to be Voltaire is to reveal at once its entire poverty from the point of view of the production of poetry. With the achievements of the previous century culminating in Racine it is perhaps not surprising that sterility should have overtaken this branch of literature. Racine is certainly an example of the tendency (common in France) to produce works incapable of further development and, in fact, it was not until the end of

the century that André Chénier (significantly enough a poet of Greek origin) managed to write beautiful and original verse, the effect of which, however, was not fully felt until the publication of his works in 1819. Apart from him – nobody. For the beginnings of the Romantic movement we have to look to prose-writers or foreign models. A French poet writing in 1815 or the years following would have heard something of German literature from Mme. de Stael (her book *De l'Allemagne* was published in a French edition in 1814); he would have encountered the troubadours and *trouvères* of his own country in Simone de Sismondi's *De la Littérature du midi de l'Europe* (1813); he would certainly know about Scott, Shakespeare, and Byron – not to mention Ossian and the horror comics of Mrs Radcliffe, 'Monk' Lewis, and Maturin. The French emigration to England during the Terror, the past cultural contacts between the two countries, the *odi et amo* relationship in which they lived, combined to make the English influence by far the most powerful force affecting French literature at this time. While Stendhal was subscribing to the *Edinburgh Review* (an event which he regarded as marking an epoch in his intellectual life), Delacroix was applying to his painting principles he had learned from Constable, and the English actors, whose performances of Shakespeare in Paris in 1822 provided one of the more picturesque episodes of the Romantic struggle to arrive – they had to be given police protection, since the Liberals regarded their appearance on the French stage as an insult to the memory of Napoleon and the Revolution – could hardly complain of a lack of publicity.

But there were French Romantics already in the field. Rousseau had set the example of an individual aesthetic. The subjectivity of his works, the importance accorded in them to passion and, above all, his attitude towards nature and the tranced feeling of unity into which he entered on contemplating it – all these things were to influence the Romantics profoundly. Chateaubriand in his *Atala* and *René* (1801 and 1802) helped to diffuse Rousseau's attitudes, while adding one or two of his own (the romantic concept of religion and history, for example). From Rousseau through Chateaubriand to Lamartine is not far. The

Méditations were published in 1820, and a poem like *Le Lac* is simply rhymed Rousseau – beautifully rhymed Rousseau, I hasten to add. It is, indeed, difficult to over-estimate the part played by Rousseau and Chateaubriand in the history of nineteenth-century poetry. In them our poet would have found all the main themes of French Romanticism (we have to wait till Baudelaire or the later Hugo for any really novel subject-matter to appear) expressed in a marvellously cadenced prose by the two most influential purveyors of ideas of their respective generations. Their works were the first demonstration of the power of the new forces which were to possess French poetry.

III

In the years between 1820 and 1830 the Romantic movement took shape. However, both Lamartine and Marceline Desbordes-Valmore, who are the first to appear on the scene, follow on from Chateaubriand. Both of them had sensitive, if not particularly strong talents, which were quite at home with the poetry of sensibility, the first type of Romantic poetry. For themes a rather arbitrary association of love, nature, and sometimes religion; for style a soft, mellifluous manner, conserving in large part the eighteenth-century vocabulary of the passions – by 1820 there was nothing very revolutionary about all this. The essential passivity of a poet like Lamartine, his willingness to abandon himself to the impact of a beautiful landscape or a beautiful woman, defines and limits his talent, though the manner was to be continued and transformed by Verlaine. His poems can hardly be called constructed, and his conception of poetry is almost that of a mere Aeolian harp. He was, of course, a considerable craftsman, but few are likely to want to read his works as a whole. He lacks the essential surprise of poetry. For a more decisive individuality we have to turn to other Romantics, whose intention of transforming their poetry was both stronger and more conscious.

In the preface to *Cromwell* (1827), which may be considered as the principal manifesto of French Romanticism, Hugo uttered the battle-cry, which is invariably produced whenever any ques-

tion of literary reform arises: 'La nature et la vérité'.* 'Mettons le marteau dans les théories, les poétiques et les systèmes', he wrote. 'Jetons bas ce vieu plâtrage qui masque la façade de l'art!' † The opposition to the old aesthetic of classicism (a classicism degraded into Laharpe's *Cours*) is total, but the constructive part of the preface is limited to the advocacy of a number of technical innovations both in poetry and drama. What is new is the urgency of the feeling, which informs Hugo's writing, that poetry and drama (for the preface to *Cromwell* is naturally more concerned with the latter) are important. The claims made for the poet's status throughout the nineteenth century begin here.

For one of the keys to an understanding of French nineteenth-century poetry is the poet's conception of the part to be played by his own work in relation to society and the universe. The idea of the poet's mission, always present in the minds of the Romantics, led them to think of him, in Shelley's words, as 'the unacknowledged legislator of mankind'. Poets are seers or law-givers, prophets, or mages, and though Baudelaire, Mallarmé, and Rimbaud were to produce more complex versions of this myth, in substance it remained the same. Moreover, this idea of a mission was to be directed as to its form by the increasing alienation of the poets from a society in the process of being transformed by the Industrial Revolution. What could a Vigny find to say to the hard-faced industrialists, *haute bourgeoisie*, and bankers of the French monarchy of the 1830s? Reacting to an unsympathetic milieu, the poets were to become ever more concerned to affirm their own necessarily aristocratic view of life, and after the disillusionment of the failed revolution of 1848 this alienation was to develop into an active revolt against society. The rise of the concept of the *poète maudit* coincides with the victory of a *bourgeoisie* that conquered society, not only (as in England) by its power, but also by its manners.

The effect of this growing separation between society and the poet is clearly to be seen in their idea of their own work.

---

* Nature and truth.

† Let us take the hammer to theories, poetics, and systems. Let us throw down this old plaster-work masking art's façade.

Lamartine had been content to regard poetry simply as a vehicle for the expression of his own personal feelings. The dissatisfaction that the younger Romantics felt with the trends of their time led them to write poetry intended to influence their contemporaries directly either from a political (and revolutionary) standpoint or else morally. Indeed, the 1820s saw far more discussion of politics than of literature, and Hugo's later political volumes (*Les Châtiments* and *L'Année terrible*, for example) were in the true Romantic tradition. The Romantics' concern with moral lessons is best expressed by Vigny:

> *Seul et dernier anneau de deux chaines brisées,*
> *Je reste. Et je soutiens encor dans les hauteurs,*
> *Parmi les maîtres purs de nos savants musées,*
> *L'IDÉAL du poète et des graves penseurs.*

Sole and last ring of two broken chains, I remain. And still I bear up on the heights, amid the pure masters of our learned museums, the poet's and the solemn thinkers' IDEAL.

Yet this concept of the poet's mission as being the propagation of the moral and political good was unsatisfactory. First, because morals and politics have a bad effect on poetry itself; Gautier's protest in this sense was made soon after 1830. Secondly, because, especially after 1848, it was no longer possible for the poet to think of society as being affected by his works. That being so, his only alternative was to exalt his art from some other point of view, proclaiming the primacy of the creation of the beautiful over all other forms of human activity (as did the devotees of Art for Art's sake), or else regarding his poetry as having some more mystic significance. From *law-giver* the poet would become *mage* (i.e. one aspiring to power through magical operations). If he could not change the world around him, he would create new worlds from language, worlds that should be no less real than the tangible one and that should, indeed, correspond to the most secret rhythms of the universe. And the production of this occult poetry would naturally widen the gap between the poet/adept and his reader/acolyte. In this way the poets of the latter half of the nineteenth century compensated themselves for the in-

creasing lack of comprehension with which they were regarded by the society around them.

IV

Of all the Romantics, Hugo is without doubt the greatest, but his greatness has been hidden by the insufficient attention paid to the last part of his work. He is not the 'garde-national épique' * which he appears to be in the school books, but a poet more akin to Blake, filling his works with monstrous cosmologies, where the terror of the abyss draws the poet's mind cascading from void to void in unending vertigo. Valéry wrote of his last poems: 'Dans la *Corde d'airain*, dans *Dieu*, dans la *Fin de Satan*, dans la pièce sur la mort de Gautier. ... le vieillard très illustre atteint le plus haut point de la puissance poétique et de la noble science du versificateur'.† Hugo's cosmic epic style can be seen in *La Trompette du Jugement*. It is a style which achieves the feat of giving imprecision to the French language. Reading it is like looking into a fog, and this is not the obscurity of a Mallarmé or of Valéry himself, where the individual phrase is clearly outlined, but an obscurity which makes it hard to focus any but the most hazy visual image:

> *Oh! quelle nuit! là, rien n'a de contour ni d'âge;*
> *Et le nuage est spectre, et le spectre est nuage.*

> Oh! What night! Nothing there has contour or age; and the cloud is a phantom and the phantom is a cloud.

These poems are rhetorical – they are highly dramatic even – but their rhetoric is broken and gasping. The rhythms pant and labour, changing with the changing of the emotions, and in this great flood of language Hugo brings to life a weird universe of absence, in which God only appears as a gulf, an imperative question. Wherever Hugo took his cosmology from (the Kabbala or Swedenborg? It does not much matter), he made it peculiarly his own, and embodied it in a series of poems which,

* The epic national guard.

† In the *Brazen Cord*, in *God*, in the *End of Satan*, in the piece on the death of Gautier ... the celebrated old man reaches the highest point of poetic power and of the verse-maker's noble art.

for epic sweep and primitive strength, have hardly their equal. Ironically they remain largely unknown, while *Ruy Blas* and *Hernani* are still performed on the stage. Of course, to praise Hugo's later poems is not to say that the well-known pieces like *L'Expiation* and *A Villequier* are not fine poetry. They, too, should be read, but with an eye to the kind of poetry that makes Hugo unique.

The works of the other Romantics present no necessity for any such revaluation. Vigny, indeed, may be thought to have been given too high a place in the past. His long philosophical poems, inculcating, as they do, a stoicism before a hostile universe, sometimes fall into a rather embarrassing bathos, which makes denigration of his talent a little too easy. But poems such as *Le Cor* or *L'Esprit pur* deserve their fame, and his style can only be fairly represented by periods rather than by the individual line. It may be a platitude to say that in his faults and virtues he resembles Wordsworth, but the English reader will find the comparison helpful. They both lack a sense of humour.

Musset, on the other hand, brought to Romanticism some of the traditional wit and *esprit gaulois* of French poetry. A poem like *A Julie* comes at the end of a long line of seventeenth- and eighteenth-century erotica. Musset's poetry is always charming and accomplished and, if there are not many people who can put up with *Les Nuits* nowadays, the poems in which he puts off the *persona* of the melancholy Romantic hero and assumes that of the Byronic boulevardier will always be read with pleasure. The colloquialism and psychological accuracy of *Une Soirée perdue* make it very modern in feeling – the reverse side of the *Lettre à M. de Lamartine*, which, however, is saved by its *naïveté*. Musset stands as the representative in his own generation of a tradition that is permanent in French poetry, and which he did not need Byron to teach him: a tradition of sentiment conveyed in a light, but classically perfected form.

Among other poets in operation between 1830 and 1850, Aloysius Bertrand may fairly be attached to the Romantics. His strange, hauntingly beautiful prose poems seem to me infinitely superior to the much-vaunted farrago produced by Isidore

Ducasse, Comte de Lautréamont (the reader can see for himself whether I am right about this). Jean-Pierre Béranger is really an older Romantic; his political songs had had an important influence on public opinion under the Restoration, and he also wrote some poems of merit, of which *Le Vieux Vagabond* is the most moving. 'Le pauvre a-t-il une patrie?' anticipates much that has happened since, and it is hard not to be touched by this sincere early statement of a truth that has since been disgraced. One other poet must be mentioned, who, though he was one of Gautier's *Jeune France* group, does not come comfortably under any heading. Gérard de Nerval, one of the greatest poets of the nineteenth century, owes his fame to a handful of works in verse and prose. In the twelve sonnets of *Les Chimères* there is as much of the miraculous as most poets achieve in a lifetime. 'Jusqu'ici rien n'a pu guérir mon cœur qui souffre toujours du mal du pays'.* 'La Muse est entrée dans mon cœur comme une déesse aux paroles dorées; elle s'en est echappée comme une pythie en jetant des cris de douleur. Seulement, ses derniers accents se sont adoucis à mesure qu'elle s'éloignait. Elle s'est détournée un instant, et j'ai revu comme en un mirage les traits adorés d'autrefois ...'.† The poetry of Nerval is commonly referred to as 'hermetic', but nothing more than these words of his is necessary to seize its inspiration. One can decode the end of a sonnet like:

> *La déesse avait fui sur sa conque dorée,*
> *La mer nous renvoyait son image adorée,*
> *Et les cieux rayonnaient sous l'écharpe d'Iris.*

The goddess had fled on her golden shell, the sea sent us back her sweet image, and the skies shone beneath Iris's scarf.

Much scholarship has in fact been expended on *Quellenforschung*, but I do not think that it adds anything more to the poem.

---

* Up to now nothing has been able to cure my heart, which still suffers from homesickness.

† The Muse entered into my heart like a goddess with golden words; she left it like a pythoness giving forth shrieks of pain. Only, her last words became softer as she went away, and I saw again as in a mirage the adored features of former days. ...

Homesickness for a land where the sea is blue and the women beautiful, a glimpse of a most fugitive beauty now lost for ever – these are the themes of this poetry, which may properly be called pure or gratuitous, since the means which it employs to effect its ends owe almost nothing to the non-poetic. The intensity is that of a style, where every word carries a dense weight of passion, and there is a total absence of rhetoric.

The urge towards a purer poetry, unconscious in Nerval, had already led Gautier to revolt against the moralizing of the Romantics. 'L'art pour nous n'est pas le moyen, mais le but; – tout artiste qui se propose autre chose que le beau n'est pas un artiste à nos yeux',* he was to write in a famous article. His own poetry is cultivated, but usually falls into an epigrammatic preciosity, which comes between it and the big attempt. It would seem that Art for Art's sake is not necessarily a battle-cry that brings inspiration with it, though Gautier found in it the means for giving a *raison d'être* to the poet's work. Leconte de Lisle, the founder of what only became the Parnassian school of poets some years after he had written his best poems, carried Gautier's ideas still further. For him art was not only superior to all other forms of human activity, but summed them up and made them incarnate. He is not a terribly good poet, but those of his poems which come off owe their success to the contrast between the stoical indifference with which he regarded nature and life (the starting-point of the famous Parnassian impassibility) and the exotic imagery he drew from mythology and landscape. Leconte de Lisle's only true successor was Hérédia, who was far more adroit at putting his ideals into practice, but his attempt to base poetry on a theory, which, for want of a better word, can be called philosophical, is highly significant. It was a step on the road towards the erection of poetry into a religious or magical operation.

v

With the publication of *Les Fleurs du mal* in 1857 this process is almost complete; at least all the elements of completion are pre-

---

* Art for us is not the means, but the end; – any artist who aims at something other than the beautiful is not an artist in our eyes.

sent. The dissociation of the artist from society had progressed so far by 1848, the year of revolutions, and the disillusionment after the failure of the hopes that year had aroused had been so bitter that, from a strong dislike of the conquering *bourgeoisie*, the French intelligentsia passed to a stage of revolt against it: a revolt which might take the form of Socialism, but which, for the majority of writers and artists, expressed itself in a withdrawal from society into the certainty of the transcendance of art. Not that Baudelaire was an adherent of Art for Art's sake. 'Dans ce livre atroce,' he wrote of *Les Fleurs du mal*, 'j'ai mis tout mon cœur, toute ma tendresse, toute ma religion (travestie), toute ma haine. Il est vrai que j'écrirai le contraire, que je jurerai mes grands dieux que c'est un livre d'art pur. ...'* Certainly his achievement had a technical side to it; Valéry's judgement on his work is well known: 'L'œuvre romantique, *en général*, supporte assez mal une lecture ralentie et hérissée des résistances d'un lecteur difficile et raffiné. ... Baudelaire était ce lecteur',† and nobody who has studied these poems would think to deny the part of the conscious artist in them (metrical innovations, fresh imagery, avoidance of obvious rhetoric, etc.). But the inspiration behind them is cosmological; Baudelaire had a system, which, it is true, can hardly be taken seriously as a philosophy, but whose existence is of the greatest importance as a directing myth of his poetry. At its base is the idea of *correspondances* set out in the poem of that name:

> *La Nature est un temple où de vivants piliers*
> *Laissent parfois sortir de confuses paroles;*
> *L'homme y passe à travers des forêts de symboles*
> *Qui l'observent avec des regards familiers.*

Nature is a temple where living pillars sometimes allow confused words to escape; man passes there through forests of symbols that watch him with familiar glances.

---

* In this dreadful book I have put all my heart, all my tenderness, all my religion (disguised), all my hatred. It is true that I shall write the contrary, that I shall swear by the great gods that it is a work of pure art.

† The work of the Romantics, in general, stands up rather badly to a slow reading, bristling with the resistance of a critical and refined reader ... Baudelaire was that reader.

And, since everything is fixed in a hierarchy of relationships, it follows that when the poet uses a metaphor or even when he simply names an object, he is invoking something *real*. His use of language is *magical*, his poems are *spells*, since they have a reality which comes from their real correspondence with the objects described. The universe has a mystical unity; no part of it can be altered without affecting the rest. From this concept of mystical unity comes the idea (which was so popular with Baudelaire and other poets in the nineteenth century) of the unity of the arts and also of the sensations (*synaesthesia*). The equivalence of colours and sounds, of music and poetry, which was to play so large a part in the discussions which went on around the Symbolist movement, is the natural consequence of this view of the universe. The exaltation of the *dandy* too, which is, however, of more importance in Baudelaire's prose than in his poetry, comes, not only from the necessity of the poet/mage's creating for himself a personality apart from the common run of men, but also from the vague feeling that this personality should be of a kind that displayed some equivalence with his creation (to the artifice of the poem corresponds the artifice of the dandy).

This system provided Baudelaire with a controlling myth or a series of controlling myths, which were not merely arbitrary, but were deeply seated in his nature. In his attitude towards women, for example, he instinctively uses the same sense of correspondences as a mechanism for his sexual sensibility. 'La femme est sans doute une lumière, un regard, une invitation au bonheur, une parole quelquefois; mais elle est surtout une harmonie générale, non-seulement dans son allure et le mouvement de ses membres, mais aussi dans les mousselines, les gazes, les vastes et chatoyantes nuées d'étoffes dont elle s'enveloppe, et qui sont comme les attributs et le piédestal de sa divinité. ...' * Evidently, for Baudelaire, these sensuous trappings of woman held

* Woman is doubtless a light, a glance, an invitation to happiness, a word sometimes; but she is above all a general harmony, not only in her carriage and the movement of her limbs, but also in the muslins, the gauzes, the vast glistening clouds of cloth, in which she swathes herself and which are as the attributes and the pedestal of her divinity.

as much charm as she herself, and this fetishism is continually displayed in those of his poems with a sexual theme, where the sensual communication with his mistress is usually achieved via her hair, her perfume, or something she is wearing (cf. *Les Bijoux*, *La Chevelure*, *Sed non satiata*, etc.). What might be called mere woman is repugnant to him: 'La femme est *naturelle*, c'est-à-dire abominable'.* The artifice that Baudelaire demands in his creation of himself he also requires in his mistress, even in his way of making love to her, a way that often seems to be that of the *voyeur*.

Sartre has recently reproached Baudelaire with his inability to create his own values. Revolting against a *bourgeois* society, but accepting its values by his denial rather than transcendence of them, paying an inverted homage to Christianity by his Satanism, for Sartre Baudelaire seems engaged in a monstrous game, erecting around himself card-houses of false revolt and false suffering, of false belief and false emotion. Now it is undoubtedly true that much of the apparatus that Baudelaire used to sustain his poetry is ridiculous as thought. The one completely puerile attitude in face of Christianity is that of the Satanist. To revolt against a system of belief, while appearing to accept its premises, is justifiable from only one point of view: that of the poet. The poet is concerned with the communication of experience and, for this communication, he must use what myths he has to hand. Moreover, these myths must be sufficiently well known to strike a resonant chord in his audience. I do not think Baudelaire was a Christian, even of an inverted kind, but he was a man of what is called religious feeling, and he wished to communicate certain things which could be expressed only in terms of Christian imagery. The question of belief does not enter into this poetic expression. Baudelaire would be quite justified in creating a mythical structure for his poems in which he himself did not believe, in the sense in which one believes in a religion. That most of his thought is valueless except in relation to his poetry I should not dispute, but it is equally true that it is not the least use considering it except in such a relationship. It is here that Sartre has

* Woman is *natural*, that is: abominable.

gone wrong; to try to separate Baudelaire's philosophy of life from his poetry is to forget that he was primarily a poet and, as such, has a right to a phoney philosophy. Perhaps Sartre is right in saying that 'ses poèmes sont comme des succédanés de la création du Bien, qu'il s'est interdite',* but anyone concerned with poetry must regard them as a good in themselves.

In fact there is one value ceaselessly affirmed in Baudelaire's poems, and from it comes most of the novelty of his poetic achievement. His definition of the Beautiful is well known: 'C'est quelque chose d'ardent et de triste, quelque chose d'un peu vague, laissant carrière à la conjecture. ... Le mystère, le regret sont aussi des caractères du Beau.' † And this uncertain objective, this mixture of the emotions represents a carrying of the romantic ideal further than it had been carried before. Baudelaire's insistence on the entry of every emotion, every passion into art, together with his love of the grotesque 'grand sourire dans un beau visage de géant'.‡ led him to create a value out of experience itself, an experience necessarily in flux, alternating between *Spleen* and *Idéal*, between God and Satan, including both the beautiful and the grotesque. This attribution of a value to the flow of life is the basic element in Romanticism, and Baudelaire pushed it to a greater extreme than it had been carried by the poets more properly called Romantics, by refusing any exclusions and by declining the idealization of the universe which is to be found in their works. The tide of experience must continue to run, whatever happens; the great enemy is boredom (*ennui*). Baudelaire described himself in *Le Voyage*:

> *Mais les vrais voyageurs sont ceux-là seuls qui partent*
> *Pour partir. ...*

> But the true travellers are only those who depart for the sake of departing.

* His poems are like substitutes for the creation of the Good, which he has forbidden himself.

† It is something passionate and sad, something a little vague, leaving room for conjecture. ... Mystery and regret are also characteristics of the Beautiful.

‡ A wide smile on a handsome giant's face.

It was the value placed upon experience (necessarily egocentric) that gave Baudelaire's universe its real unity as opposed to the mythical unity he imposed on it by his system of correspondences. And this consuming thirst made him include new themes and new images in his poetry. He was the first poet to write that *poésie des villes*, which was to become one of the chief innovations of nineteenth-century French poetry. His psychological observation of his own and other people's comportment brought a new realism into his descriptions of human behaviour (particularly as regards sexual relations), and his consciousness of the home-sickness that afflicts modern man enabled him to reach that strange tone (half-revolt, half-melancholy) which has marked so much French poetry and prose ever since. His own estrangement from society gave a new anguish to his realization of the essential loneliness of the poet, and in his poems this feeling of isolation, and the material presented by a new age and new emotions are seized upon by an aesthetic of impermanence, which in some ways is curiously near to that of the baroque. This poetry, incarnate in a style where the surprising epithet is never wanting, might be called the poetry of romantic realism, and a combination of time and quality make of Baudelaire the most revolutionary poet of the nineteenth century, the first to express the shifting sensibility of modern man.*

'Enfin Malherbe vint.' † The coming of Baudelaire has as much importance for the nineteenth century as a literary land-

---

* Marcel Aymé's attack on Baudelaire in his book *Le Confort intellectuel* seems to be due to a recognition of the basically romantic character of much of his poetry. His hostile analysis of the sonnet *La Beauté*, exaggerated as it is, makes some legitimate points about Baudelaire's vocabulary which does sometimes stray into the inflation common to all the Romantics. On the other hand, the moral strictures put into the mouth of M. Lepage seem to me purely paradoxical. Moreover, M. Aymé's Johnsonian interlocutor admits in the course of his dialogue with his creator that he finds the sonnet beautiful in spite of the faults he points out in it. That is surely enough. As any critic knows, it is only too easy to destroy the total effect of a poem by questioning individual words. Which is not to say that M. Aymé has not touched on a weak spot in Baudelaire's poetry: its frequently absurd inheritance from the Romantics.

† At last Malherbe came.

mark. Whether or not the new generation of poets needed his example to write as they did, he was their precursor, and they all paid tribute to him. Their first appearance can conveniently be dated in 1866, when the anthology *Le Parnasse contemporain* came out with poems by Verlaine and Mallarmé, and by 1870 these two poets were beginning to be known; Rimbaud was to publish *Une Saison en Enfer* in 1873, and Corbière's *Amours jaunes* date from the same year. Of these poets it is Rimbaud and Mallarmé, who continue Baudelaire's work most directly.

VI

Baudelaire's magical view of language had not led him to demand of it feats beyond its power. All he had wanted was a re-creation of experience, with no desire to put into practice the occult powers he attributed to poetry. In Rimbaud, however, the transfiguration of the poet into the demiurge is carried to its furthest limit. In him can be seen incarnate the revolt against society and the attempt to realize it in poetry. He is the poet/mage *par excellence*, and, like other mages, he envisages an asceticism: 'Je dis qu'il faut être *voyant*, se faire *voyant*. Le poète se fait *voyant* par un long, immense et déraisonné dérèglement de tous les sens.'* The anarchic side of Rimbaud's nature is complemented by a desire to create and, since it is by language that he must achieve this creation, the word necessarily takes on its full power of invocation (the primitivism of this view of language is quite in accordance with his character). By language he would destroy a world and create a world. And the change from poet to demiurge is marked by the famous statement 'Je est un autre'.†

Rimbaud's poetry is that of a man struggling to find firm ground in a world whose values he rejected, and no system entirely solves the riddle of his poignant and tormented writings.

---

* I say that it is necessary to be a *seer*, to make oneself a *seer*. The poet makes himself a *seer* by a long, vast and irrational disordering of all his senses.

† I is another.

It seems that he believed in his own myths to a dangerous point. To expect other than purely poetic results from an exaltation of poetry into sorcery could only lead to disappointment, and *Une Saison en Enfer* is probably an account of one such check, but why Rimbaud began to write and why he ceased writing at the age of nineteen or twenty remains conjectural. What is left is the marvellous incantatory power of his verse, the tender realism of a poem like *Les Premières Communions* or the nostalgia and the vision of *Matin*:

> *Le chant des cieux, la marche des peuples! Esclaves, ne maudissons pas la vie.*

> The song of the heavens, the advance of the peoples! Slaves, let us not blaspheme life.

But it would be too easy to think that Rimbaud ever succeeded in creating a certainty for himself. He was never able either to fall back on a traditional solution or to establish the foundations of his own values firmly enough to rest from his ceaseless effort towards creation. Like other poets of the time he avails himself of the myth of the city and of the myth of childhood (complementary aspects of the same nostalgia), but there is also another element in his poetry which is to be found nowhere else: an acute sense of historic movement. Over twenty years after the first Communist manifesto we can feel in Rimbaud's poetry a sense that the tribes are on the move with the old hierarchies and national states breaking down. A poem like *Qu'est-ce pour nous, mon cœur, que les nappes de sang ...* is the sharpest expression of revolutionary nihilism, just as *Matin* is the most touching hymn to revolutionary aspiration. What makes Rimbaud so near to us to-day is that he saw the break-up of civilization around him at a time when hardly anyone else saw it. For him history was *le temps des assassins*,* and he was forced to do his best about it. It is this that gives his poetry its urgent, direct quality; it was the instrument of a personal salvation. That Rimbaud was not, could not be saved by it increases the gravity of the tragedy. He was the first poet in our historic plight.

* The time of the assassins.

VII

While Rimbaud represents the claims of poetry in their most active connexion with man in history, Mallarmé is the type of the poet-contemplative, interested in the cultivation of an inner purity. Rimbaud had given himself to the creation of a world through language; Mallarmé gave himself to the creation of a language. For him it was an end sufficient in itself as virtue is sufficient. At the age of twenty-five he had written in a letter to a friend: 'Il n'y a que la Beauté; – et elle n'a qu'une expression parfaite – la Poésie'.* And Valéry has spoken of his conviction of 'l'éminente dignité de la Poésie, hors de laquelle il n'apercevait que le hasard'.† Thus the work of art was established as an absolute, incarnating something approaching the Platonic Ideas. But the poem had to be constructed from language, and how to give to language, shopsoiled from its association with the particular, the burning generality that Mallarmé desired? For his poetry differs from that of other great poets in that it moves from the general to the particular. 'Je dis: une fleur! et, hors de l'oubli où ma voix relègue aucun contour, en tant que quelque chose d'autre que les calices sus, musicalement se lève, idée même et suave, l'absente de tous bouquets'.‡ An aesthetic of absence of the particular, in which the creative act itself appears an impurity, must necessarily carry with it some obscurity. 'Toute chose sacrée et qui veut demeurer sacrée s'enveloppe de mystère'.§ The poems of Mallarmé, however, are not as difficult as they seem. The dissolution of syntax, which was for him one means of renewing language, sometimes complicates matters and gives to the poem an ambiguity that cannot be resolved in favour of any one interpretation. The *Prose pour des Esseintes* is an extreme case of a poem which does not seem meant to be

---

* There is only Beauty; – and it has only one perfect expression – Poetry.

† The eminent dignity of Poetry, outside of which he only saw chance.

‡ I say: a flower! and, out of the forgetfulness where my voice banishes any contour, inasmuch as it is something other than known calyxes, musically arises, an idea itself and fragrant, the one absent from all bouquets.

§ Every holy thing wishing to remain holy surrounds itself with mystery.

understood; there Mallarmé speaks directly of the Ideas, and his language is unavoidably a description of the unfathomable, but the sonnet for Verlaine, for instance, only seems obscure because of the great compression of language and imagery. Mallarmé also owes his reputation for coldness to his fundamental conception of poetry. Concerned as he was with the non-presence of the object, much of his imagery is drawn from the vertigo he felt before Space or the Ideal (it comes to the same thing). But the warm sensuality of a poem like *L'Après-midi d'un faune* serves to refute the legend of a poet dedicated to lunar sterility.

Dedicated, however, he was. To make of a poem at once the summit and explanation of the universe required dedication, but, as M. Raymond has pointed out, this was not an attempt which could in any sense succeed. Mallarmé could not make of language an absolute. 'Donner un sens plus pur aux mots de la tribu'*– that he could do. What was impossible was to make them the equivalent of a transcendance. Yet all was not lost; the famous salon at the rue de Rome was thronged with young writers – Valéry, Gide, and Claudel among them – who learned from Mallarmé what toil and self-abnegation the poet's task demands. Like Rimbaud, like Baudelaire, he had a directing myth that enabled him to justify his sacrifices for poetry. Withdrawn from society rather than revolting against it (but this was certainly his form of revolt), he appealed from it to eternity, and the language broke under him. Nineteenth-century poetry was bought at the price of such failures.

VIII

Verlaine's poetry shows no sign of such perilous spiritual adventures. His work is largely lyrical and resists attempts at analysis. His talent (naïve as it was) links up with the sentimental lyricism of Lamartine or Mme Desbordes-Valmore. Like them, he is given to sensibility; like theirs his poems are not the products of strength, technically perfect though they are. But he owes to Baudelaire a certain self-mocking irony in the presentation of his poetic *persona*, which had not been present in

* Give a purer meaning to the words of the tribe.

earlier poets of this type, and he extended his range to cover modern city life as well as the beauties of nature. It is curious to compare his *Art poétique* with Gautier's *Art* and see what a long way ideas on aesthetics had travelled. The jewels and statues in which Gautier chose to typify art have changed to Verlaine's misty ideal:

> *C'est des beaux yeux derrière des voiles,*
> *C'est le grand jour tremblant de midi ...*

It is lovely eyes behind veils, it is the full shimmering light of noon.

What had come between? Baudelaire: 'quelque chose d'ardent et triste, quelque chose d'un peu vague, laissant carrière à la conjecture. ...' *

It is Verlaine's wonderful skill with verse and word that most readers will choose to remember. When he tries to elaborate any other philosophy than that of the sentimentally cynical vagabond, he becomes over-pathetic. Sincere he, no doubt, was, but lines like:

> *Je ne veux plus aimer que ma mère Marie.*

I want to love no one but my mother Mary.

are positively embarrassing. However, we can forget the *fadaises* of *Sagesse* in the exquisite formality of a poem like *Clair de Lune* or the equally exquisite impressionism of *Dans l'interminable ...*

What other poets are there to talk of? Tristan Corbière wrote harsh ironic poems – some of them in the argot of the sea, others full of puns and *double-entendres*. His best poetry comes when he is speaking of his native Brittany, or when he is judging himself, as in *Paria*. His manner was to be taken up on a lighter note by Jules Laforgue, a poet who, like Corbière, died young. His poems, in turn sentimental, humorous, and tragic, were to have great influence on English and American poetry. The *persona*, which he created for himself, of the little man with a wry smile and lack of self-confidence anticipates Charlie Chaplin and Eliot (J. Alfred Prufrock attests his influence, not to mention such

---

* Something passionate and sad, something a little vague, leaving room for conjecture.

early poems of Eliot as *Conversation Galante*, which are pure Laforgue pastiche), and the mingling of images in a poem like *L'Hiver qui vient* was to be found later in the poetry of Surrealism and the humour of a Queneau or a Prévert. Laforgue and Corbière were, in fact, one possible line of development from Baudelaire and they both represent the self-critical irony which informs so much French writing. Émile Verhaeren, who was almost a very great poet, develops the poetry of the town to a point where his Flemish vision of a countryside eaten away by industrial tentacles becomes almost apocalyptic. His Socialism and intense pity for the miseries of peasant and worker give his poetry great force, even if it occasionally shows the formlessness which so displeased Rémy de Gourmont. Formless too are the vast prose poems of Lautréamont, which were to influence the Surrealists by their apparent unchaining of a purely visionary talent. These wild, often sadistic, reveries have been much overrated, but Lautréamont cannot be denied a gift of language and delirium. Towards the turn of the century a return to classicism brought about the appearance of the *École Romane*, of whom Raymond de la Tailhède is one of the more presentable members. Their inspiration was Mediterranean, and they looked back to the poets of the sixteenth century as their masters. The result was a rather Levantine *Latinità*. Nearer to Athens and Rome is Emmanuel Signoret, whose poems, sparkling with light and the southern sea, foreshadow Valéry. With this tentative reaction towards classicism the story of French nineteenth-century poetry closes.

IX

Finally, a word about this anthology. I have tried to give only complete poems, and this has necessarily meant some exclusions – notably in the case of Hugo, most of whose best works were far too long to include. I have also tried to represent fully the great poets of the time, and this has meant leaving out some others. For instance, there is no Théodore de Banville and no Sully Prudhomme, as I was unable to find a poem of theirs I liked sufficiently to justify the omission of something else. A

poem is not necessarily bad because it has figured in many antholo-gies, so the reader will find a number of very familiar poems in this book. But I hope he will also find some he does not know, but will like on acquaintance, and that he will not hold the vagaries of my taste against me. An anthology is bound to be personal, and there is nothing that can be done about it. As to the translations, it has been my aim to provide as literal a render-ing as is compatible with reasonable English prose. Occasionally I have had to be more approximate: a poet like Mallarmé, for instance, is bound to impose on his translator an interpretation which is only one of several possible versions. In one or two cases, where it has been impossible to render some play on or opposition of words, I have given an explanatory note. But I have tried to keep these down to the minimum.

My thanks are due to Mr J. M. Cohen, the general editor of this series, for his helpful advice on many aspects of this book; to Dr Joseph Chiari for checking my translations and putting his knowledge of his native language and literature at my dis-posal; to Mr Donat O'Donnell for his criticism of the intro-duction; and to Mr J. D. Scott for advising me on the translations and the introduction.

In this second edition some corrections have been made and my thanks are due to Miss Jean Stewart for pointing out a num-ber of errors in the translations and to Mme Johnson-Rébillard for solving a difficult phrase in a poem by Baudelaire.

A. H.

JEAN-PIERRE DE BÉRANGER

Le Vieux Vagabond

Dans ce fossé cessons de vivre.
Je finis vieux, infirme et las.
Les passants vont dire: Il est ivre;
Tant mieux! ils ne me plaindront pas.
J'en vois qui détournent la tête;
D'autres me jettent quelques sous.
Courez vite; allez à la fête.
Vieux vagabond, je puis mourir sans vous.

Oui, je meurs ici de vieillesse,
Parce qu'on ne meurt pas de faim.
J'espérais voir de ma détresse
L'hôpital adoucir la fin,
Mais tout est plein dans chaque hospice,
Tant le peuple est infortuné!
La rue, hélas! fut ma nourrice:
Vieux vagabond, mourons où je suis né.

The Old Tramp

Let me end my life in this ditch. I finish old and sick and tired. The passers-by will say: he is drunk; so much the better! they will not pity me. I see some turning away their heads; others throw me a few coppers. Run quickly; go to your feasting. An old tramp can die without you.

Yes, I am dying here of old age, because people do not die of hunger. I hoped to see the hospital soften the end of my distress, but everything is full up in every poor-house, so unfortunate are the common people! The street, alas, was my nurse: let an old tramp die where he was born.

1

Aux artisans, dans mon jeune âge,
J'ai dit: Qu'on m'enseigne un métier.
Va, nous n'avons pas trop d'ouvrage,
Répondaient-ils, va mendier.
Riches, qui me disiez: Travaille,
J'eus bien des os de vos repas;
J'ai bien dormi sur votre paille.
Vieux vagabond, je ne vous maudis pas.

J'aurais pu voler, moi, pauvre homme;
Mais non: mieux vaut tendre la main.
Au plus, j'ai dérobé la pomme
Qui mûrit au bord du chemin.
Vingt fois pourtant on me verrouille
Dans les cachots de par le roi.
De mon seul bien on me dépouille.
Vieux vagabond, le soleil est à moi.

Le pauvre a-t-il une patrie?
Que me font vos vins et vos blés,
Votre gloire et votre industrie,
Et vos orateurs assemblés?

In my youth I said to the craftsmen: Teach me a trade. Go away, we have not too much work, they replied; go away and beg. Rich folk, who said to me: Work, I had many a bone from your meals; I have slept well on your straw. An old tramp does not curse you.

I, poor man, could have thieved; but no: it is better to hold out my hand. At most, I stole an apple ripening on the roadside. Yet twenty times they locked me up in dungeons by order of the king. They robbed me of my only possession. The sun belongs to an old tramp.

Has the poor man a country? What do your wine and wheat, your fame and industry, and your assemblies of orators mean to

Dans vos murs ouverts à ses armes,
Lorsque l'étranger s'engraissait,
Comme un sot j'ai versé des larmes.
Vieux vagabond, sa main me nourrissait.

Comme un insecte fait pour nuire,
Hommes, que ne m'écrasiez-vous?
Ah! plutôt vous deviez m'instruire
A travailler au bien de tous.
Mis à l'abri du vent contraire,
Le ver fût devenu fourmi;
Je vous aurais chéris en frère.
Vieux vagabond, je meurs votre ennemi.

Les Souvenirs du peuple

ON parlera de sa gloire
Sous le chaume bien longtemps.
L'humble toit, dans cinquante ans,
Ne connaîtra plus d'autre histoire.

me? When the foreigner grew fat within your walls thrown open
to his arms, like a fool I shed tears. His hand used to feed an old
tramp.

Men, why did you not crush me like an insect made to harm you?
Ah! rather you should teach me to work for the good of all. Sheltered from the unkind wind, the maggot would have become an ant;
I would have loved you as a brother. As an old tramp I die your
enemy.

Memories of the Common People

BENEATH the thatch they will speak of his fame for a long time to
come. In fifty years the humble roof will know no other story.

Là viendront les villageois
Dire alors à quelque vieille:
Par des récits d'autrefois,
Mère, abrégez notre veille.
Bien, dit-on, qu'il nous ait nui,
Le peuple encor le révère,
    Oui, le révère.
Parlez-nous de lui, grand'mère;
    Parlez-nous de lui. (*bis*.)

Mes enfants, dans ce village,
Suivi de rois, il passa.
Voilà bien longtemps de ça;
Je venais d'entrer en ménage.
A pied grimpant le coteau
Où pour voir je m'étais mise,
Il avait petit chapeau
Avec redingote grise.
Près de lui je me troublai,
Il me dit: Bonjour, ma chère.
    Bonjour, ma chère.
– Il vous a parlé, grand'mère!
    Il vous a parlé!

There the villagers will come to say to some old woman: mother, shorten our evening by tales of former times. Although, they say, he harmed us, the common people still reveres him – yes, reveres him. Tell us about him, grandmother; tell us about him. (*twice*.)

My children, in this village, followed by kings he passed by. That was a very long time ago; I had just set up house. Climbing on foot the hillside where I had set myself to see, he had a little hat with a grey riding-coat. Near to him I was confused, he said to me: Good day, my dear. Good day, my dear. – He spoke to you, grandmother! He spoke to you!

L'an d'après, moi pauvre femme,
A Paris étant un jour,
Je le vis avec sa cour:
Il se rendait à Notre-Dame.
Tous les cœurs étaient contents,
On admirait son cortège.
Chacun disait: Quel beau temps!
Le ciel toujours le protège.
Son sourire était bien doux;
D'un fils Dieu le rendait père,
Le rendait père.
– Quel beau jour pour vous, grand'mère!
Quel beau jour pour vous!

Mais, quand la pauvre Champagne
Fut en proie aux étrangers,
Lui, bravant tous les dangers,
Semblait seul tenir la campagne.
Un soir, tout comme aujourd'hui,
J'entends frapper à la porte;
J'ouvre, bon Dieu! c'était lui,
Suivi d'une faible escorte.
Il s'assoit où me voilà,
S'écriant: Oh! quelle guerre!

The year after, I, poor woman, being in Paris one day, saw him
with his court: he was going to Notre Dame. All hearts were happy,
we admired his train. Everyone said: What fine weather! May
heaven always protect him. His smile was very gentle; God made
him father of a fine son, made him father. – What a fine day for you,
grandmother! What a fine day for you!

But, when poor Champagne was the prey of foreigners, he, braving every danger, seemed to hold the field alone. One evening just
as to-day, I heard a knocking at the door; I open, good God! it was
he, followed by a weak escort. He sat down where I am now, crying

Oh! quelle guerre!
– Il s'est assis là, grand'mère!
Il s'est assis là!

J'ai faim, dit-il; et bien vite
Je sers piquette et pain bis;
Puis il sèche ses habits,
Même à dormir le feu l'invite.
Au réveil, voyant mes pleurs,
Il me dit: Bonne espérance!
Je cours de tous ses malheurs
Sous Paris venger la France.
Il part; et comme un trésor
J'ai depuis gardé son verre,
Gardé son verre.
– Vous l'avez encor, grand'mère!
Vous l'avez encor!

Le voici. Mais à sa perte
Le héros fut entraîné.
Lui qu'un pape a couronné,
Est mort dans une île déserte.
Longtemps aucun ne l'a cru;
On disait: Il va paraître.
Par mer il est accouru;

out: Oh! What a war! Oh! What a war! – He sat there, grand-mother! He sat there!

I am hungry, he said; and with speed I served sour wine and brown bread; then he dried his clothes, the fire even invited him to sleep. On waking, seeing my tears, he said to me: Good courage! I hasten to avenge France of all her misfortunes beneath the walls of Paris. He went away; and since then I have kept his glass as a treasure, kept his glass. – You still have it, grandmother! You still have it!

Here it is. But the hero was swept away to his destruction. He whom a pope had crowned died on a barren island. For a long time nobody believed it; they said: He will appear. He has come by sea;

L'étranger va voir son maître.
Quand d'erreur on nous tira,
Ma douleur fut bien amère!
    Fut bien amère!
– Dieu vous bénira, grand'mère;
    Dieu vous bénira. (*bis.*)

MARCELINE DESBORDES-VALMORE

La Promenade d'automne

TE souvient-il, ô mon âme, ô ma vie,
D'un jour d'automne et pâle et languissant?
Il semblait dire un adieu gémissant
Aux bois qu'il attristait de sa mélancolie.
Les oiseaux dans les airs ne chantaient plus l'espoir;
Une froide rosée enveloppait leurs ailes,
Et, rappelant au nid leurs compagnes fidèles,
Sur des rameaux sans fleurs ils attendaient le soir.

the foreigner will see his master. When they convinced us of our
error, my sorrow was most bitter! Was most bitter! – God will
bless you, grandmother; God will bless you. (*twice.*)

The Autumn Walk

DO you remember, my soul, my life, a pale and languishing autumn
day? It seemed to say a sighing farewell to the woods which were
saddened by its melancholy. The birds in the air sang no more of
hope; a cold dew enclosed their wings, and, calling back their faithful mates to the nest, they waited for evening on boughs where
there were no flowers.

7

Les troupeaux, à regret menés aux pâturages,
   N'y trouvaient plus que des herbes sauvages;
Et le pâtre, oubliant sa rustique chanson,
Partageait le silence et le deuil du vallon;
   Rien ne charmait l'ennui de la nature;
La feuille qui perdait sa riante couleur,
Les coteaux dépouillés de leur verte parure,
Tout demandait au ciel un rayon de chaleur.

Seule, je m'éloignais d'une fête bruyante;
Je fuyais tes regards, je cherchais ma raison.
Mais la langueur des champs, leur tristesse attrayante,
A ma langueur secrète ajoutaient leur poison.
Sans but et sans espoir suivant ma rêverie,
Je portais au hasard un pas timide et lent.
L'Amour m'enveloppa de ton ombre chérie,
Et, malgré la saison, l'air me parut brûlant.
Je voulais, mais en vain, par un effort suprême,
En me sauvant de toi, me sauver de moi-même.
Mon œil, voilé de pleurs, à la terre attaché,
Par un charme invincible en fut comme arraché.

The flocks, regretfully led to pasture, found only wild grasses there; and the herd, forgetting his rustic song, shared the silence and mourning of the valley. Nothing charmed away nature's tedium. The leaf losing its laughing colour, the hillsides stripped of their green ornaments, everything asked heaven for one gleam of warmth.

I went away alone from a noisy merry-making; I fled your glances, I looked for my own reason: but the languor of the fields, their attractive melancholy added their poison to my own secret languor. Aimless and hopeless, following my thoughts, I carried my slow and timid steps where chance led me; Love covered me with your beloved shadow, and despite the time of year, the air seemed to burn me.

I wished, but in vain, by a last effort, to save myself from myself, by saving myself from you; my eye, clouded with tears and fixed on the ground, was torn away as if by an invincible spell. Through

A travers les brouillards, une image légère
Fit palpiter mon sein de tendresse et d'effroi;
Le soleil reparaît, l'environne, l'éclaire,
Il entr'ouvre les cieux. ... Tu parus devant moi.
Je n'osai te parler: interdite, rêveuse,
Enchaînée et soumise à ce trouble enchanteur,
Je n'osai te parler: pourtant j'étais heureuse;
Je devinais ton âme, et j'entendis mon cœur.

    Mais, quand ta main pressa ma main tremblante,
Quand un frisson léger fit tressaillir mon corps,
Quand mon front se couvrit d'un rougeur brûlante,
    Dieu! qu'est-ce donc que je sentis alors?
J'oubliai de te fuir, j'oubliai de te craindre,
Pour la première fois ta bouche osa se plaindre;
Ma douleur à la tienne osa se révéler,
Et mon âme vers toi fut prête à s'exhaler!
    Il m'en souvient! T'en souvient-il, ma vie,
        De ce tourment délicieux,
De ces mots arrachés à ta mélancolie:
    «Ah! si je souffre, on souffre aux cieux!»

the mists a delicate image made my breast pulse with tenderness and fear; the sun reappears, surrounds and lights it up; the sun half-opens the heavens. ... You appeared before me. I did not dare to speak to you; I was abashed and meditative, enthralled and submissive to this enchanting confusion; I did not dare to speak to you, yet I was happy; I guessed your soul and I listened to my heart.

But, when your hand pressed my trembling hand, when a slight shudder made my body shake, when my forehead was covered with a burning blush, God! what did I feel then? I forgot to flee you, I forgot to fear you; for the first time your mouth dared to complain, my suffering dared to reveal itself to yours and my soul was on the point of breathing itself forth towards you. I remember! My life, do you remember that delicious torture, those words torn from your melancholy: 'Ah! if I suffer, they must suffer in heaven!'

Des bois nul autre aveu ne troubla le silence.
Ce jour fut de nos jours le plus beau, le plus doux;
Prêt à s'éteindre, enfin il s'arrêta sur nous,
Et sa fuite à mon cœur présagea ton absence.

    L'âme du monde éclaira notre amour;
Je vis ses derniers feux mourir sous un nuage;
Et dans nos cœurs brisés, désunis sans retour,
    Il n'en reste plus que l'image!

ALPHONSE DE LAMARTINE

Le Lac

Ainsi, toujours poussés vers de nouveaux rivages,
Dans la nuit éternelle emportés sans retour,
Ne pourrons-nous jamais sur l'océan des âges
    Jeter l'ancre un seul jour?

Ô lac! l'année à peine a fini sa carrière,
Et, près des flots chéris qu'elle devait revoir,
Regarde! je viens seul m'asseoir sur cette pierre
    Où tu la vis s'asseoir!

No other confession disturbed the silence of the woods. That day was the loveliest and sweetest of our days; ready to vanish, at the last it lingered on us, and its flight foreshadowed your absence to my heart: the world's soul lit up our love; I saw its last fires die away beneath a cloud; and only its image remains in our broken hearts that are parted for ever.

The Lake

So, always impelled towards new shores, carried for ever into eternal night, can we never cast anchor in time's ocean for a single day?

O lake! The year has hardly finished its course, and behold! I come alone to sit upon this stone where you saw her sit, near the beloved waves that she was to have seen once more!

Tu mugissais ainsi sous ces roches profondes;
Ainsi tu te brisais sur leurs flancs déchirés;
Ainsi le vent jetait l'écume de tes ondes
      Sur ses pieds adorés.

Un soir, t'en souvient-il? nous voguions en silence;
On n'entendait au loin, sur l'onde et sous les cieux,
Que le bruit des rameurs qui frappaient en cadence
      Tes flots harmonieux.

Tout à coup des accents inconnus à la terre
Du rivage charmé frappèrent les échos;
Le flot fut attentif, et la voix qui m'est chère
      Laissa tomber ces mots:

«Ô temps, suspends ton vol! et vous, heures propices,
      Suspendez votre cours!
Laissez-nous savourer les rapides délices
      Des plus beaux de nos jours!

«Assez de malheureux ici-bas vous implorent:
      Coulez, coulez pour eux;
Prenez avec leurs jours les soins qui les dévorent;
      Oubliez les heureux.

Thus you murmured beneath these steep rocks; thus you broke upon their torn sides; thus the wind threw the foam from your waves on her adorable feet.

One evening, do you remember? we were sailing noiselessly; we only heard far off, on the water and beneath the skies, the sound of rowers rhythmically striking the melodious waves.

All at once strains unknown to earth struck the echoes of the spell-bound shore; the waves were attentive, and the voice dear to me let fall these words:

'O time, suspend your flight! And you, propitious hours, suspend your course! Let us taste the swift delights of the fairest of our days!

'Enough unhappy beings pray to you down here on earth: flow on, flow on for them; together with their days take away the cares that consume them; forget those that are happy.

«Mais je demande en vain quelques moments encore,
      Le temps m'échappe et fuit;
Je dis à cette nuit: « Sois plus lente»; et l'aurore
      Va dissiper la nuit.

«Aimons donc, aimons donc! de l'heure fugitive,
      Hâtons-nous, jouissons!
L'homme n'a point de port, le temps n'a point de rive:
      Il coule, et nous passons!»

Temps jaloux, se peut-il que ces moments d'ivresse,
Où l'amour à longs flots nous verse le bonheur,
S'envolent loin de nous de la même vitesse
      Que les jours de malheur?

Hé quoi! n'en pourrons-nous fixer au moins la trace?
Quoi! passés pour jamais? quoi! tout entiers perdus?
Ce temps qui les donna, ce temps qui les efface
      Ne nous les rendra plus?

Éternité, néant, passé, sombres abîmes,
Que faites-vous des jours que vous engloutissez?
Parlez: nous rendrez-vous ces extases sublimes
      Que vous nous ravissez?

'But in vain I ask for a few more moments; time escapes me and
flees away; I say to this night: "Go more slowly"; and dawn will
scatter the night.

'Let us love then, let us love! Let us hasten to enjoy the fleeting
hour! Man has no harbour, time has no shore: it flows on, and we
pass by!'

Jealous time, can it be that these moments of intoxication, when
love pours us happiness in long draughts, fly far away from us with
the same speed as days of misfortune?

What! Can we not preserve their trace at least? What! Gone for
ever? What! All quite lost? The time that gave them, the time that
blots them out will give them back to us no more?

Eternity, nothingness, past – dark abysses – what do you do with
the days you swallow up? Speak: will you give us back those sublime raptures that you snatch from us?

O lac! rochers muets! grottes! forêt obscure!
Vous que le temps épargne ou qu'il peut rajeunir,
Gardez de cette nuit, gardez, belle nature,
        Au moins le souvenir!

Qu'il soit dans ton repos, qu'il soit dans tes orages,
Beau lac, et dans l'aspect de tes riants coteaux,
Et dans ces noirs sapins, et dans ces rocs sauvages
        Qui pendent sur tes eaux!

Qu'il soit dans le zéphyr qui frémit et qui passe,
Dans les bruits de tes bords par tes bords répétés,
Dans l'astre au front d'argent qui blanchit ta surface
        De ses molles clartés!

Que le vent qui gémit, le roseau qui soupire,
Que les parfums légers de ton air embaumé,
Que tout ce qu'on entend, l'on voit ou l'on respire,
        Tout dise: «Ils ont aimé!»

O lake! Silent rocks! Caves! Dark forest! You whom time spares or can make young again, keep at least the memory of that night; keep it, fair landscape!

Let it be in your calms or in your storms, sweet lake, and in the sight of your laughing hillsides, and in these black pines, and in these wild rocks overhanging your waters!

Let it be in the breeze trembling and passing by, in the sounds of your shores and their echoes, in the silver-browed star that whitens your surface with its soft lights!

Let the moaning wind, the sighing reed, the light perfumes of your scented air, let everything that is heard, seen, or breathed, let everything say: 'They loved!'

Tristesse

Ramenez-moi, disais-je, au fortuné rivage
Où Naples réfléchit dans une mer d'azur
Ses palais, ses coteaux, ses astres sans nuage,
Où l'oranger fleurit sous un ciel toujours pur.
Que tardez-vous? Partons! Je veux revoir encore
Le Vésuve enflammé sortant du sein des eaux;
Je veux de ses hauteurs voir se lever l'aurore;
Je veux, guidant les pas de celle que j'adore,
Redescendre en rêvant de ces riants coteaux.
Suis-moi dans les détours de ce golfe tranquille:
Retournons sur ces bords à nos pas si connus,
Aux jardins de Cynthie, au tombeau de Virgile,
Près des débris épars du temple de Vénus:
Là, sous les orangers, sous la vigne fleurie
Dont le pampre flexible au myrte se marie
Et tresse sur ta tête une voûte de fleurs,
Au doux bruit de la vague ou du vent qui murmure,
Seuls avec notre amour, seuls avec la nature,
La vie et la lumiere auront plus de douceurs.

Sorrow

Take me back, I said, to the happy shore where Naples reflects its palaces, its hillsides, and its cloudless stars in a blue sea, where the orange-tree blooms beneath a sky that is always clear. Why do you delay? Let us depart! I want to see once again flaming Vesuvius rising from the bosom of the waves; from its heights I want to see the dawn rise; I want to come down those laughing slopes once again in a dream, guiding the steps of her whom I adore.

Follow me among the windings of this calm bay: let us return to those shores so well known to our footsteps, to Cynthia's gardens, to Virgil's tomb, near the scattered ruins of the temple of Venus: there, beneath the orange-trees, beneath the flowering vine whose lithe stem is united to the myrtle and weaves a vault of flowers above your head, there, to the gentle noise of the waves or of the murmuring wind, alone with our love, alone with nature, life and light will have more sweetness.

De mes jours pâlissants le flambeau se consume,
Il s'éteint par degrés au souffle du malheur,
Ou s'il jette parfois une faible lueur,
C'est quand ton souvenir dans mon sein le rallume.
Je ne sais si les dieux me permettront enfin
D'achever ici-bas ma pénible journée:
Mon horizon se borne, et mon œil incertain
Ose l'étendre à peine au delà d'une année.
      Mais s'il faut périr au matin,
S'il faut, sur une terre au bonheur destinée,
     Laisser échapper de ma main
     Cette coupe que le destin
Semblait avoir pour moi de roses couronnée,
Je ne demande aux dieux que de guider mes pas
Jusqu'aux bords qu'embellit ta mémoire chérie,
De saluer de loin ces fortunés climats,
Et de mourir aux lieux où j'ai goûté la vie!

The torch of my paling days burns itself out, it goes out gradually at the breath of misfortune, or, if sometimes it throws a faint
light, it is when your memory rekindles it in my breast. I do not
know if at last the gods will allow me to conclude my wearisome
day down here on earth: my horizon is confined, and my uncertain
eye hardly dares to stretch it beyond a year. But if I must die in the
morning, if, in a land appointed for happiness, I must let fall from
my hand this cup which fate seemed to have crowned with roses for
me, I only ask the gods to guide my steps to shores made more
beautiful by your beloved memory, to hail from afar those happy
climes, and to die in the places where I tasted life.

Élégie

CUEILLONS, cueillons la rose au matin de la vie;
Des rapides printemps respire au moins les fleurs;
Aux chastes voluptés abandonnons nos cœurs;
Aimons-nous sans mesure, ô mon unique amie!

Quand le nocher battu par les flots irrités
Voit son fragile esquif menacé du naufrage,
Il tourne ses regards aux bords qu'il a quittés,
Et regrette trop tard les loisirs du rivage.
Ah! qu'il voudrait alors, au toit de ses aïeux,
Près des objets chéris présents à sa mémoire,
Coulant des jours obscurs, sans périls et sans gloire,
N'avoir jamais laissé son pays ni ses dieux!

Ainsi l'homme, courbé sous le poids des années,
Pleure son doux printemps qui ne peut revenir.
«Ah! rendez-moi, dit-il, ces heures profanées!
Ô dieux! dans leur saison j'oubliai d'en jouir.»

Elegy

LET us gather, let us gather the rose in the morning of life; at least breathe the flowers of fleeting Springs; let us abandon our hearts to chaste pleasures; let us love without limit, O my only friend!

When the boatman beaten by angry waves sees his frail bark threatened by shipwreck, he turns his glance to the shores he has left and regrets too late the land's leisure. Ah! how he then wishes he had never forsaken his country or his gods, passing obscure days without danger or fame beneath the roof of his fathers near the beloved objects that are present in his memory!

So man, bent beneath the weight of the years, weeps for his sweet Spring that cannot return. 'Ah! give me back, he says, those hours I profaned! O gods! I forgot to enjoy them in their season.' He

Il dit: la mort répond; et ces dieux qu'il implore
Le poussant au tombeau sans se laisser fléchir,
Ne lui permettent pas de se baisser encore
Pour ramasser ces fleurs qu'il n'a pas su cueillir.

Aimons-nous, ô ma bien-aimée!
Et rions des soucis qui bercent les mortels.
Pour le frivole appât d'une vaine fumée,
La moitié de leurs jours, hélas! est consumée
Dans l'abandon des biens réels.
A leur stérile orgueil ne portons point envie;
Laissons le long espoir aux maîtres des humains!
Pour nous, de notre heure incertains,
Hâtons-nous d'épuiser la coupe de la vie
Pendant qu'elle est entre nos mains.

Soit que le laurier nous couronne,
Et qu'aux fastes sanglants de l'altière Bellone
Sur le marbre ou l'airain on inscrive nos noms;
Soit que des simples fleurs que la beauté moissonne
L'amour pare nos humbles fronts,
Nous allons échouer, tous, au même rivage:

speaks; death replies; and those gods to whom he prays, pushing
him into the grave without relenting, do not let him stoop again to
pick up those flowers which he has not known how to gather.

O my beloved, let us love one another! And let us laugh at the
cares that cradle mortal men. For the foolish lure of empty smoke
half their days, alas! are used up in neglect of the real wealth. Let us
not envy their sterile pride; let us leave far-off hopes to the masters
of men! For us, uncertain of our hour, let us hasten to empty life's
cup while it is in our hands.

Whether the bays crown us and our names are inscribed on
marble or brass in the bloody annals of proud Bellona; or whether
love adorns our humble brows with the simple flowers harvested by
beauty, we shall all be cast away on the same shore: at the moment

Qu'importe, au moment du naufrage,
Sur un vaisseau fameux d'avoir fendu les airs,
Ou sur une barque légère
D'avoir, passager solitaire,
Rasé timidement le rivage des mers?

ALFRED DE VIGNY

Le Cor

Poème

I

J'AIME le son du Cor, le soir, au fond des bois,
Soit qu'il chante les pleurs de la biche aux abois,
Ou l'adieu du chasseur que l'écho faible accueille
Et que le vent du nord porte de feuille en feuille.

Que de fois, seul dans l'ombre à minuit demeuré,
J'ai souri de l'entendre, et plus souvent pleuré!
Car je croyais ouïr de ces bruits prophétiques
Qui précédaient la mort des Paladins antiques.

of shipwreck what does it matter whether we have cleft the air on a famous ship or timidly skirted the sea-shore, the sole traveller on a light bark?

The Horn

A poem

I

I LOVE the horn's sound in the evening in the depth of the woods, whether it sings the tears of the doe at bay, or the hunter's farewell greeted by the faint echo and carried from leaf to leaf by the north wind.

How many times, lingering alone in the shade at midnight, have I smiled to hear it and more often wept! For I thought to hear those prophetic sounds that preceded the death of the old Paladins.

Ô montagnes d'azur! ô pays adoré!
Rocs de la Frazona, cirque du Marboré,
Cascades qui tombez des neiges entraînées,
Sources, gaves, ruisseaux, torrents des Pyrénées;

Monts gelés et fleuris, trône des deux saisons,
Dont le front est de glace et le pied de gazons!
C'est là qu'il faut s'asseoir, c'est là qu'il faut entendre
Les airs lointains d'un Cor mélancolique et tendre.

Souvent un voyageur, lorsque l'air est sans bruit,
De cette voix d'airain fait retentir la nuit;
A ses chants cadencés autour de lui se mêle
L'harmonieux grelot du jeune agneau qui bêle.

Une biche attentive, au lieu de se cacher,
Se suspend immobile au sommet du rocher,
Et la cascade unit, dans une chute immense,
Son éternelle plainte au chant de la romance.

Âmes des Chevaliers, revenez-vous encor?
Est-ce vous qui parlez avec la voix du Cor?
Roncevaux! Roncevaux! dans ta sombre vallée
L'ombre du grand Roland n'est donc pas consolée!

O blue mountains! O beloved country! Rocks of the Frazona,
valley of the Marboré, waterfalls coming down from the moving
snows, springs, burns, streams, torrents of the Pyrenees;
Frozen and flowered mountains, throne of both seasons, whose
brow is made of ice and foot of grass! It is there one must sit, it is
there one must hear the far-off notes of a tender, melancholy Horn.
Often a traveller, when the air is still, makes night resound with
that brazen voice; around him is mingled with his rhythmic song
the melodious bell of the young bleating lamb.
An attentive doe stays motionless on top of a rock instead of hiding, and the cascade in its huge fall joins its eternal complaint to the
song of the ballad.
Souls of the Knights, do you still linger here? Is it you who speak
with the voice of the Horn? Roncesvalles! Roncesvalles! In your
dark valley great Roland's shade has found no rest!

2

Tous les preux étaient morts, mais aucun n'avait fui.
Il reste seul debout, Olivier près de lui;
L'Afrique sur les monts l'entoure et tremble encore.
«Roland, tu vas mourir, rends-toi, criait le More,

«Tous tes Pairs sont couchés dans les eaux des torrents .
Il rugit comme un tigre, et dit: «Si je me rends,
Africain, ce sera lorsque les Pyrénées
Sur l'onde avec leurs corps rouleront entraînées.»

«Rends-toi donc, répond-il, ou meurs, car les voilà.»
Et du plus haut des monts un grand rocher roula.
Il bondit, il roula jusqu'au fond de l'abîme,
Et de ses pins, dans l'onde, il vint briser la cime.

«Merci, cria Roland; tu m'as fait un chemin.»
Et jusqu'au pied des monts le roulant d'une main,
Sur le roc affermi comme un géant s'élance,
Et, prête à fuir, l'armée à ce seul pas balance.

2

All the valiant were dead, but none had fled. He alone remains
standing, Oliver near him; on the hills Africa surrounds him and
still trembles. 'Roland, you are going to die, yield,' cried the Moor,
'All your Peers are laid low in the waters of the streams.' He
roared like a tiger, and said: 'If I yield, African, it will be when the
Pyrenees tumble carried away on the water with their bodies.'
'– Yield then, he answers, or die, for there they are.' And from
the top of the mountains a great rock fell. It bounced, rolled to the
bottom of the abyss and broke the crest of its pines in the water.
'Thanks, cried Roland; you have made me a path.' And rolling
it with one hand to the foot of the mountains, he springs like a giant
on the steady rock, and the army ready to flee sways at this single
step.

3

Tranquilles cependant, Charlemagne et ses preux
Descendaient la montagne et se parlaient entre eux.
A l'horizon déjà, par leurs eaux signalées,
De Luz et d'Argelès se montraient les vallées.

L'armée applaudissait. Le luth du troubadour
S'accordait pour chanter les saules de l'Adour;
Le vin français coulait dans la coupe étrangère;
Le soldat, en riant, parlait à la bergère.

Roland gardait les monts; tous passaient sans effroi.
Assis nonchalamment sur un noir palefroi
Qui marchait revêtu de housses violettes,
Turpin disait, tenant les saintes amulettes:

«Sire, on voit dans le ciel des nuages de feu;
Suspendez votre marche; il ne faut tenter Dieu.
Par monsieur saint Denis, certes ce sont des âmes
Qui passent dans les airs sur ces vapeurs de flammes.

3

Meanwhile Charlemagne and his knights were calmly descending
the mountains and talking among themselves. The valleys of Luz
and Argelès, marked out by their streams, were already visible on
the horizon.

The army applauded. The troubadour's lute was tuned to sing
the willows of the Adour; French wine flowed in foreign cups;
laughing, the soldier spoke to the shepherdess.

Roland was guarding the mountains; they all passed over without fear. Carelessly seated on a black palfrey that walked clothed in
violet trappings, Turpin said, holding the holy amulets:

'Sire, we see clouds of fire in the sky; halt your march; you must
not tempt God. By Saint Denis, for sure these are souls passing by
in the air on those flaming mists.

«Deux éclairs ont relui, puis deux autres encor.»
Ici l'on entendit le son lointain du Cor.
L'Empereur étonné, se jetant en arrière,
Suspend du destrier la marche aventurière.

«Entendez-vous? dit-il. — Oui, ce sont des pasteurs
Rappelant les troupeaux épars sur les hauteurs,
Répondit l'archevêque, ou la voix étouffée
Du nain vert Obéron qui parle avec sa Fée.»

Et l'Empereur poursuit; mais son front soucieux
Est plus sombre et plus noir que l'orage des cieux.
Il craint la trahison, et, tandis qu'il y songe,
Le Cor éclate et meurt, renaît et se prolonge.

«Malheur! c'est mon neveu! malheur! car si Roland
Appelle à son secours, ce doit être en mourant.
Arrière, chevaliers, repassons la montagne!
Tremble encor sous nos pieds, sol trompeur de
    l'Espagne!»

'Two flashes of lightning have shone, then two others again.'
Here they heard the distant sound of the Horn. The astonished Emperor, throwing himself back, halts the bold march of his charger.
'Do you hear?' said he. '— Yes, those are herdsmen calling in the flocks scattered on the heights, answered the archbishop, or the muffled voice of the green dwarf Oberon talking to his fairy queen.'
And the Emperor goes on his way; but his careworn brow is darker and blacker than the storm of the skies. He fears treason, and, while he thinks of it, the Horn bursts forth and dies, is reborn and prolonged.
'Ill luck! it is my nephew! ill luck! for if Roland calls for help, he must be dying. Back, knights, let us pass back over the mountains! Tremble once more beneath our feet, deceitful soil of Spain!'

4

Sur le plus haut des monts s'arrêtent les chevaux;
L'écume les blanchit; sous leurs pieds, Roncevaux
Des feux mourants du jour à peine se colore.
A l'horizon lointain fuit l'étendard du More.

«Turpin, n'as-tu rien vu dans le fond du torrent?
– J'y vois deux chevaliers: l'un mort, l'autre expirant.
Tous deux sont écrasés sous une roche noire;
Le plus fort, dans sa main, élève un Cor d'ivoire,
Son âme en s'exhalant nous appela deux fois.»

Dieu! que le son du Cor est triste au fond des bois!

La Colère de Samson

Le désert est muet, la tente est solitaire.
Quel pasteur courageux la dressa sur la terre
Du sable et des lions? – La nuit n'a pas calmé
La fournaise du jour dont l'air est enflammé.

4

On the very highest of the mountains the horses stop; they are white with foam; beneath their feet Roncesvalles is hardly tinted by the dying fires of day. On the far horizon flees the banner of the Moor.

'Turpin, do you see nothing in the depth of the stream? – I see two knights there: one dead, the other dying. Both are crushed beneath a black rock; the stronger raises an ivory Horn in his hand, his soul in going forth called us twice.'

God! how sad the Horn's sound is in the depth of the woods!

The Wrath of Samson

The desert is dumb, the tent is solitary. What courageous shepherd planted it on the land of sand and lions? Night has not quieted the furnace of the day that heats the air. On the horizon a light wind

Un vent léger s'élève à l'horizon et ride
Les flots de la poussière ainsi qu'un lac limpide.
Le lin blanc de la tente est bercé mollement;
L'œuf d'autruche allumé veille paisiblement,
Des voyageurs voilés intérieure étoile,
Et jette longuement deux ombres sur la toile.

L'une est grande et superbe, et l'autre est à ses pieds:
C'est Dalila, l'esclave, et ses bras sont liés
Aux genoux réunis du maître jeune et grave
Dont la force divine obéit à l'esclave.
Comme un doux léopard elle est souple, et répand
Ses cheveux dénoués aux pieds de son amant.
Ses grands yeux, entr'ouverts comme s'ouvre l'amande,
Sont brûlants du plaisir que son regard demande
Et jettent, par éclats, leurs mobiles lueurs.
Ses bras fins tout mouillés de tièdes sueurs,
Ses pieds voluptueux qui sont croisés sous elle,
Ses flancs plus élancés que ceux de la gazelle,
Pressés de bracelets, d'anneaux, de boucles d'or,
Sont bruns; et, comme il sied aux filles de Hatsor,

rises and wrinkles the waves of dust like a clear lake. The tent's white linen is rocked softly; the lighted ostrich egg, inner star of the veiled travellers, keeps watch peacefully, and throws two elongated shadows on the cloth.

One is great and proud, and the other is at its feet: that is Dalila, the slave, and her arms are bound to the joined knees of her stern young master whose divine strength obeys the slave. She is lithe as a gentle leopard, and spreads her unbound hair at her lover's feet. Her large eyes, half-open as the almond opens, burn with the pleasure that her glance demands, and throw forth their moving lights in a sudden blaze. Her slim arms quite moist with warm sweat, her sensuous feet, which are crossed beneath her, her sides more slender than the gazelle's, clasped with bracelets, rings, and golden buckles, are brown; and, as is fitting for the daughters of Hatsor, both her

Ses deux seins, tout chargés d'amulettes anciennes,
Sont chastement pressés d'étoffes Syriennes.

Les genoux de Samson fortement sont unis
Comme les deux genoux du colosse Anubis.
Elle s'endort sans force et riante et bercée
Par la puissante main sous sa tête placée.
Lui, murmure le chant funèbre et douloureux
Prononcé dans la gorge avec des mots hébreux.
Elle ne comprend pas la parole étrangère,
Mais le chant verse un somme en sa tête légère.

«Une lutte éternelle en tout temps, en tout lieu
Se livre sur la terre, en présence de Dieu,
Entre la bonté d'Homme et la ruse de Femme.
Car la Femme est un être impur de corps et d'âme.

«L'Homme a toujours besoin de caresse et d'amour,
Sa mère l'en abreuve alors qu'il vient au jour,
Et ce bras le premier l'engourdit, le balance
Et lui donne un désir d'amour et d'indolence.
Troublé dans l'action, troublé dans le dessein,
Il rêvera partout à la chaleur du sein,

breasts, loaded with ancient amulets, are chastely held in by Syrian cloths.

Samson's knees are strongly joined like the two knees of the colossus Anubis. She slumbers powerless and laughing and rocked by the powerful hand placed beneath her head. He murmurs the ill-omened and melancholy song pronounced in the throat with Hebrew words. She does not understand the foreign tongue, but the song pours sleep into her light head.

'An eternal struggle in every time and place is carried on on earth, in God's presence, between Man's goodness and the wiles of Woman. For Woman is a being impure in body and soul.

'Man always needs caresses and love, his mother quenches his thirst for them when he comes to the light of day, and this arm is the first to benumb him, to rock him, and give him a desire for love and idleness. Disturbed in his actions, disturbed in his plans, every-where he will dream of the breast's warmth, of night songs, of

Aux chansons de la nuit, aux baisers de l'aurore,
A la lèvre de feu que sa lèvre dévore,
Aux cheveux dénoués qui roulent sur son front,
Et les regrets du lit, en marchant, le suivront.
Il ira dans la ville, et là les vierges folles
Le prendront dans leurs lacs aux premières paroles.
Plus fort il sera né, mieux il sera vaincu,
Car plus le fleuve est grand et plus il est ému.
Quand le combat que Dieu fit pour la créature
Et contre son semblable et contre la Nature
Force l'Homme à chercher un sein où reposer,
Quand ses yeux sont en pleurs, il lui faut un baiser.
Mais il n'a pas encor fini toute sa tâche:
Vient un autre combat plus secret, traître et lâche;
Sous son bras, sur son cœur se livre celui-là;
Et, plus ou moins, la Femme est toujours DALILA.

«Elle rit et triomphe; en sa froideur savante,
Au milieu de ses sœurs elle attend et se vante
De ne rien éprouver des atteintes du feu.
A sa plus belle amie elle en a fait l'aveu:

dawn kisses, of the fiery lip consumed by his own, of unbound hair sweeping his brow, and, while he walks, longings for the bed will follow him. He will go to the town, and there the foolish virgins will take him in their snares at the first word. The stronger he is born, the easier he will be conquered, for the greater the river the more turbulent it is. When the battle, which God made for his creature, both against his fellow and against Nature, forces Man to seek a breast on which to rest, when his eyes are in tears, he must have a kiss. But he has not yet finished all his labour: there comes another battle, more secret, treacherous, and cowardly; this one takes place under his guard, on his heart; and, more or less, the woman is always DALILA.

'She laughs and triumphs; in her knowing coldness, in the midst of her sisters she waits and boasts of feeling nothing of the fire's pangs. She has confessed it to her loveliest friend: "She makes her-

«Elle se fait aimer sans aimer elle-même.
«Un maître lui fait peur. C'est le plaisir qu'elle aime,
«L'Homme est rude et le prend sans savoir le donner.
«Un sacrifice illustre et fait pour étonner
«Rehausse mieux que l'or, aux yeux de ses pareilles,
«La beauté qui produit tant d'étranges merveilles
«Et d'un sang précieux sait arroser ses pas.»

– «Donc ce que j'ai voulu, Seigneur, n'existe pas! –
Celle à qui va l'amour et de qui vient la vie,
Celle-là, par orgueil, se fait notre ennemie.
La Femme est à present pire que dans ces temps
Où, voyant les humains, Dieu dit: «Je me repens!»
Bientôt, se retirant dans un hideux royaume,
La Femme aura Gomorrhe et l'Homme aura Sodome,
Et, se jetant de loin un regard irrité,
Les deux sexes mourront chacun de son côté.

«Eternel! Dieu des forts! vous savez que mon âme
N'avait pour aliment que l'amour d'une femme,
Puisant dans l'amour seul plus de sainte vigueur
Que mes cheveux divins n'en donnaient à mon cœur.

self loved without loving. A master frightens her. It is the pleasure
she loves. Man is rough and takes it without knowing how to give.
A noble sacrifice and one made to astonish is better than gold to
heighten, in the eyes of her fellows, the beauty that causes so many
strange prodigies and knows how to sprinkle her steps with precious
blood."
   – 'So what I have wished for, Lord, does not exist! She to whom
love goes and from whom life comes, she through pride becomes
our enemy. Woman is now worse than in those times when God,
seeing mankind, said: "I repent!" Soon, withdrawing into a
hideous kingdom, Woman will have Gomorrha and Man will have
Sodom, and, throwing angry glances at one another from a distance,
both sexes will die, each by itself.
   'O Eternal! God of the strong! you know that my soul had only
the love of a woman for food, drawing from love alone more holy
strength than my divine hair gave to my heart. – Judge us. – There

— Jugez-nous. — La voilà sur mes pieds endormie!
Trois fois elle a vendu mes secrets et ma vie,
Et trois fois a versé des pleurs fallacieux
Qui n'ont pu me cacher la rage de ses yeux;
Honteuse qu'elle était plus encor qu'étonnée
De se voir découverte ensemble et pardonnée;
Car la bonté de l'Homme est forte, et sa douceur
Écrase, en l'absolvant, l'être faible et menteur.

«Mais enfin je suis las. — J'ai l'âme si pesante
Que mon corps gigantesque et ma tête puissante
Qui soutiennent le poids des colonnes d'airain
Ne la peuvent porter avec tout son chagrin.
Toujours voir serpenter la vipère dorée
Qui se traîne en sa fange et s'y croit ignorée!
Toujours ce compagnon dont le cœur n'est pas sûr,
La Femme, enfant malade et douze fois impur!
Toujours mettre sa force à garder sa colère
Dans son cœur offensé, comme en un sanctuaire
D'où le feu s'échappant irait tout dévorer,
Interdire à ses yeux de voir ou de pleurer,

she is asleep at my feet! Three times she has sold my secrets and my
life, and three times shed deceitful tears which could not hide from
me the rage in her eyes; ashamed as she was, still more than astonished, to see herself both discovered and pardoned at the same time;
for the goodness of Man is strong, and his gentleness crushes, by
pardoning, the feeble, lying creature.

'But after all I am tired. — My soul is so heavy, that my giant body
and powerful head, that bear up the weight of brazen columns, cannot carry it with all its grief. Always to see the gilded viper creeping, dragging itself in its dirt, and thinking itself undiscovered! Always this companion, whose heart is not trustworthy. Woman, a
sick child, and twelve times impure! Always to spend one's strength
in keeping wrath within the offended heart as in a sanctuary whence,
if the fire escaped, it would consume everything, to forbid one's
eyes to see or to weep; it is too much! — God, if he wishes, can

C'est trop! – Dieu, s'il le veut, peut balayer ma cendre.
J'ai donné mon secret, Dalila va le vendre.
Qu'ils seront beaux les pieds de celui qui viendra
Pour m'annoncer la mort! – Ce qui sera, sera!»

Il dit et s'endormit près d'elle jusqu'à l'heure
Où les guerriers, tremblant d'être dans sa demeure,
Payant au poids de l'or chacun de ses cheveux,
Attachèrent ses mains et brulèrent ses yeux,
Le traînèrent sanglant et chargé d'une chaîne
Que douze grands taureaux ne tiraient qu'avec peine,
Le placèrent debout, silencieusement,
Devant Dagon, leur Dieu, qui gémit sourdement
Et deux fois, en tournant, recula sur sa base
Et fit pâlir deux fois ses prêtres en extase;
Allumèrent l'encens, dressèrent un festin
Dont le bruit s'entendait du mont le plus lointain,
Et près de la génisse aux pieds du Dieu tuée
Placèrent Dalila, pâle prostituée,
Couronnée, adorée et reine du repas,
Mais tremblante et disant: «IL NE ME VERRA PAS!»

sweep away my ashes, I have betrayed my secret, Dalila will sell it.
How beautiful will be the feet of him who comes to announce my
death to me! – What has to be, will be!'
    He spoke and slept beside her till the hour when the warriors,
trembling to be in his dwelling, and paying its weight in gold for
each of his hairs, bound his hands and burned out his eyes, dragged
him bleeding and loaded with a chain that twelve great bulls only
pulled with difficulty and placed him standing upright, silently, in
front of Dagon, their God, who groaned hollowly and twice, turning round, tottered upon his plinth and twice made his ecstatic
priests turn pale; then they lighted the incense, prepared a banquet,
whose noise was heard from the furthest mountain, and near the
heifer killed at the feet of the God placed Dalila, the pale prostitute,
crowned, worshipped, and queen of the feast, but trembling and
saying: 'HE WILL NOT SEE ME!'

Terre et Ciel! avez-vous tressailli d'allégresse
Lorsque vous avez vu la menteuse maîtresse
Suivre d'un œil hagard les yeux tachés de sang
Qui cherchaient le soleil d'un regard impuissant,
Et quand enfin Samson, secouant les colonnes
Qui faisaient le soutien des immenses Pylônes,
Écrasa d'un seul coup sous les débris mortels
Ses trois mille ennemis, leurs dieux et leurs autels?
Terre et Ciel! punissez par de telles justices
La trahison ourdie en des amours factices,
Et la délation du secret de nos cœurs
Arraché dans nos bras par des baisers menteurs!

La Bouteille à la mer

Conseil à un jeune homme inconnu

I

COURAGE, ô faible enfant, de qui ma solitude
Reçoit ces chants plaintifs, sans nom, que vous jetez
Sous mes yeux ombragés du camail de l'étude.
Oubliez les enfants par la mort arrêtés;

Earth and Heaven! did you start for joy when you saw the false
mistress with a wild eye follow the bloodstained eyes that sought
the sun with a powerless gaze, and when at last Samson, shaking the
pillars that held up the huge Pylons, crushed with a single blow beneath the deadly ruins his three thousand enemies, their gods, and
their altars?

Earth and Heaven! punish by such acts of justice the treason
plotted in feigned love, and the betrayal of our hearts' secrets, torn
from our arms by lying kisses!

The Bottle in the Sea

Advice to an unknown young man

COURAGE, O weak child, from whom my solitude receives these
plaintive, nameless songs which you throw beneath my eyes
shadowed by study's hood. Forget the children halted by death;

Oubliez Chatterton, Gilbert et Malfilâtre;
De l'œuvre d'avenir saintement idolâtre,
Enfin oubliez l'homme en vous-même. – Écoutez:

2

Quand un grave marin voit que le vent l'emporte
Et que les mâts brisés pendent tous sur le pont,
Que dans son grand duel la mer est la plus forte
Et que par des calculs l'esprit en vain répond;
Que le courant l'écrase et le roule en sa course,
Qu'il est sans gouvernail, et partant sans ressource,
Il se croise les bras dans un calme profond.

3

Il voit les masses d'eau, les toise et les mesure,
Les méprise en sachant qu'il en est écrasé,
Soumet son âme au poids de la matière impure
Et se sent mort ainsi que son vaisseau rasé.
– A de certains moments, l'âme est sans résistance;
Mais le penseur s'isole et n'attend d'assistance
Que de la forte foi dont il est embrasé.

forget Chatterton, Gilbert and Malfilâtre; lastly, while sacredly idol-
izing future achievement, forget the man within yourself. – Listen:
    When a stern sailor sees the wind carrying him away and the
broken masts all hanging over the bridge, that the sea is the stronger
in their great duel, and that it is in vain the mind answers by reckonings; that the current crushes him and rolls him in its course, that he
is without a rudder and hence without help, he folds his arms in a
deep calm.
    He sees the masses of water, scans them, and measures them,
scorns them, while knowing he is overwhelmed by them, submits
his soul to the weight of vile matter and feels himself dead like his
dismasted ship. – At certain moments the soul has no resistance; but
the thinker stands apart and only expects help from the strong faith
with which he is aflame.

4

Dans les heures du soir, le jeune Capitaine
A fait ce qu'il a pu pour le salut des siens.
Nul vaisseau n'apparaît sur la vague lointaine,
La nuit tombe, et le brick court aux rocs indiens.
– Il se résigne, il prie; il se recueille, il pense
A Celui qui soutient les pôles et balance
L'équateur hérissé des longs méridiens.

5

Son sacrifice est fait; mais il faut que la terre
Recueille du travail le pieux monument.
C'est le journal savant, le calcul solitaire,
Plus rare que la perle et que le diamant;
C'est la carte des flots faite dans la tempête,
La carte de l'écueil qui va briser sa tête:
Aux voyageurs futurs sublime testament.

6

Il écrit: «Aujourd'hui, le courant nous entraîne,
Désemparés, perdus, sur la Terre-de-Feu.
Le courant porte à l'est. Notre mort est certaine:
Il faut cingler au nord pour bien passer ce lieu.

In the evening hours the young Captain has done what he could
for the safety of his crew. No vessel appears on the distant wave,
night falls, and the brig runs on the Indian rocks. – He resigns himself and prays; he meditates and thinks of Him who sustains the
poles and sways the equator bristling with long meridians.

His sacrifice is made; but earth must inherit the pious monument
of toil. This is the scholar's journal, the lonely reckoning, rarer
than pearl or diamond; it is the chart of the waves made in the
storm, the chart of the reef that will shatter his head: a sublime testament to future travellers.

He writes: 'To-day we are swept by the tide disabled and lost on
Tierra del Fuego. The tide carries us to the east. Our death is certain: one must stem to the north to pass this place in safety. – En-

– Ci-joint est mon journal, portant quelques études
Des constellations des hautes latitudes.
Qu'il aborde, si c'est la volonté de Dieu!»

7

Puis, immobile et froid, comme le cap des Brumes
Qui sert de sentinelle au détroit Magellan,
Sombre comme ces rocs au front chargé d'écumes,
Ces pics noirs dont chacun porte un deuil castillan,
Il ouvre une bouteille et la choisit très forte,
Tandis que son vaisseau, que le courant emporte,
Tourne en un cercle étroit comme un vol de milan.

8

Il tient dans une main cette vieille compagne,
Ferme, de l'autre main, son flanc noir et terni.
Le cachet porte encor le blason de Champagne,
De la mousse de Reims son col vert est jauni.
D'un regard, le marin en soi-même rappelle
Quel jour il assembla l'équipage autour d'elle,
Pour porter un grand toste au pavillon béni.

closed is my journal, containing some studies of the constellations of high latitudes. Let it reach shore, if it is the will of God!'

Then, motionless and cold, like the Cape of Mists that serves as a sentinel to the Magellan Straits, sombre as those rocks with foam-laden brows, those black peaks each of which wears Castilian mourning, he opens a bottle, choosing a very strong one, while his ship, carried away by the current, turns in a narrow circle like a hawk's flight.

He holds this old companion in one hand and closes with the other its black tarnished side. The seal still bears the badge of Champagne, its green neck is yellow with the foam of Rheims. With a glance the sailor recalls the day he gathered the crew around it to drink a solemn toast to the hallowed flag.

9

On avait mis en panne, et c'était grande fête;
Chaque homme sur son mât tenait le verre en main;
Chacun à son signal se décrouvrit la tête,
Et répondit d'en haut par un hourra soudain.
Le soleil souriant dorait les voiles blanches;
L'air ému répétait ces voix mâles et franches,
Ce noble appel de l'homme à son pays lointain.

10

Après le cri de tous, chacun rêve en silence.
Dans la mousse d'Aï luit l'éclair d'un bonheur;
Tout au fond de son verre il aperçoit la France.
La France est pour chacun ce qu'y laissa son cœur:
L'un y voit son vieux père assis au coin de l'âtre,
Comptant ses jours d'absence; à la table du pâtre,
Il voit sa chaise vide à côté de sa sœur.

11

Un autre y voit Paris, où sa fille penchée
Marque avec le compas tous les souffles de l'air,
Ternit de pleurs la glace où l'aiguille est cachée,
Et cherche à ramener l'aimant avec le fer.

They had heaved to and there was great merry-making; each man on his mast held a glass in his hand; each man uncovered his head at his signal, and answered from aloft by a sudden hurrah. The smiling sun gilded the white sails; the moving air repeated those clear, virile voices, that noble call of man to his distant country.

After the general shout each one silently dreams. In Aï's foam shines the gleam of happiness; right in the bottom of his glass he sees France. France is for each one what his heart left there: one sees his old father seated in the corner of the hearth, counting his days of absence; at the shepherd's table he sees his empty chair beside his sister.

Another sees Paris, where his daughter, stooping over it, records with the compass every breath of air, dulls with tears the glass where the needle is hidden and seeks to lead the magnet back with

Un autre y voit Marseille. Une femme se lève,
Court au port et lui tend un mouchoir de la grève,
Et ne sent pas ses pieds enfoncés dans la mer.

12

Ô superstition des amours ineffables,
Murmures de nos cœurs qui nous semblez des voix,
Calculs de la science, ô décevantes fables!
Pourquoi nous apparaître en un jour tant de fois?
Pourquoi vers l'horizon nous tendre ainsi des pièges?
Espérances roulant comme roulent les neiges;
Globes toujours pétris et fondus sous nos doigts!

13

Où sont-ils à présent? Où sont ces trois cents braves?
Renversés par le vent dans les courants maudits,
Aux harpons indiens ils portent pour épaves
Leurs habits déchirés sur leurs corps refroidis.
Les savants officiers, la hache à la ceinture,
Ont péri les premiers en coupant la mâture;
Ainsi de ces trois cents il n'en reste que dix!

iron. Another sees Marseilles. A woman gets up, runs to the port,
and waves a handkerchief to him from the beach, not feeling her
feet plunging in the sea.

O the superstition of unspeakable loves, murmurs of our hearts
that seem voices to us, reckonings of science, O deceitful fables!
Why appear to us so many times in one day? Why lay snares for us
on the horizon in this way? Hopes rolling as the snows roll; spheres
ever moulded and melting beneath our fingers!

Where are they now? Where are these three hundred brave men?
Thrown by the wind into the accursed tides, they carry for flotsam
to the Indian harpoons the torn clothes on their chilled bodies. The
skilful officers, axes at their belts, died first cutting away the masts;
so of these three hundred there only remain ten!

14

Le Capitaine encor jette un regard au pôle
Dont il vient d'explorer les détroits inconnus:
L'eau monte à ses genoux et frappe son épaule;
Il peut lever au ciel l'un de ses deux bras nus.
Son navire est coulé, sa vie est révolue:
Il lance la Bouteille à la mer, et salue
Les jours de l'avenir qui pour lui sont venus.

15

Il sourit en songeant que ce fragile verre
Portera sa pensée et son nom jusqu'au port,
Que d'une île inconnue il agrandit la terre,
Qu'il marque un nouvel astre et le confie au sort,
Que Dieu peut bien permettre à des eaux insensées
De perdre des vaisseaux, mais non pas des pensées,
Et qu'avec un flacon il a vaincu la mort.

16

Tout est dit. A présent, que Dieu lui soit en aide!
Sur le brick englouti l'onde a pris son niveau.
Au large flot de l'est le flot de l'ouest succède,
Et la Bouteille y roule en son vaste berceau.
Seule dans l'Océan, la frêle passagère

The Captain once again throws a glance towards the pole, whose unknown straits he has been exploring: the water rises to his knees and strikes his shoulder; he can raise one of his bare arms to the sky. His ship is sunk, his life is past: he hurls the Bottle into the sea, and salutes the days to come which have arrived for him.

He smiles thinking that this brittle glass will bear his thoughts and his name to harbour, that he enlarges the earth by an unknown island, that he notes a new star and entrusts it to fate, that God may well allow the wild waters to destroy ships, but not thoughts, and that with a flask he has conquered death.

Everything is said. Now God be his help! The sea has become evel again over the brig it swallowed up. The wave from the west follows on the broad wave from the east, and the Bottle wallows there in its vast cradle. Alone in the ocean the frail traveller has no

N'a pas pour se guider une brise légère;
— Mais elle vient de l'arche et porte le rameau.

17

Les courants l'emportaient, les glaçons la retiennent
Et la couvrent des plis d'un épais manteau blanc.
Les noirs chevaux de mer la heurtent, puis reviennent
La flairer avec crainte, et passent en soufflant.
Elle attend que l'été, changeant ses destinées,
Vienne ouvrir le rempart des glaces obstinées,
Et vers la ligne ardente elle monte en roulant.

18

Un jour, tout était calme, et la mer Pacifique,
Par ses vagues d'azur, d'or et de diamant,
Renvoyait ses splendeurs au soleil du tropique.
Un navire y passait majestueusement.
Il a vu la Bouteille aux gens de mer sacrée:
Il couvre de signaux sa flamme diaprée,
Lance un canot en mer et s'arrête un moment.

light breeze to guide it; but it comes from the ark and bears the
olive-branch.

The tides bore it away, the ice-floes keep it back and cover it with
the folds of a thick white cloak. The black sea-horses knock against
it, then return to sniff it fearfully and pass on snorting. It waits until
summer, changing its fate, comes to open the barrier of the stub-
born ice, and ascends pitching towards the burning line.

One day everything was calm, and the Pacific Ocean reflected the
splendours of the tropical sun from its waves of blue, gold, and diamond. A ship was passing majestically by. She has seen the Bottle,
a sacred object for people of the sea: she covers her multi-coloured
pennon with signals, launches a boat in the sea, and heaves to for a
moment.

19

Mais on entend au loin le canon des corsaires;
Le négrier va fuir s'il peut prendre le vent.
Alerte! et coulez bas ces sombres adversaires!
Noyez or et bourreaux du couchant au levant!
La frégate reprend ses canots et les jette
En son sein, comme fait la sarigue inquiète,
Et par voile et vapeur vole et roule en avant.

20

Seule dans l'Océan, seule toujours! – Perdue
Comme un point invisible en un mouvant désert,
L'aventurière passe errant dans l'étendue,
Et voit tel cap secret qui n'est pas découvert.
Tremblante voyageuse à flotter condamnée,
Elle sent sur son col que depuis une année
L'algue et les goémons lui font un manteau vert.

21

Un soir enfin, les vents qui soufflent des Florides
L'entraînent vers la France et ses bords pluvieux.
Un pêcheur accroupi sous des rochers arides
Tire dans ses filets le flacon précieux.

But far off the pirates' cannon is heard; the slaver is going to flee if she can take the wind. Look out! and sink those dark enemies deep! Drown gold and torturers from the west to the east! The frigate takes up her boats again and throws them into her bosom, as the opossum does with its little ones when disturbed, and by sail and steam she flies and rolls forward.

Alone in the Ocean, always alone! – Lost like an invisible speck in a moving desert, the adventurer passes on wandering in the expanse, and sees some secret undiscovered cape. The trembling voyager, condemned to float on, feels hanging on its neck the green cloak, that for a year algae and seaweeds have made for it.

One evening, at last, the winds that blow from Florida sweep it towards France and her rainy shores. A fisherman squatting beneath barren rocks draws the precious flagon up in his nets. He runs, seeks

Il court, cherche un savant et lui montre sa prise,
Et, sans l'oser ouvrir, demande qu'on lui dise
Quel est cet élixir noir et mystérieux.

22

Quel est cet elixir! Pêcheur, c'est la science,
C'est l'élixir divin que boivent les esprits,
Trésor de la pensée et de l'expérience,
Et si tes lourds filets, ô pêcheur, avaient pris
L'or qui toujours serpente aux veines du Mexique,
Les diamants de l'Inde et les perles d'Afrique,
Ton labeur de ce jour aurait eu moins de prix.

23

Regarde. – Quelle joie ardente et sérieuse!
Une gloire de plus luit sur la nation.
Le canon tout-puissant et la cloche pieuse
Font sur les toits tremblants bondir l'émotion.
Aux héros du savoir plus qu'à ceux des batailles
On va faire aujourd'hui de grandes funérailles.
Lis ce mot sur les murs: «Commémoration!»

out a scholar, and shows him his catch, and, without daring to open
it, asks to be told what this dark mysterious elixir is.

What is this elixir! Fisherman, it is knowledge, it is the divine
elixir which minds drink, the treasure of thought and experience,
and if your heavy nets, O fisherman, had taken the gold that still
crawls in the veins of Mexico, the diamonds of India and the pearls
of Africa, this day's toil would have been worth less.

Look. – What solemn ardent joy! One more fame shines on the
nation. The all-powerful cannon and the pious bell make emotion
leap over the trembling roofs. A great funeral will be made to-day
for the heroes of knowledge more than for those of battles. Read
this word on the walls: 'Commemoration!'

24

Souvenir éternel! gloire à la découverte
Dans l'homme ou la nature égaux en profondeur,
Dans le Juste et le Bien, source à peine entr'ouverte,
Dans l'Art inépuisable, abîme de splendeur!
Qu'importe oubli, morsure, injustice insensée,
Glaces et tourbillons de notre traversée?
Sur la pierre des morts croît l'arbre de grandeur.

25

Cet arbre est le plus beau de la terre promise,
C'est votre phare à tous, penseurs laborieux!
Voguez sans jamais craindre ou les flots ou la brise
Pour tout trésor scellé du cachet précieux.
L'or pur doit surnager, et sa gloire est certaine.
Dites en souriant comme ce capitaine:
«Qu'il aborde, si c'est la volonté des Dieux!»

26

Le vrai Dieu, le Dieu fort est le Dieu des idées!
Sur nos fronts où le germe est jeté par le sort,
Répandons le savoir en fécondes ondées;
Puis, recueillant le fruit tel que de l'âme il sort,

Eternal memory! honour to discovery of man or nature, equal in depth, of the Just or the Good, a spring hardly half-open, of inexhaustible Art, abyss of splendour! What do forgetfulness, wounds, or senseless injustice, the ice-floes and whirlwinds of our ocean crossing, matter? On the tombstone of the dead the tree of greatness grows.

This tree is the fairest of the promised land, it is a beacon for all of you, laborious thinkers! Sail without ever fearing either the waves or the breeze, stamped with the precious seal for your only treasure. The pure gold must float and its fame is certain. Say smiling like this Captain: 'Let it reach shore, if it is the will of the Gods!'

The true God, the strong God is the God of ideas! On our brows where the seed is thrown by fate let us spread knowledge in fertile showers; then, gathering the fruit as it comes forth from the soul,

Tout empreint du parfum des saintes solitudes,
Jetons l'œuvre à la mer, la mer des multitudes:
— Dieu la prendra du doigt pour la conduire au port.

Le Mont des Oliviers

I

ALORS il était nuit, et Jésus marchait seul,
Vêtu de blanc ainsi qu'un mort de son linceul;
Les disciples dormaient au pied de la colline.
Parmi les oliviers, qu'un vent sinistre incline,
Jésus marche à grands pas en frissonant comme eux;
Triste jusqu'à la mort, l'œil sombre et ténébreux,
Le front baissé, croisant les deux bras sur sa robe
Comme un voleur de nuit cachant ce qu'il dérobe;
Connaissant les rochers mieux qu'un sentier uni,
Il s'arrête en un lieu nommé Gethsémani.
Il se courbe, à genoux, le front contre la terre;
Puis regarde le ciel en appelant: «Mon Père!»

marked by the perfume of holy solitudes, let us throw the work into the sea, the sea of the masses: — God will take it with his finger to bring it to port.

The Mount of Olives

I

THEN it was night, and Jesus walked alone, dressed in white like a dead man in his shroud; the disciples were asleep at the foot of the hill. Among the olives bent by a dismal wind Jesus walks with long strides shivering like them; sad unto death, his eye dark and shadowy, his brow bent, crossing both arms over his gown like a thief of the night hiding what he steals; knowing the rocks better than a beaten path, he halts in a place called Gethsemane. He bows on his knees, his forehead against the ground; then looks at the sky and calls: 'My Father!'

– Mais le ciel reste noir, et Dieu ne répond pas.
Il se lève étonné, marche encore à grands pas,
Froissant les oliviers qui tremblent. Froide et lente
Découle de sa tête une sueur sanglante.
Il recule, il descend, il crie avec effroi:
«Ne pourriez-vous prier et veiller avec moi?»
Mais un sommeil de mort accable les apôtres.
Pierre à la voix du maître est sourd comme les autres.
Le Fils de l'Homme alors remonte lentement;
Comme un pasteur d'Égypte, il cherche au firmament
Si l'Ange ne luit pas au fond de quelque étoile.
Mais un nuage en deuil s'étend comme le voile
D'une veuve, et ses plis entourent le désert.
Jésus, se rappelant ce qu'il avait souffert
Depuis trente-trois ans, devint homme, et la crainte
Serra son cœur mortel d'une invincible étreinte.
Il eut froid. Vainement il appela trois fois:
«Mon Père!» – Le vent seul répondit à sa voix.
Il tomba sur le sable assis et, dans sa peine,
Eut sur le monde et l'homme une pensée humaine.

But the sky remains dark and God does not answer. He rises
astonished, again walks with long strides, brushing the trembling
olives. A bloody sweat flows down from his head cold and slow.
He draws back, he descends and shouts in terror: 'Could you not
pray and watch with me?'
But a deathly sleep overwhelms the apostles. Peter is deaf to his
master's voice, like the others. Then the Son of Man climbs up
again slowly; like an Egyptian shepherd, he searches the sky to see
if the Angel does not shine in the depth of some star. But a cloud
the colour of mourning spreads out like a widow's veil, and its folds
enclose the desert. Jesus, remembering what he had suffered for
thirty-three years, became a man, and fear squeezed his mortal
heart with an unconquerable grip. He was cold. In vain he called
three times: 'My Father!' – The wind alone answered his voice. He
fell sitting on the sand, and, in his agony, had mortal thoughts on
the world and on man.

– Et la Terre trembla, sentant la pesanteur
Du Sauveur qui tombait aux pieds du Créateur.

2

Jésus disait : «Ô Père, encor laissez-moi vivre!
Avant le dernier mot ne ferme pas mon livre!
Ne sens-tu pas le monde et tout le genre humain
Qui souffre avec ma chair et frémit dans ta main?
C'est que la Terre a peur de rester seule et veuve,
Quand meurt celui qui dit une parole neuve;
Et que tu n'as laissé dans son sein desséché
Tomber qu'un mot du ciel par ma bouche épanché.
Mais ce mot est si pur, et sa douceur est telle,
Qu'il a comme enivré la famille mortelle
D'une goutte de vie et de divinité,
Lorsqu'en ouvrant les bras j'ai dit: «Fraternité.»

«Père, oh! si j'ai rempli mon douloureux message,
Si j'ai caché le Dieu sous la face du Sage,
Du Sacrifice humain si j'ai changé le prix,
Pour l'offrande des corps recevant les esprits,

And the Earth trembled, feeling the weight of the Saviour falling at the Creator's feet.

2

Jesus said: 'O Father, still let me live! Do not close my book before the last word! Do you not feel the world and the whole of mankind suffering with my flesh and shuddering in your hand? Because Earth is afraid to remain solitary and widowed when the man dies who speaks a new word; and because you have let only one word from Heaven, given forth by my mouth, fall on its withered breast. But this word is so pure and its sweetness is such that it almost intoxicated the human family with a drop of life and divinity, when opening my arms I said: "Fraternity."

'Father, oh! if I have fulfilled my grievous message, if I have hidden the God beneath the face of the Sage, if I have changed the value of human Sacrifice, receiving spirits for the offering of bodies,

Substituant partout aux choses le symbole,
La parole au combat, comme au trésor l'obole,
Aux flots rouges du sang les flots vermeils du vin,
Aux membres de la chair le pain blanc sans levain;
Si j'ai coupé les temps en deux parts, l'une esclave
Et l'autre libre; – au nom du Passé que je lave
Par le Sang de mon corps qui souffre et va finir:
Versons-en la moitié pour laver l'avenir!
Père Libérateur! jette aujourd'hui, d'avance,
La moitié de ce sang d'amour et d'innocence
Sur la tête de ceux qui viendront en disant:
«Il est permis pour tous de tuer l'innocent.»
Nous savons qu'il naîtra, dans le lointain des âges,
Des dominateurs durs escortés de faux sages,
Qui troubleront l'esprit de chaque nation
En donnant un faux sens à ma rédemption.
– Hélas! je parle encor que déjà ma parole
Est tournée en poison dans chaque parabole;
Éloigne ce calice impur et plus amer
Que le fiel, ou l'absinthe, ou les eaux de la mer.
Les verges qui viendront, la couronne d'épine,
Les clous des mains, la lance au fond de ma poitrine,

everywhere substituting the symbol for things, the word for the
battle, the obol for the treasure, wine's crimson waves for the red
waves of blood, the white unleavened bread for the limbs of the flesh;
if I divided time into two parts, the one enslaved and the other
free; – in the name of the Past which I wash with the Blood of my
body suffering and about to die: let us pour the half of it to wash
the future! Liberating Father! to-day cast in advance half of this
blood of love and innocence on their head who shall come saying:
"It is lawful for all to kill the innocent." We know that in the distance of ages there will be born harsh oppressors escorted by false
philosophers, who will disturb every nation's spirit by giving a
false meaning to my redemption.

'Alas! I speak though already my word is turned into poison in
every parable; take away this impure cup bitterer than gall or worm-
wood or the waters of the sea. The rods to come, the crown of
thorns, the nails for the hands, the lance in the depth of my breast, in

Enfin toute la croix qui se dresse et m'attend,
N'ont rien, mon Père, oh! rien qui m'épouvante autant!
Quand les Dieux veulent bien s'abattre sur les mondes,
Ils n'y doivent laisser que des traces profondes,
Et si j'ai mis le pied sur ce globe incomplet
Dont le gémissement sans repos m'appelait,
C'était pour y laisser deux Anges à ma place
De qui la race humaine aurait baisé la trace,
La Certitude heureuse et l'Espoir confiant
Qui, dans le Paradis, marchent en souriant.
Mais je vais la quitter, cette indigente terre,
N'ayant que soulevé ce manteau de misère
Qui l'entoure à grands plis, drap lugubre et fatal,
Que d'un bout tient le Doute et de l'autre le Mal.

«Mal et Doute! En un mot je puis les mettre en poudre;
Vous les aviez prévus, laissez-moi vous absoudre
De les avoir permis. – C'est l'accusation
Qui pèse de partout sur la Création! –
Sur son tombeau désert faisons monter Lazare.
Du grand secret des morts qu'il ne soit plus avare

short, the whole cross which is raised and awaits me, have nothing,
my Father, oh! nothing which frightens me so much! When Gods
intend to swoop upon worlds, they must only leave deep prints behind, and if I set foot on this imperfect sphere, whose restless groaning called to me, it was to leave two Angels in my place whose footprints the human race would have kissed, happy Certainty and confident Hope who walk smiling in Paradise. But I am going to leave
this wretched earth, having only raised the cloak of misery sur-
rounding it in great folds, the gloomy and fatal cloth whose one end
is held by Doubt and the other by Evil.

'Evil and Doubt! With one word I can reduce them to dust; you
had foreseen them, let me absolve you from having allowed them. –
This is the indictment that weighs everywhere on the Creation! –
Let us make Lazarus climb on his desert tomb. Let him no longer

Et de ce qu'il a vu donnons-lui souvenir:
Qu'il parle. – Ce qui dure et ce qui doit finir,
Ce qu'a mis le Seigneur au cœur de la Nature,
Ce qu'elle prend et donne à toute créature,
Quels sont, avec le Ciel, ses muets entretiens,
Son amour ineffable et ses chastes liens;
Comment tout s'y détruit et tout s'y renouvelle,
Pourquoi ce qui s'y cache et ce qui s'y révèle;
Si les astres des cieux tour à tour éprouvés
Sont comme celui-ci coupables et sauvés;
Si la Terre est pour eux ou s'ils sont pour la Terre;
Ce qu'a de vrai la fable et de clair le mystère,
D'ignorant le savoir et de faux la raison;
Pourquoi l'âme est liée en sa faible prison;
Et pourquoi nul sentier entre deux larges voies,
Entre l'ennui du calme et des paisibles joies
Et la rage sans fin des vagues passions,
Entre la léthargie et les convulsions;
Et pourquoi pend la Mort comme une sombre épée
Attristant la Nature à tout moment frappée; –

be sparing of the great secret of the dead and let us grant him
memory of what he has seen: let him speak.

'What lasts and what must end, what the Lord has placed at the
heart of Nature, what she takes and gives to every created thing,
what are her silent conversations with Heaven, her unspeakable
love and her chaste bonds; how everything there is destroyed and
renewed, the reason for what is hidden and revealed; if the stars of
the sky put to the test in turn are like this one guilty and redeemed;
if Earth is made for them or they are made for the Earth; what is
true in fable and clear in mystery, ignorant in knowledge and false
in reason; why the soul is bound in her weak prison; and why there
is no path between two broad roads, between the tedium of tranquillity and peaceful pleasures and the endless fury of random passions, between lethargy and convulsions; and why Death hangs like
a dark sword afflicting Nature and striking it at every moment; –

Si le Juste et le Bien, si l'Injuste et le Mal
Sont de vils accidents en un cercle fatal,
Ou si de l'univers ils sont les deux grands pôles,
Soutenant Terre et Cieux sur leurs vastes épaules;
Et pourquoi les Esprits du mal sont triomphants
Des maux immérités de la mort des enfants;
– Et si les Nations sont des Femmes guidées
Par les étoiles d'or des divines idées
Ou de folles enfants sans lampes dans la nuit,
Se heurtant et pleurant et que rien ne conduit;
– Et si, lorsque des temps l'horloge périssable
Aura jusqu'au dernier versé ses grains de sable,
Un regard de vos yeux, un cri de votre voix,
Un soupir de mon cœur, un signe de ma croix,
Pourra faire ouvrir l'ongle aux Peines Eternelles,
Lâcher leur proie humaine et reployer leurs ailes:
– Tout sera révélé dès que l'homme saura
De quels lieux il arrive et dans quels il ira.»

3

Ainsi le divin Fils parlait au divin Père.
Il se prosterne encore, il attend, il espère. ...

if Justice and Good, Injustice and Evil are base accidents in a fatal
circle, or if they are the two great poles of the universe, bearing
Earth and Heaven on their huge shoulders; and why evil Spirits
triumph over the undeserved ills of the death of children; – and if
Nations are Women guided by the golden stars of the divine ideas
or foolish children without lamps in the night, knocking themselves
and weeping and led by nothing; – and if, when the perishable glass
of time has poured its grains of sand to the last, a glance of your
eyes, a cry of your voice, a sigh of my heart, a sign of my cross, can
make the eternal Torments open their claws, leave their human prey
and fold their wings again: – all will be revealed as soon as man
knows from what place he comes and to what place he will go.'

3

So the divine Son spoke to the divine Father. He bows himself
again, he waits and hopes. ... But he gives up and says: 'May your

47

Mais il renonce et dit: «Que votre volonté
Soit faite et non la mienne, et pour l'Éternité!»
Une terreur profonde, une angoisse infinie
Redoublent sa torture et sa lente agonie.
Il regarde longtemps, longtemps cherche sans voir.
Comme un marbre de deuil tout le ciel était noir;
La Terre sans clartés, sans astre et sans aurore,
Et sans clartés de l'âme ainsi qu'elle est encore,
Frémissait. – Dans le bois il entendit des pas,
Et puis il vit rôder la torche de Judas.

LE SILENCE

S'il est vrai qu'au Jardin sacré des Écritures,
Le Fils de l'Homme ait dit ce qu'on voit rapporté;
Muet, aveugle et sourd au cri des créatures,
Si le Ciel nous laissa comme un monde avorté,
Le juste opposera le dédain à l'absence
Et ne répondra plus que par un froid silence
Au silence éternel de la Divinité.

will be done and not mine, and for Eternity!' A deep terror, an
infinite anguish redouble his torture and his slow agony. For a long
time he gazes, for a long time searches without seeing. The whole
sky was black, like a funeral marble; the Earth without light, without stars, and without dawn, and without light of the soul, as it still
is, trembled. – In the wood he heard steps, and then he saw the
torch of Judas prowling.

THE SILENCE

If it is true that, in the holy Garden of the Scriptures, the Son of
Man said what we see reported; if Heaven, dumb, blind, and deaf to
the creatures' cry, left us like an aborted world, the just man will
oppose absence with disdain and will only reply by cold silence to
the eternal silence of the Deity.

L'Esprit pur

A Éva

1

Si l'orgueil prend ton cœur quand le peuple me nomme,
Que de mes livres seuls te vienne ta fierté.
J'ai mis sur le cimier doré du gentilhomme
Une plume de fer qui n'est pas sans beauté.
J'ai fait illustre un nom qu'on m'a transmis sans gloire.
Qu'il soit ancien, qu'importe? Il n'aura de mémoire
Que du jour seulement où mon front l'a porté.

2

Dans le caveau des miens plongeant mes pas nocturnes,
J'ai compté mes aïeux, suivant leur vieille loi.
J'ouvris leurs parchemins, je fouillai dans leurs urnes
Empreintes sur le flanc des sceaux de chaque Roi.
A peine une étincelle a relui dans leur cendre.
C'est en vain que d'eux tous le sang m'a fait descendre;
Si j'écris leur histoire, ils descendront de moi.

The Pure Spirit

To Eva

If pride takes your heart when the people name me, let your arrogance come from my books alone. I have placed on the gentleman's gilded crest an iron plume that is not without beauty. I have made illustrious a name that was left to me without fame. What does it matter that it is old? It will only be remembered from the day my brow bore it.

Plunging my nightly steps into my people's vault, I counted my ancestors according to their ancient law. I opened their parchments, I ransacked their caskets stamped on the side with the seals of every King. Hardly a spark shone in their ashes. In vain my blood has made me descend from all of them; if I write their history, they will descend from me.

3

Ils furent opulents, seigneurs de vastes terres,
Grands chasseurs devant Dieu, comme Nemrod, jaloux
Des beaux cerfs qu'ils lançaient des bois héréditaires
Jusqu'où voulait la mort les livrer à leurs coups;
Suivant leur forte meute à travers deux provinces,
Coupant les chiens du Roi, déroutant ceux des Princes,
Forçant les sangliers et détruisant les loups;

4

Galants guerriers sur terre et sur mer, se montrèrent
Gens d'honneur en tout temps comme en tous lieux,
      cherchant
De la Chine au Pérou les Anglais, qu'ils brûlèrent
Sur l'eau qu'ils écumaient du Levant au Couchant;
Puis, sur leur talon rouge, en quittant les batailles,
Parfumés et blessés revenaient à Versailles
Jaser à l'Œil-de-bœuf avant de voir leur champ.

5

Mais les champs de la Beauce avaient leurs cœurs, leurs
      âmes,
Leurs soins. Ils les peuplaient d'innombrables garçons,

They were rich, the lords of vast lands, great hunters before God, like Nimrod, jealous of the lovely stags they started from their hereditary woods to where death would deliver them to their blows; following their strong cry of hounds across two provinces, cutting off the King's hounds, turning those of the Princes, forcing the boars and exterminating the wolves;

Gallant warriors on land and sea, they showed themselves men of honour in all times and places, from China to Peru searching out the English, burning them on the water they scoured from East to West; then on their red heels, leaving battles behind, they returned perfumed and wounded to Versailles to chat at the Œil-de-bœuf before going to see their fields.

But the fields of the Beauce had their hearts, their souls, their care. They populated them with innumerable boys, with daughters

De filles qu'ils donnaient aux chevaliers pour femmes,
Dignes de suivre en tout l'exemple et les leçons;
Simples et satisfaits si chacun de leur race
Apposait saint Louis en croix sur sa cuirasse,
Comme leurs vieux portraits qu'aux murs noirs nous
    plaçons.

6

Mais aucun, au sortir d'une rude campagne,
Ne sut se recueillir, quitter le destrier,
Dételer pour un jour ses palefrois d'Espagne,
Ni des coursiers de chasse enlever l'étrier
Pour graver quelque page et dire en quelque livre
Comme son temps vivait et comment il sut vivre,
Dès qu'ils n'agissaient plus, se hâtant d'oublier.

7

Tous sont morts en laissant leur nom sans auréole,
Mais sur le Livre d'or voilà qu'il est écrit,
Disant: «Ici passaient deux races de la Gaule
Dont le dernier vivant monte au temple et s'inscrit,
Non sur l'obscur amas des vieux noms inutiles,
Des orgueilleux méchants et des riches futiles,
Mais sur le pur tableau des titres de l'ESPRIT.»

whom they gave to the knights for wives, worthy to follow their example and lessons in all things; simply satisfied if each one of their race placed St Louis in a cross on his breastplate, like their old portraits which we hang on blackened walls.

But none, coming from a hard campaign, knew how to lose himself in meditation, leave his charger, unsaddle his Spanish palfreys for a day, or take the stirrups from his hunting horses to engrave some page and say in some book how his time lived and how he lived himself; as soon as they ceased to act, they hurried to forget.

They are all dead, leaving their name without fame, but in the Golden Book here is what is written, saying: 'Here two races of Gaul passed by, whose last descendant climbs to the temple and inscribes his name, not in the obscure heap of useless old names, of proud evildoers and the futile rich, but on the pure tablet of the SPIRIT's title-deeds.'

8

Ton règne est arrivé, PUR ESPRIT, roi du monde!
Quand ton aile d'azur dans la nuit nous surprit,
Déesse de nos mœurs, la guerre vagabonde
Régnait sur nos aïeux. Aujourd'hui, c'est l'ÉCRIT,
L'ÉCRIT UNIVERSEL, parfois impérissable,
Que tu graves au marbre ou traces sur le sable,
Colombe au bec d'airain! VISIBLE SAINT-ESPRIT!

9

Seul et dernier anneau de deux chaînes brisées,
Je reste. Et je soutiens encor dans les hauteurs,
Parmi les maîtres purs de nos savants musées,
L'IDÉAL du poète et des graves penseurs.
J'éprouve sa durée en vingt ans de silence,
Et toujours, d'âge en âge, encor je vois la France
Contempler mes tableaux et leur jeter des fleurs.

10

Jeune postérité d'un vivant qui vous aime!
Mes traits dans vos regards ne sont pas effacés;
Je peux en ce miroir *me connaître moi-même*,
Juge toujours nouveau de nos travaux passés!

Your kingdom has come, PURE SPIRIT, king of the world!
When your blue wing surprised us in the night, goddess of our
ways, roving war reigned over our ancestors. To-day it is the
WRITTEN WORD, the UNIVERSAL WRITTEN WORD, sometimes
imperishable, that you engrave in marble or trace on sand, dove
with the brazen beak! VISIBLE HOLY SPIRIT!

Sole and last ring of two broken chains, I remain. And still I bear
up on the heights, amid the pure masters of our learned museums,
the poet's and solemn thinkers' IDEAL. In twenty years of silence
I test its duration, and ever from age to age I see France gaze on my
pictures and throw flowers on them.

Young posterity of a man who loves you! In your gaze my features are not blotted out; in this mirror, this ever-new judge of our
past works, I can *know myself*! Waves of friends reborn! May my

Flots d'amis renaissants! Puissent mes destinées
Vous amener à moi, de dix en dix années,
Attentifs à mon œuvre, et pour moi c'est assez!

VICTOR HUGO

Puisque j'ai mis ma lèvre …

PUISQUE j'ai mis ma lèvre à ta coupe encor pleine,
Puisque j'ai dans tes mains posé mon front pâli,
Puisque j'ai respiré parfois la douce haleine
De ton âme, parfum dans l'ombre enseveli,

Puisqu'il me fut donné de t'entendre me dire
Les mots où se répand le cœur mystérieux,
Puisque j'ai vu pleurer, puisque j'ai vu sourire
Ta bouche sur ma bouche et tes yeux sur mes yeux;

Puisque j'ai vu briller sur ma tête ravie
Un rayon de ton astre, hélas! voilé toujours,
Puisque j'ai vu tomber dans l'onde de ma vie
Une feuille de rose arrachée à tes jours,

fate lead you to me, from decade to decade, attentive to my work,
and that is enough for me!

Since I have put my lip …

SINCE I have put my lip to your still brimming cup, since I have
placed my pale brow in your hands, since I have sometimes breathed
the sweet breath of your soul, a perfume buried in the shadow,

Since it was given to me to hear you say the words in which the
mysterious heart pours itself forth, since I have seen weep, since I
have seen smile your mouth on my mouth and your eyes on my
eyes;

Since over my enraptured head I have seen a beam of your star
shine, alas! always veiled, since I have seen a rose leaf snatched from
your days fall into my life's sea,

Je puis maintenant dire aux rapides années:
– Passez! passez toujours! je n'ai plus à vieillir!
Allez-vous-en avec vos fleurs toutes fanées;
J'ai dans l'âme une fleur que nul ne peut cueillir!

Votre aile en le heurtant ne fera rien répandre
Du vase où je m'abreuve et que j'ai bien rempli.
Mon âme a plus de feu que vous n'avez de cendre!
Mon cœur a plus d'amour que vous n'avez d'oubli!

Nuits de Juin

L'été, lorsque le jour a fui, de fleurs couverte
La plaine verse au loin un parfum enivrant;
Les yeux fermés, l'oreille aux rumeurs entr'ouverte,
On ne dort qu'à demi d'un sommeil transparent.

Les astres sont plus purs, l'ombre paraît meilleure;
Un vague demi-jour teint le dôme éternel;
Et l'aube douce et pâle, en attendant son heure,
Semble toute la nuit errer au bas du ciel.

Now I can say to the swift years: – pass by! ever pass by! I have
nothing more to age! Away with you and your withered flowers;
in my soul I have a flower that none may pluck!
 Your wing brushing it will cause nothing to spill from the cup
where I quench my thirst and that I have filled right up. My soul
has more fire than you have ashes! My heart has more love than you
have forgetfulness!

June Nights

In summer, when day has fled, the plain covered with flowers pours
out far away an intoxicating scent; eyes shut, ears half open to
noises, we only half sleep in a transparent slumber.
 The stars are purer, the shade seems pleasanter; a hazy half-day
colours the eternal dome; and the sweet pale dawn awaiting her
hour seems to wander all night at the bottom of the sky.

L'Expiation

2

WATERLOO! Waterloo! Waterloo! morne plaine!
Comme une onde qui bout dans une urne trop pleine,
Dans ton cirque de bois, de coteaux, de vallons,
La pâle mort mêlait les sombres bataillons.
D'un côté c'est l'Europe et de l'autre la France.
Choc sanglant! des héros Dieu trompait l'espérance;
Tu désertais, victoire, et le sort était las.
Ô Waterloo! je pleure et je m'arrête, hélas!
Car ces derniers soldats de la dernière guerre
Furent grands; ils avaient vaincu toute la terre,
Chassé vingt rois, passé les Alpes et le Rhin,
Et leur âme chantait dans les clairons d'airain!

Le soir tombait; la lutte était ardente et noire.
Il avait l'offensive et presque la victoire;
Il tenait Wellington acculé sur un bois.
Sa lunette à la main, il observait parfois

The Atonement

2

WATERLOO! Waterloo! Waterloo! dismal plain! Like a sea boiling in too full a cauldron, in your arena of woods, of hills, of valleys, pale death mingled the dark battalions. On one side is Europe, on the other France. A bloody clash! God deceived the heroes' hopes; victory, you deserted, and fate was tired. O Waterloo! I weep and halt, alas! For those last soldiers of the last war were great; they had conquered the whole earth, expelled twenty kings, crossed the Alps and the Rhine, and their soul sung in the brazen trumpets!

Evening was falling; the struggle was fierce and dark. He had the offensive and almost victory; he held Wellington pinned down against a wood. His spy-glass in his hand, sometimes he watched

Le centre du combat, point obscur où tressaille
La mêlée, effroyable et vivante broussaille,
Et parfois l'horizon, sombre comme la mer.
Soudain, joyeux, il dit: Grouchy! – C'était Blücher.
L'espoir changea de camp, le combat changea d'âme,
La mêlée en hurlant grandit comme une flamme.
La batterie anglaise écrasa nos carrés.
La plaine, où frissonnaient nos drapeaux déchirés,
Ne fut plus, dans les cris des mourants qu'on égorge,
Qu'un gouffre flamboyant, rouge comme une forge;
Gouffre où les régiments comme des pans de murs
Tombaient, où se couchaient comme des épis mûrs
Les hauts tambour-majors aux panaches énormes,
Où l'on entrevoyait des blessures difformes!
Carnage affreux! moment fatal! L'homme inquiet
Sentit que la bataille entre ses mains pliait.
Derrière un mamelon la garde était massée.
La garde, espoir suprême et suprême pensée!
– Allons! faites donner la garde, cria-t-il. –
Et, lanciers, grenadiers aux guêtres de coutil,

the centre of the fight, the hidden point where the hand-to-hand fighting trembled like a terrible living thicket, and sometimes the horizon dark as the sea. Suddenly he said joyfully: Grouchy! – It was Blücher.

Hope changed sides, the battle changed its spirit, howling the hand-to-hand fighting grew like a flame. The English artillery crushed our squares. The plain where our torn flags shivered, in the shrieks of the slaughtered dying, was no more than a flaming gulf red as a forge; a gulf where regiments fell like slabs of walls, where the tall drum-majors with their vast plumes lay down like ears of ripe corn, where monstrous wounds were glimpsed! A frightful slaughter! Fatal moment! Anxiously the man felt the battle bending beneath his hands. Behind a mound the guard was massed, the guard, his last hope and last thought! 'Come! throw in the guard,' he cried. –

And lancers, grenadiers with canvas gaiters, dragoons that Rome

Dragons que Rome eût pris pour des légionnaires,
Cuirassiers, canonniers qui traînaient des tonnerres,
Portant le noir colback ou le casque poli,
Tous, ceux de Friedland et ceux de Rivoli,
Comprenant qu'ils allaient mourir dans cette fête,
Saluèrent leur dieu, debout dans la tempête.
Leur bouche, d'un seul cri, dit: vive l'Empereur!
Puis, à pas lents, musique en tête, sans fureur,
Tranquille, souriant à la mitraille anglaise,
La garde impériale entra dans la fournaise.
Hélas! Napoléon, sur sa garde penché,
Regardait, et, sitôt qu'ils avaient débouché
Sous les sombres canons crachant des jets de souffre,
Voyait, l'un après l'autre, en cet horrible gouffre,
Fondre ces régiments de granit et d'acier
Comme fond une cire au souffle d'un brasier.
Ils allaient, l'arme au bras, front haut, graves, stoïques.
Pas un ne recula. Dormez, morts héroïques!
Le reste de l'armée hésitait sur leurs corps
Et regardait mourir la garde. – C'est alors

would have taken for legionnaries, cuirassiers, gunners dragging
the thunders, wearing the black busby or the polished helmet, all,
the men of Friedland and of Rivoli, knowing that they were going
to die at this banquet, hailed their god, standing upright in the
storm. Their mouth with one shout said: Long live the Emperor!
Then, with slow steps, bands at their head, without frenzy, calmly
smiling at the English grapeshot, the imperial guard entered the
furnace.

Alas! Napoleon, leaning over his guard, watched and, as soon as
they had come out beneath the dark cannon spitting jets of sulphur,
he saw those regiments of granite and steel melt one after another
in that horrible gulf, as wax melts at the blast from a brazier. They
went on, arms supported, heads high, grave, and stoical. Not one
recoiled. Sleep, heroic dead! The remainder of the army hesitated
above their bodies and watched the guard die.

Qu'élevant tout à coup sa voix désespérée,
La Déroute, géante à la face effarée
Qui, pâle, épouvantant les plus fiers bataillons,
Changeant subitement les drapeaux en haillons,
A de certains moments, spectre fait de fumées,
Se lève grandissante au milieu des armées,
La Déroute apparut au soldat qui s'émeut,
Et, se tordant les bras, cria: Sauve qui peut!
Sauve qui peut! – affront! horreur! – toutes les bouches
Criaient; à travers champs, fous, éperdus, farouches,
Comme si quelque souffle avait passé sur eux,
Parmi les lourds caissons et les fourgons poudreux,
Roulant dans les fossés, se cachant dans les seigles,
Jetant shakos, manteaux, fusils, jetant les aigles,
Sous les sabres prussiens, ces vétérans, ô deuil!
Tremblaient, hurlaient, pleuraient, couraient! – En un
  clin d'œil,
Comme s'envole au vent une paille enflammée,
S'évanouit ce bruit qui fut la grande armée,
Et cette plaine, hélas! où l'on rêve aujourd'hui,
Vit fuir ceux devant qui l'univers avait fui!

It was then that, suddenly raising her despairing voice, Defeat, the giantess with the scared face, who, frightening the proudest battalions, all at once changing the flags into tatters, at certain moments, like a ghost made of smoke, rises palely towering in the midst of armies, Defeat appeared to the nervous soldier and, wringing her hands, cried: Save himself who may!

Save himself who may! – shame! horror! – all mouths shrieked; through the fields, mad, dismayed, wild, as if some breath had passed over them, among the heavy tumbrils and the dusty ammunition wagons, rolling in the ditches, hiding in the rye-fields, throwing away shakoes, cloaks, muskets, throwing away the eagles, beneath the Prussian sabres those veterans, O grief! trembled, howled, wept, and ran! – In the twinkling of an eye this noise which was the *Grande Armée* vanished as burning straw flies away on the wind, and this plain, alas! where we dream to-day saw the men flee before whom the universe had fled! Forty years have passed, and this

Quarante ans sont passés, et ce coin de la terre,
Waterloo, ce plateau funèbre et solitaire,
Ce champ sinistre où Dieu mêla tant de néants,
Tremble encor d'avoir vu la fuite des géants!

Napoléon les vit s'écouler comme un fleuve;
Hommes, chevaux, tambours, drapeaux; — et dans
    l'épreuve
Sentant confusément revenir son remords,
Levant les mains au ciel, il dit: Mes soldats morts,
Moi vaincu! mon empire est brisé comme verre.
Est-ce le châtiment cette fois, Dieu sévère?
Alors parmi les cris, les rumeurs, le canon,
Il entendit la voix qui lui répondait: Non!

Demain, dès l'aube ...

DEMAIN, dès l'aube, à l'heure où blanchit la campagne,
Je partirai. Vois-tu, je sais que tu m'attends.
J'irai par la forêt, j'irai par la montagne.
Je ne puis demeurer loin de toi plus longtemps.

corner of earth, Waterloo, this dismal solitary plateau, this ill-omened field where God mingled so many nothings, still trembles to have seen the flight of the giants!

Napoleon saw them flow away like a river; men, horses, drums, and flags; — and in his trial, feeling remorse confusedly return, raising his hands to heaven, he said: My soldiers dead, myself conquered! My empire is smashed like glass. Is it the punishment this time, O severe God? Then among the shrieks, the clamours, and the cannon he heard the voice answering him: No!

To-morrow at dawn ...

TO-MORROW at dawn, the hour when the countryside whitens, I shall depart. You see, I know you are waiting for me. I shall go through the forest, I shall go over the mountain. I cannot remain away from you any longer.

Je marcherai les yeux fixés sur mes pensées,
Sans rien voir au dehors, sans entendre aucun bruit,
Seul, inconnu, le dos courbé, les mains croisées,
Triste, et le jour pour moi sera comme la nuit.

Je ne regarderai ni l'or du soir qui tombe,
Ni les voiles au loin descendant vers Harfleur,
Et quand j'arriverai, je mettrai sur ta tombe
Un bouquet de houx vert et de bruyère en fleur.

A Villequier

MAINTENANT que Paris, ses pavés et ses marbres,
Et sa brume et ses toits sont bien loin de mes yeux;
Maintenant que je suis sous les branches des arbres,
Et que je puis songer à la beauté des cieux;

Maintenant que du deuil qui m'a fait l'âme obscure
　　Je sors, pâle et vainqueur,
Et que je sens la paix de la grande nature
　　Qui m'entre dans le cœur;

    I shall walk with eyes fixed on my thoughts, without seeing anything outside, without hearing any noise, alone, unknown, back bent, hands folded, sorrowful, and day for me shall be as night.

    I shall gaze neither at the falling gold of evening nor at the far-off sails dropping down towards Harfleur, and when I arrive, I shall place on your grave a bunch of green holly and flowering heather.

At Villequier

NOW that Paris, its pavements and its marbles, and its mist and its roofs, are far from my eyes; now that I am beneath the branches of the trees, and that I can think of the beauty of the heavens;

    Now that I emerge, pale and victorious, from the grief which made my soul dark, and I feel great nature's peace entering my heart;

Maintenant que je puis, assis au bord des ondes,
Ému par ce superbe et tranquille horizon,
Examiner en moi les vérités profondes
Et regarder les fleurs qui sont dans le gazon;

Maintenant, ô mon Dieu! que j'ai ce calme sombre
      De pouvoir désormais
Voir de mes yeux la pierre où je sais que dans l'ombre
      Elle dort pour jamais;

Maintenant qu'attendri par ces divins spectacles,
Plaines, forêts, rochers, vallons, fleuve argenté,
Voyant ma petitesse et voyant vos miracles,
Je reprends ma raison devant l'immensité;

Je viens à vous, Seigneur, père auquel il faut croire;
      Je vous porte, apaisé,
Les morceaux de ce cœur tout plein de votre gloire
      Que vous avez brisé;

Now that, seated beside the waves, stirred by this proud, calm horizon, I can examine deep truths within myself and gaze at the flowers in the grass;

Now, O my God! that I have the dark tranquillity of being able henceforward to see with my eyes the stone where I know she sleeps for ever in the shade;

Now that, softened by these heavenly sights, plains, forests, rocks, valleys, and silvery river, seeing my pettiness and seeing your marvels, I recover my reason in face of the immensity of Nature;

I come to you, Lord, father in whom we must believe; appeased, I bring to you the pieces of this heart, full of your glory, which you shattered;

Je viens à vous, Seigneur! confessant que vous êtes
Bon, clément, indulgent et doux, ô Dieu vivant!
Je conviens que vous seul savez ce que vous faites,
Et que l'homme n'est rien qu'un jonc qui tremble au vent;

Je dis que le tombeau qui sur les morts se ferme
   Ouvre le firmament;
Et que ce qu'ici-bas nous prenons pour le terme
   Est le commencement;

Je conviens à genoux que vous seul, père auguste,
Possédez l'infini, le réel, l'absolu;
Je conviens qu'il est bon, je conviens qu'il est juste
Que mon cœur ait saigné, puisque Dieu l'a voulu!

Je ne résiste plus à tout ce qui m'arrive
   Par votre volonté.
L'âme de deuils en deuils, l'homme de rive en rive,
   Roule à l'éternité.

Nous ne voyons jamais qu'un seul côté des choses;
L'autre plonge dans la nuit d'un mystère effrayant.
L'homme subit le joug sans connaître les causes.
Tout ce qu'il voit est court, inutile et fuyant.

I come to you, Lord! confessing that you are good, merciful, indulgent, and gentle, O living God! I grant that you alone know
what you are doing, and that man is nothing but a reed trembling in
the wind;

I say that the tomb closing upon the dead opens the sky; and that
what we take for the end down here on earth is the beginning;

On my knees I grant that you alone, august father, possess the
infinite, the real, the absolute; I grant that it is good, I grant that it
is just that my heart bled, since God willed it!

I make no more resistance to anything that happens to me by
your will. The soul from grief to grief, man from shore to shore,
travels to eternity.

We only ever see a single side of things; the other plunges into
the night of a fearful mystery. Man submits to the yoke without
knowing the cause. All that he sees is brief, useless, and fleeting.

Vous faites revenir toujours la solitude
      Autour de tous ses pas.
Vous n'avez pas voulu qu'il eût la certitude
      Ni la joie ici-bas!

Dès qu'il possède un bien, le sort le lui retire.
Rien ne lui fut donné, dans ses rapides jours,
Pour qu'il s'en puisse faire une demeure, et dire:
C'est ici ma maison, mon champ et mes amours!

Il doit voir peu de temps tout ce que ses yeux voient;
      Il vieillit sans soutiens.
Puisque ces choses sont, c'est qu'il faut qu'elles soient;
      J'en conviens, j'en conviens!

Le monde est sombre, ô Dieu! l'immuable harmonie
Se compose des pleurs aussi bien que des chants;
L'homme n'est qu'un atome en cette ombre infinie,
Nuit où montent les bons, où tombent les méchants.

Je sais que vous avez bien autre chose à faire
      Que de nous plaindre tous,
Et qu'un enfant qui meurt, désespoir de sa mère,
      Nous vous fait rien, à vous.

Still you make solitude return about all his steps. You have not wished him to have certainty or joy down here on earth!

As soon as he possesses a treasure, fate takes it away from him again. In his swift days, nothing was given him to make his dwelling of, and say: here are my home, my field, and my loves!

All that his eyes see he must see for a short time; he grows old without support. Since these things are, they must be; I grant it, I grant it!

The world is dark, O God! the unchangeable harmony is made of tears as well as of songs; man is only an atom in this infinite shadow, the night where the good ascend and the wicked fall.

I know that you have other things to do than to pity us all, and that a dying child, the despair of its mother, means nothing to you.

Je sais que le fruit tombe au vent qui le secoue,
Que l'oiseau perd sa plume et la fleur son parfum;
Que la création est une grande roue
Qui ne peut se mouvoir sans écraser quelqu'un;

Les mois, les jours, les flots des mers, les yeux qui
pleurent,
Passent sous le ciel bleu;
Il faut que l'herbe pousse et que les enfants meurent;
Je le sais, ô mon Dieu!

Dans vos cieux, au-delà de la sphère des nues,
Au fond de cet azur immobile et dormant,
Peut-être faites-vous des choses inconnues
Où la douleur de l'homme entre comme élément.

Peut-être est-il utile à vos desseins sans nombre
Que des êtres charmants
S'en aillent, emportés par le tourbillon sombre
Des noirs événements.

Nos destins ténébreux vont sous des lois immenses
Que rien ne déconcerte et que rien n'attendrit.
Vous ne pouvez avoir de subites clémences
Qui dérangent le monde, ô Dieu, tranquille esprit!

I know that the fruit falls in the wind that shakes it, that the bird
loses its feather and the flower its scent; that the creation is a great
wheel which cannot move without crushing somebody;

The months, the days, the waves of the sea, the weeping eyes
pass by beneath the blue sky; the grass must grow and children die;
I know it, O my God!

In your heavens, beyond the cloudy sphere, in the depth of that
motionless slumbering blue, perhaps you create unknown things
where man's suffering enters as an ingredient.

Perhaps it is useful to your numberless plans that charming creatures should pass away, carried off by the sombre whirlwind of dark
events.

Our shadowy destinies move under vast laws that nothing dis-
concerts or softens. You cannot have sudden mercies that upset the
world, O God, calm spirit!

Je vous supplie, ô Dieu! de regarder mon âme,
   Et de considérer
Qu'humble comme un enfant et doux comme une femme,
   Je viens vous adorer!

Considérez encor que j'avais, dès l'aurore,
Travaillé, combattu, pensé, marché, lutté,
Expliquant la nature à l'homme qui l'ignore,
Éclairant toute chose avec votre clarté;

Que j'avais, affrontant la haine et la colère,
   Fait ma tâche ici-bas,
Que je ne pouvais pas m'attendre à ce salaire,
   Que je ne pouvais pas

Prévoir que, vous aussi, sur ma tête qui ploie
Vous appesantiriez votre bras triomphant,
Et que, vous qui voyiez comme j'ai peu de joie,
Vous me reprendriez si vite mon enfant!

Qu'une âme ainsi frappée à se plaindre est sujette,
   Que j'ai pu blasphémer,
Et vous jeter mes cris comme un enfant qui jette
   Une pierre à la mer!

 I implore you, O God! to look upon my soul, and to consider that I come to worship you as humbly as a child and as gently as a woman!

 Consider again that since dawn I had worked, fought, thought, marched, and struggled, explaining nature to man, to whom it is unknown and lighting all things with your light;

 That, braving hatred and anger, I had performed my task down here on earth, that I could not expect this reward, that I could not

 Foresee that you, too, would make your triumphant arm heavy upon my inclining head, and that you, who saw what little joy I have, would take back my child so quickly!

 That a soul so stricken is liable to complain, that I may have blasphemed and thrown my cries to you like a child throwing a stone into the sea!

Considérez qu'on doute, ô mon Dieu! quand on souffre,
Que l'œil qui pleure trop finit par s'aveugler,
Qu'un être que son deuil plonge au plus noir du gouffre,
Quand il ne vous voit plus, ne peut vous contempler,

Et qu'il ne se peut pas que l'homme, lorsqu'il sombre
       Dans les afflictions,
Ait présente à l'esprit la sérénité sombre
       Des constellations!

Aujourd'hui, moi qui fus faible comme une mère,
Je me courbe à vos pieds devant vos cieux ouverts.
Je me sens éclairé dans ma douleur amère
Par un meilleur regard jeté sur l'univers.

Seigneur, je reconnais que l'homme est en délire
       S'il ose murmurer;
Je cesse d'accuser, je cesse de maudire,
       Mais laissez-moi pleurer!

Hélas! laissez les pleurs couler de ma paupière,
Puisque vous avez fait les hommes pour cela!
Laissez-moi me pencher sur cette froide pierre
Et dire à mon enfant: Sens-tu que je suis là?

    Consider, O my God! that we doubt when we suffer, that the eye which weeps too much ends by becoming blind, that a creature who is plunged to the darkest of the abyss by his sorrow, cannot gaze upon you, when he sees you no more,
    And that it cannot be that man, when he sinks into affliction, has in his mind the dark serenity of the constellations!
    To-day I, who was weak as a mother, bend at your feet before your open heavens. I feel myself lightened in my bitter grief by a more favourable glance cast on the universe.
    Lord, I recognize that man is raving if he dares to complain; I give up accusation, I give up curses, but let me weep!
    Alas! let the tears flow from my eyelids, since you have made men for that! Let me bend over this cold stone and say to my child: Do you feel that I am there?

Laissez-moi lui parler, incliné sur ses restes,
          Le soir, quand tout se tait,
Comme si, dans sa nuit rouvrant ses yeux célestes,
          Cet ange m'écoutait!

Hélas! vers le passé tournant un œil d'envie,
Sans que rien ici-bas puisse m'en consoler,
Je regarde toujours ce moment de ma vie
Où je l'ai vue ouvrir son aile et s'envoler.

Je verrai cet instant jusqu'à ce que je meure,
          L'instant, pleurs superflus!
Où je criai: L'enfant que j'avais tout à l'heure,
          Quoi donc! je ne l'ai plus!

Ne vous irritez pas que je sois de la sorte,
Ô mon Dieu! cette plaie a si longtemps saigné!
L'angoisse dans mon âme est toujours la plus forte,
Et mon cœur est soumis, mais n'est pas résigné.

Let me speak to her, bent over her remains, in the evening when
all is silent, as if, reopening her heavenly eyes in her night, that
angel heard me!

Alas! turning an eye of desire towards the past without anything
down here on earth being able to comfort me, I still see that moment
of my life when I watched her open her wing and fly away.

I shall see that moment until I die, the moment, unwanted tears!
when I cried: The child that I had just now, what! I have it no
longer!

Do not be angered that I behave thus, O my God! this wound
has bled so long! Anguish is still the stronger in my soul, and my
heart is submissive, but not resigned.

Ne vous irritez pas! fronts que la deuil réclame,
  Mortels sujets aux pleurs.
Il nous est malaisé de retirer notre âme
  De ces grandes douleurs.

Voyez-vous, nos enfants nous sont bien nécessaires,
Seigneur; quand on a vu dans sa vie, un matin
Au milieu des ennuis, des peines, des misères,
Et de l'ombre que fait sur nous notre destin,

Apparaître un enfant, tête chère et sacrée,
  Petit être joyeux,
Si beau, qu'on a cru voir s'ouvrir à son entrée
  Une porte des cieux;

Quand on a vu, seize ans, de cet autre soi-même
Croître la grâce aimable et la douce raison,
Lorsqu'on a reconnu que cet enfant qu'on aime
Fait le jour dans notre âme et dans notre maison,

Que c'est la seule joie ici-bas qui persiste
  De tout ce qu'on rêva,
Considérez que c'est une chose bien triste
  De le voir qui s'en va!

Do not be angered: brows claimed by grief, mortals liable to tears. It is difficult for us to redeem our soul from these great sorrows.

You see, our children are most necessary to us, Lord; when you have seen one morning in your life, in the midst of the boredom, the suffering, the wretchedness, and the shadow our fate casts upon us,

A child appear, a dear sacred head, a joyful little creature, so fair that you thought to see a gate of heaven open at its coming;

When you have seen for sixteen years the lovable charm and sweet reason of this other self grow, when you have realized that this child you love makes the daylight in our soul and in our home,

That it is the only lasting joy down here on earth of all that you dreamed, consider how sad a thing it is to see it pass away!

Booz endormi

Booz s'était couché de fatigue accablé;
Il avait tout le jour travaillé dans son aire;
Puis avait fait son lit à sa place ordinaire;
Booz dormait auprès des boisseaux pleins de blé.

Ce vieillard possédait des champs de blés et d'orge;
Il était, quoique riche, à la justice enclin;
Il n'avait pas de fange en l'eau de son moulin,
Il n'avait pas d'enfer dans le feu de sa forge.

Sa barbe était d'argent comme un ruisseau d'avril.
Sa gerbe n'était point avare ni haineuse;
Quand il voyait passer quelque pauvre glaneuse:
– Laissez tomber exprès des épis, disait-il.

Cet homme marchait pur loin des sentiers obliques,
Vêtu de probité candide et de lin blanc;
Et, toujours du côté des pauvres ruisselant,
Ses sacs de grains semblaient des fontaines publiques.

Booz Sleeping

Booz had lain down overwhelmed by fatigue; he had worked all day on his threshing-floor; then had made his bed in his usual place; Booz slept beside bushels full of corn.

This old man owned fields of corn and barley; though rich, he was given to justice; he had no dirt in the water of his mill, he had no inferno in the fire of his forge.

His beard was silver like an April stream. His sheaves of corn were not mean or hateful; when he saw some poor woman pass gleaning: – 'Let some ears fall on purpose,' he said.

This man walked pure far from crooked paths, dressed in shining righteousness and white linen; and his sacks of grain seemed public fountains, ever pouring forth towards the poor.

Booz était bon maître et fidèle parent ;
Il était généreux, quoiqu'il fût économe ;
Les femmes regardaient Booz plus qu'un jeune homme,
Car le jeune homme est beau, mais le vieillard est grand.

Le vieillard, qui revient vers la source première,
Entre aux jours éternels et sort des jours changeants ;
Et l'on voit de la flamme aux yeux des jeunes gens,
Mais dans l'œil du vieillard on voit de la lumière.

*

Donc, Booz dans la nuit dormait parmi les siens.
Près des meules, qu'on eût prises pour des décombres,
Les moissoneurs couchés faisaient des groupes sombres ;
Et ceci se passait dans des temps très anciens.

Les tribus d'Israël avaient pour chef un juge ;
La terre, où l'homme errait sous la tente, inquiet
Des empreintes de pieds de géant qu'il voyait,
Était encor mouillée et molle du déluge.

*

Booz was a good master and faithful kinsman; he was generous,
though he was sparing; women looked at Booz more than at a
young man, for the young man is fair, but the old man is great.

The old man returning towards the first fountain-head enters on
eternal days and emerges from changing days; and flame is seen in
the eyes of young folk, but in the old man's eyes we see light.

*

So Booz in the night slept among his people. Near the mill-stones
which you would have taken for ruins, the sleeping harvesters made
dark groups; and this took place in times long past.

The tribes of Israel had a judge for head; the earth, where men
wandered with tents, troubled by the giants' footprints which they
saw, was still damp and soft from the flood.

*

Comme dormait Jacob, comme dormait Judith,
Booz, les yeux fermés, gisait sous la feuillée;
Or, la porte du ciel s'étant entre-bâillée
Au-dessus de sa tête, un songe en descendit.

Et ce songe était tel, que Booz vit un chêne
Qui, sorti de son ventre, allait jusqu'au ciel bleu;
Une race y montait comme une longue chaîne;
Un roi chantait en bas, en haut mourait un dieu.

Et Booz murmurait avec la voix de l'âme:
«Comment se pourrait-il que de moi ceci vînt?
Le chiffre de mes ans a passé quatre-vingt,
Et je n'ai pas de fils, et je n'ai plus de femme.

«Voilà longtemps que celle avec qui j'ai dormi,
O Seigneur! a quitté ma couche pour la vôtre;
Et nous sommes encor tout mêlés l'un à l'autre,
Elle à demi vivante et moi mort à demi.

«Une race naîtrait de moi! Comment le croire?
Comment se pourrait-il que j'eusse des enfants?

As Jacob slept, as Judith slept, Booz, his eyes shut, lay beneath the bower; now, the gate of heaven having half-opened above his head, a dream came down from it.

And this dream was such that Booz saw an oak, which, issuing from his stomach, went up to the blue sky; a people ascended it like a long chain; a king was singing at the bottom, a god dying at the top.

And Booz murmured with the voice of the soul: 'How could it be that this came from me? The number of my years has passed eighty, and I have no son and I have no longer a wife.

'It is a long time ago that she with whom I slept, O Lord! left my bed for yours; and we are still mingled the one to the other, she half living and I half dead.

'A people to be born of me! How should I believe it? How could

Quand on est jeune, on a des matins triomphants;
Le jour sort de la nuit comme d'une victoire;

«Mais vieux, on tremble ainsi qu'à l'hiver le bouleau;
Je suis veuf, je suis seul, et sur moi le soir tombe,
Et je courbe, ô mon Dieu! mon âme vers la tombe,
Comme un bœuf ayant soif penche son front vers l'eau.»

Ainsi parlait Booz dans le rêve et l'extase,
Tournant vers Dieu ses yeux par le sommeil noyés;
Le cèdre ne sent pas une rose à sa base,
Et lui ne sentait pas une femme à ses pieds.

*

Pendant qu'il sommeillait, Ruth, une moabite,
S'était couchée aux pieds de Booz, le sein nu,
Espérant on ne sait quel rayon inconnu,
Quand viendrait du réveil la lumière subite.

Booz ne savait point qu'une femme était là,
Et Ruth ne savait point ce que Dieu voulait d'elle.
Un frais parfum sortait des touffes d'asphodèle;
Les souffles de la nuit flottaient sur Galgala.

it be that I should have children? When we are young, we have
triumphant mornings, day emerges from night as from a victory;
  'But, old, we tremble like the birch-tree in winter. I am a
widower, I am alone, and evening falls upon me, and I bend, O my
God! my soul towards the tomb, as a thirsty ox inclines his brow
towards the water.'
  So Booz spoke in dream and ecstasy, turning his eyes, drowned
by sleep, towards God; the cedar does not feel a rose at its base, and
he did not feel a woman at his feet.

*

While he slept, Ruth, a Moabite, had lain down at the feet of Booz,
with naked breast, hoping we know not what unknown gleam,
when the sudden light of awakening should come.
  Booz did not know that a woman was there, and Ruth did not
know what God wanted of her; a cool perfume came from the tufts
of asphodel; the breath of night floated over Galgala.

L'ombre était nuptiale, auguste et solennelle;
Les anges y volaient sans doute obscurément,
Car on voyait passer dans la nuit, par moment,
Quelque chose de bleu qui paraissait une aile.

La respiration de Booz qui dormait,
Se mêlait au bruit sourd des ruisseaux sur la mousse.
On était dans le mois où la nature est douce,
Les collines ayant des lys sur leur sommet.

Ruth songeait et Booz dormait; l'herbe était noire;
Les grelots des troupeaux palpitaient vaguement;
Une immense bonté tombait du firmament;
C'était l'heure tranquille où les lions vont boire.

Tout reposait dans Ur et dans Jérimadeth;
Les astres émaillaient le ciel profond et sombre;
Le croissant fin et clair parmi ces fleurs de l'ombre
Brillait à l'occident, et Ruth se demandait,

Immobile, ouvrant l'œil à moitié sous ses voiles,
Quel dieu, quel moissonneur de l'éternel été,
Avait, en s'en allant, négligemment jeté
Cette faucille d'or dans le champ des étoiles.

The shadow was nuptial, august, and solemn; doubtless angels flew darkly there, for from time to time there was seen to pass in the night something blue that seemed to be a wing.

The breathing of the sleeping Booz mingled with the hollow sound of streams upon the moss. It was in the month when nature is gentle; the hills had lilies on their tops.

Ruth mused and Booz slept; the grass was dark; the bells of the flocks vaguely quivered; a vast beneficence fell from the sky; it was the quiet hour when lions go to drink.

Everything slept in Ur and in Jerimadeth; the stars enamelled the deep, dark sky; the small bright crescent shone in the west among those flowers of the shade, and Ruth asked herself,

Lying motionless and half-opening her eye beneath her veils, what god, what harvester of the eternal summer, departing, had negligently thrown down this golden sickle in the field of stars.

La Trompette du Jugement

*

JE vis dans la nuée un clairon monstrueux.

Et ce clairon semblait, au seuil profond des cieux,
Calme, attendre le souffle immense de l'archange.

Ce qui jamais ne meurt, ce qui jamais ne change,
L'entourait. A travers un frisson, on sentait
Que ce buccin fatal, qui rêve et qui se tait,
Quelque part, dans l'endroit où l'on crée, où l'on sème,
Avait été forgé par quelqu'un de suprême
Avec de l'équité condensée en airain.
Il était là, lugubre, effroyable, serein.
Il gisait sur la brume insondable qui tremble,
Hors du monde, au delà de tout ce qui ressemble
A la forme de quoi que ce soit.

                                                Il vivait.

Il semblait un réveil songeant près d'un chevet.

The Trumpet of Judgement

*

I SAW a monstrous trumpet in the clouds.

And this trumpet seemed calmly to await the vast breath of the
archangel on the steep threshold of the skies.

What never dies, what never changes surrounded it. With a
shudder one felt that this fatal horn, dreaming and silent, somewhere, in the place where there is creation and sowing of seed, had
been forged by someone supreme out of justice condensed into
brass. It was there, dismal, terrible, and calm. It lay on the trembling, unfathomable mist out of the world, beyond everything resembling any form whatever.

It was alive.

It seemed an alarum clock musing near the head of a bed.

Oh! quelle nuit! là, rien n'a de contour ni d'âge;
Et le nuage est spectre, et le spectre est nuage.

*

Et c'était le clairon de l'abîme.

Une voix

Un jour en sortira qu'on entendra sept fois.
En attendant, glacé, mais écoutant, il pense;
Couvant le châtiment, couvant la récompense;
Et toute l'épouvante éparse au ciel est sœur
De cet impénétrable et morne avertisseur.

Je le considérais dans les vapeurs funèbres
Comme on verrait se taire un coq dans les ténèbres.
Pas un murmure autour du clairon souverain.
Et la terre sentait le froid de son airain,
Quoique, là, d'aucun monde on ne vît les frontières.

Et l'immobilité de tous les cimetières,
Et le sommeil de tous les tombeaux, et la paix
De tous les morts couchés dans la fosse, étaient faits

Oh! What night! Nothing there has contour or age; and the
cloud is a phantom and the phantom is a cloud.

*

And it was the trumpet of the abyss.

One day a voice will come forth from it that will be heard seven
times. Meanwhile, frozen but listening, it thinks; hatching punish-
ments, hatching rewards; and all the fear scattered in the sky is this
impenetrably dreary watchman's sister.

I contemplated it in the sinister mists as you might a cock silent
in the shadows. Not a murmur around the sovereign trumpet. And
the earth felt the chill of its brass, though there the frontiers of no
world were to be seen.

And the stillness of all the graveyards and the slumber of all the
tombs and the peace of all the dead sleeping in the grave were made

Du silence inouï qu'il avait dans la bouche;
Ce lourd silence était pour l'affreux mort farouche
L'impossibilité de faire faire un pli
Au suaire cousu sur son front par l'oubli.
Ce silence tenait en suspens l'anathème.
On comprenait que tant que ce clairon suprême
Se tairait, le sépulcre, obscur, roidi, béant,
Garderait l'attitude horrible du néant,
Que la momie aurait toujours sa bandelette,
Que l'homme irait tombant du cadavre au squelette,
Et que ce fier banquet radieux, ce festin
Que les vivants gloutons appellent le destin,
Toute la joie errante en tourbillons de fêtes,
Toutes les passions de la chair satisfaites,
Gloire, orgueil, les héros ivres, les tyrans soûls,
Continueraient d'avoir pour but et pour dessous
La pourriture, orgie offerte aux vers convives;
Mais qu'à l'heure où soudain, dans l'espace sans rives,
Cette trompette vaste et sombre sonnerait,
On verrait, comme un tas d'oiseaux d'une forêt,
Toutes les âmes, cygne, aigle, éperviers, colombes,
Frémissantes, sortir du tremblement des tombes,

out of the unheard-of silence that was in its mouth; for the wild and awful dead this heavy silence was the impossibility of making a fold in the shroud sewn over his brow by forgetfulness. This silence held the anathema in suspense. It was understood that, as long as this last trumpet was silent, the dark, stiff, gaping grave would keep the horrible posture of nothingness, that the mummy would still have its winding-cloth, that man would go on falling from corpse to skeleton, and that this proud shining banquet, this feast which living gluttons call destiny, all the joy wandering in whirlpools of merry-making, all the satisfied passions of the flesh, fame, pride, the tipsy heroes, the drunken tyrants would continue to have, for end and base, decay, the orgy offered to worms for guests; but that at the hour when suddenly in boundless space this vast dark trumpet sounded you would see, like a flock of birds from a forest, all the souls, swan, eagle, sparrow-hawks, doves shivering emerge from

Et tous les spectres faire un bruit de grandes eaux,
Et se dresser, et prendre à la hâte leurs os,
Tandis qu'au fond, au fond du gouffre, au fond du rêve,
Blanchissant l'absolu, comme un jour qui se lève,
Le front mystérieux du juge apparaîtrait!

*

Ce clairon avait l'air de savoir le secret.

On sentait que le râle énorme de ce cuivre
Serait tel qu'il ferait bondir, vibrer, revivre
L'ombre, le plomb, le marbre, et qu'à ce fatal glas,
Toutes les surdités voleraient en éclats;
Que l'oubli sombre, avec sa perte de mémoire,
Se lèverait au son de la trompette noire;
Que dans cette clameur étrange, en même temps
Qu'on entendrait frémir tous les cieux palpitants,
On entendrait crier toutes les consciences;
Que le sceptique au fond de ses insouciances,
Que le voluptueux, l'athée et le douteur,
Et le maître tombé de toute sa hauteur,

the trembling tombs, and all the ghosts, making a noise like great waters, rise up and hastily take their bones upon them, while in the depth, in the depth of the gulf, in the depth of dream, whitening the absolute like rising day, the mysterious brow of the judge would appear.

*

This trumpet had the air of knowing the secret.

One felt that this copper's vast rattle would be such as to cause shadow, lead, and marble to leap, vibrate, and live again, and that at this fatal knell all deafness would fly into splinters; that black forgetfulness with its loss of memory would rise up at the sound of the dark trumpet; that at the same time in this strange clamour all the throbbing skies would be heard to shiver, all consciences to shriek; that the sceptic in the depth of his carelessness, the voluptuary, the atheist, and the doubter, and the master fallen from all his

Sentiraient ce fracas traverser leurs vertèbres;
Que ce déchirement céleste des ténèbres
Ferait dresser quiconque est soumis à l'arrêt;
Que qui n'entendit pas le remords, l'entendrait;
Et qu'il réveillerait, comme un choc à la porte,
L'oreille la plus dure et l'âme la plus morte,
Même ceux qui, livrés au rire, aux vains combats,
Aux vils plaisirs, n'ont point tenu compte ici-bas
Des avertissements de l'ombre et du mystère,
Même ceux que n'a point réveillés sur la terre
Le tonnerre, ce coup de cloche de la nuit!

Oh! dans l'esprit de l'homme où tout vacille et fuit,
Où le verbe n'a pas un mot qui ne bégaie,
Où l'aurore apparaît, hélas! comme une plaie,
Dans cet esprit, tremblant dès qu'il ose augurer,
Oh! comment concevoir, comment se figurer
Cette vibration communiquée aux tombes,
Cette sommation aux blêmes catacombes
Du ciel ouvrant sa porte et du gouffre ayant faim,
Le prodigieux bruit de Dieu disant: Enfin!

arrogance would feel this din pierce their spine; that this heavenly
rending of the shades would make whosoever is subject to judgement start up; that he who heard no remorse would hear it; and
that, like a blow on the gate, it would awaken the hardest ear and
the deadest soul, even those who, given over to laughter, vain dis-
putes, and base pleasures, took no heed down here of the warnings of
the shadow and mystery, even those on earth whom the thunder, that
bell-stroke of the night, has not awakened!

Oh! In man's mind where everything wavers and flees, where
language has no unstammered word, where dawn appears, alas!
like a wound, in this mind trembling as soon as it dares prophesy,
oh! how to conceive, how imagine this movement imparted to
tombs, this summons to the pale catacombs of the sky opening its
gate and of the hungry gulf, the stupendous noise of God saying:
At last!

Oui, c'est vrai, – c'est du moins jusque-là que l'œil
    plonge, –
C'est l'avenir, – du moins tel qu'on le voit en songe, –
Quand le monde atteindra son but, quand les instants,
Les jours, les mois, les ans, auront rempli le temps,
Quand tombera du ciel l'heure immense et nocturne,
Cette goutte qui doit faire déborder l'urne,
Alors, dans le silence horrible, un rayon blanc,
Long, pâle, glissera, formidable et tremblant,
Sur ces haltes de nuit qu'on nomme cimetières;
Les tentes frémiront, quoiqu'elles soient des pierres,
Dans tous ces sombres camps endormis; et, sortant
Tout à coup de la brume où l'univers l'attend,
Ce clairon, au-dessus des êtres et des choses,
Au-dessus des forfaits et des apothéoses,
Des ombres et des os, des esprits et des corps,
Sonnera la diane effrayante des morts.

Ô lever en sursaut des larves pêle-mêle!
Oh! la Nuit réveillant la mort, sa sœur jumelle!

Pensif, je regardais l'incorruptible airain.

*

    Yes, it is true – at least it is as far as the eye plunges – it is the
future – at least as we see it in a dream; – when the world reaches
its end, when the seconds, days, months, and years have filled up
time, when the huge nocturnal hour falls from the sky, that drop
which is to make the urn overflow, then in the horrible silence a
long, pale, white beam will slide, shivering dreadfully, over those
night halts we call cemeteries; although they are stones, the tents
will shudder in all those dark, sleeping camps; and, emerging all at
once from the mist where the universe awaits it, this trumpet will
sound the terrifying reveille of the dead over creatures and things,
crimes and apotheoses, shades and bones, minds and bodies.
    O suddenly to raise up a confusion of worms! Oh! Night awak-
ening death, her twin sister!
    Thoughtfully I gazed on the incorruptible brass.

*

Les volontés sans loi, les passions sans frein,
Toutes les actions de tous les êtres, haines,
Amours, vertus, fureurs, hymnes, cris, plaisirs, peines,
Avaient laissé, dans l'ombre où rien ne remuait,
Leur pâle empreinte autour de ce bronze muet;
Une obscure Babel y tordait sa spirale.

Sa dimension vague, ineffable, spectrale,
Sortant de l'éternel, entrait dans l'absolu.
Pour pouvoir mesurer ce tube, il eût fallu
Prendre la toise au fond du rêve, et la coudée
Dans la profondeur trouble et sombre de l'idée;
Un de ses bouts touchait le bien, l'autre le mal;
Et sa longueur allait de l'homme à l'animal,
Quoiqu'on ne vît point là d'animal et point d'homme;
Couché sur terre, il eût joint Éden à Sodome.

Son embouchure, gouffre où plongeait mon regard,
Cercle de l'Inconnu ténébreux et hagard,
Pleine de cette horreur que le mystère exhale,
M'apparaissait ainsi qu'une offre colossale
D'entrer dans l'ombre où Dieu même est évanoui.
Cette gueule, avec l'air d'un redoutable ennui,

Lawless wills, passions without restraint, all actions of all beings,
hatreds, virtues, rages, hymns, shrieks, pleasures, pains, had left
their pale mark around this mute bronze in the shadow where nothing moved; a dark Babel twisted its spiral there. Its vague, unspeakable, phantasmic size, emerging from the eternal, entered into the
absolute. To be able to measure this tube, you would have had to
take the yardstick in the depth of dream and the cubit in the dark,
troubled gulf of the idea; one of its ends touched good, the other
evil; and its length went from man to the animal, though there was
no animal to be seen and no man; laid on earth it would have joined
Eden to Sodom.

Its mouth, the gulf where my gaze plunged, shadowy wild circle
of the unknown, full of horror breathed forth by mystery, appeared
to me like an immense offer to enter into the shade where God himself vanishes. That muzzle, with the air of fearful tedium, drearily

Morne, s'élargissait sur l'homme et la nature;
Et cette épouvantable et muette ouverture
Semblait le bâillement noir de l'éternité.

*

Au fond de l'immanent et de l'illimité,
Parfois, dans les lointains sans nom de l'Invisible,
Quelque chose tremblait de vaguement terrible,
Et brillait et passait, inexprimable éclair.
Toutes les profondeurs des mondes avait l'air
De méditer, dans l'ombre où l'ombre se répète,
L'heure où l'on entendrait de cette âpre trompette
Un appel aussi long que l'infini jaillir.
L'immuable semblait d'avance en tressaillir.

Des porches de l'abîme, antres hideux, cavernes
Que nous nommons enfers, puits, gehennams, avernes,
Bouches d'obscurité qui ne prononcent rien,
Du vide, où ne flottait nul souffle aérien,
Du silence où l'haleine osait à peine éclore,
Ceci se dégageait pour l'âme: Pas encore.

grew greater over man and nature, and the terrible dumb opening
seemed the dark yawn of eternity.

*

In the depth of the immanent and of the limitless, sometimes, in the
nameless distances of the Invisible, something vaguely terrible
trembled and shone and passed by like an unutterable lightning
flash. In the shadow where shadow is multiplied all the deeps of the
worlds appeared to muse on the hour when a call as long drawn out
as the infinite would be heard to burst from this harsh trumpet. The
immutable seemed to quake for it in advance.

From the porches of the abyss, the hideous caves, the caverns
that we call hells, pits, gehennas, avernuses, mouths of darkness saying nothing, from the void where floated no airy breath, from the
silence where the breath dared hardly respire, this was revealed to
the soul: Not yet.

Par instants, dans ce lieu triste comme le soir,
Comme on entend le bruit de quelqu'un qui vient voir,
On entendait le pas boiteux de la justice;
Puis cela s'effaçait. Des vermines, le vice,
Le crime, s'approchaient, et, fourmillement noir,
Fuyaient. Le clairon sombre ouvrait son entonnoir.
Un groupe d'ouragans dormait dans ce cratère.
Comme cet organum des gouffres doit se taire
Jusqu'au jour monstrueux où nous écarterons
Les clous de notre bière au-dessus de nos fronts,
Nul bras ne le touchait dans l'invisible sphère;
Chaque race avait fait sa couche de poussière
Dans l'orbe sépulcral de son évasement;
Sur cette poudre l'œil lisait confusément
Ce mot: RIEZ, écrit par le doigt d'Épicure;
Et l'on voyait, au fond de la rondeur obscure,
La toile d'araignée horrible de Satan.

Des astres qui passaient murmuraient: «Souviens-t'en!
Prie!» et la nuit portait cette parole à l'ombre.

From time to time in this place melancholy as evening, as we
hear the sound of someone coming to look, we heard the limping
step of justice; then it disappeared. Vermin, vice, crime approached
and fled in a dark swarm. The dark trumpet opened its funnel. A
cluster of storms slept in that crater; since this organ of the gulfs
must be silent, until the monstrous day when we push aside the nails
of our coffin above our foreheads, not an arm touched it in the invisible sphere; every people had made its layer of dust in the sepulchral globe of its mouth; on this powder the eye read confusedly the
word: LAUGH, traced by Epicurus's finger; and Satan's horrible
spider's web was to be seen in the depth of the dark hollow.

Passing stars whispered: 'Remember! Pray!' And night bore
those words to the shade.

Et je ne sentais plus ni le temps ni le nombre.

*

Une sinistre main sortait de l'infini.

Vers la trompette, effroi de tout crime impuni,
Qui doit faire à la mort un jour lever la tête,
Elle pendait, énorme, ouverte, et comme prête
A saisir ce clairon qui se tait dans la nuit,
Et qu'emplit le sommeil formidable du bruit.
La main, dans la nuée et hors de l'Invisible,
S'allongeait. A quel être était-elle? Impossible
De le dire, en ce morne et brumeux firmament.
L'œil dans l'obscurité ne voyait clairement
Que les cinq doigts béants de cette main terrible;
Tant l'être, quel qu'il fût, debout dans l'ombre horrible,
– Sans doute, quelque archange ou quelque séraphin
Immobile, attendant le signe de la fin, –
Plongeait profondément, sous les ténébreux voiles,
Du pied dans les enfers, du front dans les étoiles!

And I felt no more time or number.

*

An ominous hand came out of the infinite.

Towards the trumpet, terror of all unpunished crime, which must one day make death raise its head, it hung enormous, open and as though ready to seize this bugle silent in the night and filled with the dreadful slumber of sound. The hand was extended in the clouds and out of the invisible. To what being did it belong? Impossible to tell in this dreary, misty sky. In the darkness the eye only saw clearly the five gaping fingers of this terrible hand; the being, whoever he was, standing in the horrible shadow – doubtless some archangel or some seraph motionlessly awaiting the sign of the end – beneath the shadowy veils plunged his foot so deep into the pit, his brow so deep among the stars!

A Théophile Gautier

Ami, poète, esprit, tu fuis notre nuit noire,
Tu sors de nos rumeurs pour entrer dans la gloire;
Et désormais ton nom rayonne aux purs sommets.
Moi qui t'ai connu jeune et beau, moi qui t'aimais,
Moi qui, plus d'une fois, dans nos altiers coups d'aile,
Éperdu, m'appuyais sur ton âme fidèle,
Moi, blanchi par les jours sur ma tête neigeant,
Je me souviens des temps écoulés, et songeant
A ce jeune passé qui vit nos deux aurores,
A la lutte, à l'orage, aux arènes sonores,
A l'art nouveau qui s'offre, au peuple criant: oui,
J'écoute ce grand vent sublime évanoui.

Fils de la Grèce antique et de la jeune France,
Ton fier respect des morts fut rempli d'espérance;
Jamais tu ne fermas les yeux à l'avenir.
Mage à Thèbes, druide au pied du noir menhir,
Flamine aux bords du Tibre et brahme aux bords du
    Gange,
Mettant sur l'arc du dieu la flèche de l'archange,

To Théophile Gautier

Friend, poet, spirit, you flee our dark night; you emerge from our clamours to enter into fame, and henceforward your name will shine on the pure hilltops. I who knew you when you were young and handsome, I who loved you; I who more than once, when dismayed in our proud flights, supported myself on your faithful soul; I, whitened by the days snowing upon my head; I recall times gone by, and, thinking of that recent past which saw the dawn of both of us, of the struggle, of the storm, of the resounding arenas, of the new art being offered, and the people crying: yes, I hear that vast sublime wind that has passed away.

Son of ancient Greece and modern France, your proud respect for the dead was filled with hope; you never shut your eyes to the future. A mage in Thebes, a druid at the foot of the dark menhir, a flamen on Tiber's banks, and a Brahim on those of the Ganges, placing the archangel's arrow in the god's bow, haunting the bed-

D'Achille et de Roland hantant les deux chevets,
Forgeur mystérieux et puissant, tu savais
Tordre tous les rayons dans une seule flamme;
Le couchant rencontrait l'aurore dans ton âme;
Hier croisait demain dans ton fécond cerveau;
Tu sacrais le vieil art aïeul de l'art nouveau;
Tu comprenais qu'il faut, lorsqu'une âme inconnue
Parle au peuple, envolée en éclairs dans la nue,
L'écouter, l'accepter, l'aimer, ouvrir les cœurs;
Calme, tu dédaignais l'effort vil des moqueurs
Écumant sur Eschyle et bavant sur Shakspeare;
Tu savais que ce siècle a son air qu'il respire,
Et que, l'art ne marchant qu'en se transfigurant,
C'est embellir le beau que d'y joindre le grand.
Et l'on t'a vu pousser d'illustres cris de joie
Quand le Drame a saisi Paris comme une proie.
Quand l'antique hiver fut chassé par Floréal,
Quand l'astre inattendu du moderne idéal
Est venu tout à coup, dans le ciel qui s'embrase,
Luire, et quand l'Hippogriffe a relayé Pégase!

*

sides of both Achilles and Roland, like a smith of mysterious power you knew how to twist all sunbeams into a single flame; in your soul the sunset met the dawn; yesterday encountered to-morrow in your fertile brain; you consecrated ancient art, ancestor of the new; you understood that, when an unknown soul speaks to the people, flying away in lightnings to the clouds, we must hear it, accept it, love it, open our hearts to it; you calmly scorned the base attempt of the mockers drooling on Aeschylus and dribbling on Shakespeare; you knew that this age has its own air which it breathes, and that, since art only progresses by transforming itself, to join the great to the beautiful makes it more beautiful still. And you were seen to utter noble cries of joy, when the drama seized Paris like a prey, when old winter was expelled by Spring, when the unexpected star of the modern ideal suddenly came to shine in the glowing sky, and when the hippogriff took Pegasus's place.

*

Je te salue au seuil sévère du tombeau.
Va chercher le vrai, toi qui sus trouver le beau.
Monte l'âpre escalier. Du haut des sombres marches,
Du noir pont de l'abîme on entrevoit les arches;
Va! meurs! la dernière heure est le dernier degré.
Pars, aigle, tu vas voir des gouffres à ton gré;
Tu vas voir l'absolu, le réel, le sublime.
Tu vas sentir le vent sinistre de la cime
Et l'éblouissement du prodige éternel.
Ton olympe, tu vas le voir du haut du ciel,
Tu vas du haut du vrai voir l'humaine chimère,
Même celle de Job, même celle d'Homère,
Âme, et du haut de Dieu tu vas voir Jéhovah.
Monte! esprit! Grandis, plane, ouvre tes ailes, va!

Lorsqu'un vivant nous quitte, ému, je le contemple,
Car entrer dans la mort, c'est entrer dans le temple
Et quand un homme meurt, je vois distinctement
Dans son ascension mon propre avènement.
Ami, je sens du sort la sombre plénitude;
J'ai commencé la mort par de la solitude,

On the severe threshold of the tomb I salute you. Go to seek truth, you who knew how to find beauty. Climb the harsh staircase. From the top of the dark steps the arches of the black bridge over the abyss can just be seen; Go! Die! The last hour is the last step! Depart, eagle, you will see gulfs to your taste; you will see the absolute, the real, the sublime, feel the ominous wind of the summit and the dizziness of perpetual wonder. You will see your Olympus from the height of heaven; you will see human unreality from the height of truth, even Job's, even Homer's unreality, soul, and you will see Jehovah from the height of God. Soar! Spirit! Tower, hover, open your wings, go!

When a living being leaves us, I gaze upon him with emotion, for to enter into death is to enter into the temple; and when a man dies, in his ascent I clearly see my own accession. Friend, I feel the dark plenitude of fate; I have begun death by solitude; I see my

Je vois mon profond soir vaguement s'étoiler.
Voici l'heure où je vais, aussi moi, m'en aller.
Mon fil trop long frissonne et touche presque au glaive;
Le vent qui t'emporta doucement me soulève,
Et je vais suivre ceux qui m'aimaient, moi banni.
Leur œil fixe m'attire au fond de l'infini.
J'y cours. Ne fermez pas la porte funéraire.

Passons; car c'est la loi; nul ne peut s'y soustraire;
Tout penche; et ce grand siècle avec tous ses rayons
Entre en cette ombre immense où pâles nous fuyons.
Oh! quel farouche bruit font dans le crépuscule
Les chênes qu'on abat pour le bûcher d'Hercule!
Les chevaux de la Mort se mettent à hennir,
Et sont joyeux, car l'âge éclatant va finir;
Ce siècle altier, qui sut dompter le vent contraire,
Expire ... Ô Gautier! toi, leur égal et leur frère,
Tu pars après Dumas, Lamartine et Musset.
L'onde antique est tarie où l'on rajeunissait;
Comme il n'est plus de Styx, il n'est plus de Jouvence.
Le dur faucheur avec sa large lame avance

own deep evening vaguely covered with stars; here is the hour when
I too shall depart; my extenuated thread shudders and almost touches
the sword; the wind that carried you away lifts me gently, and I
shall follow those who loved me when I was banished. Their fixed
eye draws me to the depth of the infinite. I hasten. Do not shut the
funereal door.

Let us pass by, for it is the law; no one can escape it; everything
declines, and this great age with all its luminaries enters that vast
shadow, where palely we vanish. Oh! What a wild sound the oaks
being cut for Hercules's pyre make in the twilight! Death's horses
begin to neigh and are joyful, for the brilliant age is ending; this
proud century, which knew how to conquer the opposing wind, is
dying. ... O Gautier, you their equal and their brother, depart after
Dumas, Lamartine, and Musset. The ancient wave, where men grew
young again, is dried up; since there is no more Styx, there is no
more fountain of youth, and the harsh reaper, thoughtfully, step by

Pensif et pas à pas vers le reste du blé;
C'est mon tour; et la nuit emplit mon œil troublé
Qui, devinant, hélas, l'avenir des colombes,
Pleure sur des berceaux et sourit à des tombes.

Ave, Dea; moriturus te salutat

A Judith Gautier

LA mort et la beauté sont deux choses profondes
Qui contiennent tant d'ombre et d'azur qu'on dirait
Deux sœurs également terribles et fécondes
Ayant la même énigme et le même secret.

Ô femmes, voix, regards, cheveux noirs, tresses blondes,
Brillez, je meurs! Ayez l'éclat, l'amour, l'attrait,
Ô perles que la mer mêle à ses grandes ondes,
Ô lumineux oiseaux de la sombre forêt!

Judith, nos deux destins sont plus près l'un de l'autre
Qu'on ne croirait, à voir mon visage et le vôtre;
Tout le divin abîme apparaît dans vos yeux,

step advances with his broad blade towards the remainder of the corn; it is my turn; and night fills my anxious eye which, guessing, alas! the future of doves, weeps over cradles and smiles at tombs.

Ave, Dea; moriturus te salutat

To Judith Gautier

DEATH and beauty are two deep things which hold so much shade and light, that one might say they were two sisters equally terrible and fertile, holding the same enigma and the same secret.

O women, voices, looks, black hair, blonde plaits, shine, I am dying! Hold brightness, love, fascination, O pearls that the sea mingles with its great waves, O shining birds of the dark forest!

Judith, our two fates are nearer one another than one would think, to see my face and yours: the whole divine abyss appears in your eyes,

Et moi, je sens le gouffre étoilé dans mon âme;
Nous sommes tous les deux voisins du ciel, madame,
Puisque vous êtes belle et puisque je suis vieux.

ALOYSIUS BERTRAND

Le Maçon

> Le maître Maçon. – Regardez ces
> bastions, ces contreforts: on les
> dirait construits pour l'éternité.
> SCHILLER. – Guillaume Tell.

L E maçon Abraham Knupfer chante, la truelle à la main, dans les airs échafaudé, si haut que, lisant les vers gothiques du bourdon, il nivelle de ses pieds et l'église aux trente arc-boutants, et la ville aux trente églises.

Il voit les tarasques de pierre vomir l'eau des ardoises dans l'abîme confus des galeries, des fenêtres, des pendentifs, des clochetons, des tourelles, des toits et des char-

And I feel the starry gulf in my soul; we are both neighbours of heaven, Madame, since you are beautiful and I am old.

The Mason

> The Master Mason. – Look at these
> bastions, these buttresses: one
> would say they were built for
> eternity.
> SCHILLER, *William Tell.*

T HE mason Abraham Knupfer is singing, trowel in hand, scaffolded so high in the air that, reading the Gothic verses on the great bell, he puts his feet on a level with both the church with thirty buttresses and the town with thirty churches.

He sees the stone monsters vomit the water from the slates into the confused abyss of galleries, windows, pendentives, bell-towers,

pentes, que tache d'un point gris l'aile échancrée et immobile du tiercelet.

Il voit les fortifications qui se découpent en étoile, la citadelle qui se rengorge comme une géline dans un tourteau, les cours des palais où le soleil tarit les fontaines, et les cloîtres des monastères où l'ombre tourne autour des piliers.

Les troupes impériales se sont logées dans le faubourg. Voilà qu'un cavalier tambourine là-bas. Abraham Knupfer distingue son chapeau à trois cornes, ses aiguillettes de laine rouge, sa cocarde traversée d'une ganse, et sa queue nouée d'un ruban.

Ce qu'il voit encore, ce sont des soudards qui, dans le parc empanaché de gigantesques ramées, sur de larges pelouses d'émeraude, criblent de coups d'arquebuse un oiseau de bois fiché à la pointe d'un mai.

turrets, roofs, and timber work, which the slanting motionless wing of the falcon marks with a grey spot.

He sees the fortifications outlined in a star, the citadel cocking itself up like a hen in a pie, the palace courtyards where the sun dries up the fountains and the monastery cloisters where the shadow turns around the pillars.

The imperial troops are quartered in the suburb. There is a horseman beating a drum down there. Abraham Knupfer makes out his tricorn hat, his shoulder-knots of red wool, his cockade crossed with a gimp, and his pigtail knotted with a ribbon.

He sees more: there are old soldiers who, in the park adorned with huge leafy branches, on broad emerald lawns, riddle with arquebus shots a wooden bird fixed to the top of a maypole.

Et le soir, quand la nef harmonieuse de la cathédrale s'endormit couchée les bras en croix, il aperçut de l'échelle, à l'horizon, un village incendié par des gens de guerre, qui flamboyait comme une comète dans l'azur.

Le Nain

— Toi, à cheval!
— Eh! pourquoi pas? j'ai si souvent galopé sur un lévrier du laird de Linlithgow!

Ballade écossaise

J'AVAIS capturé de mon séant, dans l'ombre de mes courtines, ce furtif papillon, éclos d'un rai de la lune ou d'une goutte de rosée.

Phalène palpitante qui, pour dégager ses ailes captives entre mes doigts, me payait une rançon de parfums!

And in the evening, when the melodious nave of the cathedral went to sleep lying with its arms in a cross, he saw from his ladder, on the horizon, a village, set on fire by soldiers, flaming like a comet in the blue sky.

The Dwarf

— You on horseback!
— Well, why not? I have galloped so often on the Laird of Linlithgow's greyhound!

Scottish Ballad

SITTING up, I had captured in the shadow of my curtains this furtive butterfly hatched from moonshine or a drop of dew.

The throbbing moth which, to free its wings imprisoned between my fingers, paid me a ransom of perfume!

Soudain la vagabonde bestiole s'envolait, abandonnant dans mon giron, – ô horreur! – une larve monstrueuse et difforme à tête humaine!

– «Où est ton âme, que je chevauche! – Mon âme, haquenée boiteuse des fatigues du jour, repose maintenant sur la litière dorée des songes.»

Et elle s'échappait d'effroi, mon âme, à travers la livide toile d'araignée du crépuscule, par-dessus de noirs horizons dentelés de noirs clochers gothiques.

Mais le nain, pendu à sa fuite hennissante, se roulait comme un fuseau dans les quenouillées de sa blanche crinière.

Suddenly, the wandering little beast flew away, leaving in my lap – O horror – a monstrous and misshapen maggot with a human head!
– 'Where is your soul that I may ride it! – My soul, that nag lame from the labours of the day, is now resting on the golden litter of dreams.'
And for fright my soul escaped through the livid spider's web of the twilight, over dark horizons notched with dark Gothic belfries.
But the dwarf, hanging on to its neighing flight, rolled himself like a spindle in the distaff-fuls of its white mane.

Le Deuxième Homme

> Et nunc, Domine, tolle, quaeso,
> animam meam a me, quia melior est
> mihi mors quam vita.
>
> Jonas, cap. 4, v. 3.
>
> J'en jure par la mort, dans un monde
> pareil,
> Non, je ne voudrais pas rajeunir d'un
> soleil.
>
> ALPHONSE DE LAMARTINE.
> – *Méditations.*

ENFER! – Enfer et paradis! – cris de désespoir! cris de joie! – blasphèmes des reprouvés! concerts des élus! – âmes des morts, semblables aux chênes de la montagne déracinés par les démons! âmes des morts, semblables aux fleurs de la vallée cueillies par les anges!

Soleil, firmament, terre et homme, tout avait commencé, tout avait fini. Une voix sécoua le néant. – «Soleil? appela cette voix, du seuil de la radieuse Jérusalem. –

The Second Man

> Et nunc, Domine, tolle, quaeso,
> animam meam a me, quia melior est
> mihi mors quam vita.
>
> Jonah, ch. 4, v. 3
>
> I swear by death that in such a
> world, no, I would not wish to live
> a single sun again.
>
> ALPHONSE DE LAMARTINE. – *Meditations.*

HELL! – Hell and paradise! – cries of despair! cries of joy! – blasphemies of the damned! harmonies of the elect! – souls of the dead like mountain oaks uprooted by demons! souls of the dead like flowers of the valley gathered by angels!

Sun, sky, earth, and man, everything had begun, everything had finished. A voice shook the void. – 'Sun?' called this voice from the threshold of radiant Jerusalem. – 'Sun?' repeated the echoes of in-

Soleil? répétèrent les échos de l'inconsolable Josaphat.» —
Et le soleil ouvrit ses cils d'or sur le chaos des mondes.

Mais le firmament pendait comme un lambeau d'étendard. — «Firmament? appela cette voix, du seuil de la
radieuse Jérusalem. — Firmament? répétèrent les échos de
l'inconsolable Josaphat.» — Et le firmament déroula aux
vents ses plis de pourpre et d'azur.

Mais la terre voguait à la dérive, comme un navire
foudroyé qui ne porte dans ses flancs que des cendres et
des ossements. — «Terre? appela cette voix, du seuil de la
radieuse Jérusalem. — Terre? répétèrent les échos de
l'inconsolable Josaphat.» — Et la terre ayant jeté l'ancre,
la nature s'assit, couronnée de fleurs, sous le porche de
montagnes aux cent mille colonnes.

Mais l'homme manquait à la creation, et tristes étaient
la terre et la nature, l'une de l'absence de son roi, l'autre
de l'absence de son époux. — «Homme? appela cette voix,
du seuil de la radieuse Jérusalem. — Homme? répétèrent les

consolable Josaphat. — And the sun opened its golden lashes on
the chaos of worlds.

But the sky hung like a rag torn from a standard. — 'Sky?' called
this voice from the threshold of radiant Jerusalem. — 'Sky?' repeated
the echoes of inconsolable Josaphat. — And the sky unrolled its
folds of purple and blue to the winds.

But the earth was sailing adrift, like a ship struck by lightning,
that bears in its sides only ashes and bones. — 'Earth?' called this
voice from the threshold of radiant Jerusalem. — 'Earth?' repeated the
echoes of inconsolable Josaphat. — And earth having cast anchor,
nature sat down crowned with flowers beneath the porch of mountains with the hundred thousand columns.

But man was lacking to the creation, and earth and nature were
sad, the one for the absence of her king, the other for the absence of
her husband. — 'Man?' called this voice from the threshold of radiant
Jerusalem. — 'Man?' repeated the echoes of inconsolable Josaphat. —

échos de l'inconsolable Josaphat.» – Et l'hymne de
délivrance et de grâces ne brisa point le sceau dont la mort
avait plombé les lèvres de l'homme endormi pour l'éternité
dans le lit du sépulcre.

«Ainsi soit-il! dit cette voix, et le seuil de la radieuse
Jérusalem se voila de deux sombres ailes. – Ainsi soit-il!
répétèrent les échos, et l'inconsolable Josaphat se remit à
pleurer.» – Et la trompette de l'archange sonna d'abîme
en abîme, tandis que tout croulait avec un fracas et une
ruine immense: le firmament, la terre, et le soleil, faute
de l'homme, cette pierre angulaire de la création!

GÉRARD DE NERVAL

Une Allée du Luxembourg

ELLE a passé, la jeune fille
Vive et preste comme un oiseau:
A la main une fleur qui brille,
A la bouche un refrain nouveau.

And the hymn of deliverance and thanks did not break the seal with
which death had sealed the lips of man sleeping for eternity in the
bed of the tomb.

'So be it!' said this voice, and the threshold of radiant Jerusalem
was veiled by two dark wings. – 'So be it!' repeated the echoes, and
inconsolable Josaphat began to weep again. – And the archangel's
trumpet sounded from abyss to abyss, while everything crumbled
with great noise and ruin: the sky, the earth, and the sun, for want
of man, that corner-stone of the creation!

An Alley in the Luxembourg Gardens

THE young girl passed by as lively and quick as a bird: in her hand
a shining flower, in her mouth a new song.

C'est peut-être la seule au monde
Dont le cœur au mien répondrait,
Qui venant dans ma nuit profonde
D'un seul regard l'éclaircirait!

Mais non, – ma jeunesse est finie …
Adieu, doux rayon qui m'as lui, –
Parfum, jeune fille, harmonie …
Le bonheur passait, – il a fui!

El Desdichado

JE suis le ténébreux, – le veuf, – l'inconsolé,
Le prince d'Aquitaine à la tour abolie:
Ma seule *étoile* est morte, – et mon luth constellé
Porte le *soleil* noir de la *Mélancolie*.

Dans la nuit du tombeau, toi qui m'as consolé,
Rends-moi le Pausilippe et la mer d'Italie,
La *fleur* qui plaisait tant à mon cœur désolé,
Et la treille où le pampre à la rose s'allie.

She is, perhaps, the only one in the world whose heart would
answer mine, who, coming into my deep night, would light it up
with a single glance.

But no, – my youth is over. … Farewell, sweet beam that shone
on me, – perfume, young girl, melody. … Happiness passed by, – it
has fled!

El Desdichado

I AM the shadow, the widower, the unconsoled, the Aquitanian prince
with the ruined tower: my only *star* is dead, and my star-strewn
lute bears the *black sun* of *Melancholy*.

You who consoled me, in the night of the tomb, give me
back Posilipo and the Italian sea, the *flower* which pleased my grief-
stricken heart so much, and the arbour where the vine joins with the
rose.

Suis-je Amour ou Phébus? … Lusignan ou Biron?
Mon front est rouge encor du baiser de la reine;
J'ai rêvé dans la grotte où nage la sirène. …

Et j'ai deux fois vainqueur traversé l'Achéron:
Modulant tour à tour sur la lyre d'Orphée
Les soupirs de la sainte et les cris de la fée.

Myrtho

JE pense à toi, Myrtho, divine enchanteresse,
Au Pausilippe altier, de mille feux brillant,
A ton front inondé des clartés d'Orient,
Aux raisins noirs mêlés avec l'or de ta tresse.

C'est dans ta coupe aussi que j'avais bu l'ivresse,
Et dans l'éclair furtif de ton œil souriant,
Quand aux pieds d'Iacchus on me voyait priant,
Car la Muse m'a fait l'un des fils de la Grèce.

Am I Love or Phoebus? … Lusignan or Biron? My brow is still
red from the queen's kiss; I have dreamed in the cave where the
siren swims. …
   And I have twice crossed Acheron victoriously: tuning in turn on
Orpheus's lyre the sighs of the saint and the fairy's cries.

Myrtho

I THINK of you, Myrtho, divine sorceress, of proud Posilipo shining with a thousand fires, of your brow flooded with the lights of
the East, of the black grapes mingled with the gold of your plait.
   It was in your cup too that I had drunk intoxication and in the
stealthy lightning of your smiling eye, when I was seen praying at
the feet of Iacchus, for the Muse made me one of the sons of
Greece.

Je sais pourquoi là-bas le volcan s'est rouvert …
C'est qu'hier tu l'avais touché d'un pied agile,
Et de cendres soudain l'horizon s'est couvert.

Depuis qu'un duc normand brisa tes dieux d'argile,
Toujours, sous les rameaux du laurier de Virgile,
Le pâle hortensia s'unit au myrte vert!

Horus

Le dieu Kneph en tremblant ébranlait l'univers:
Isis, la mère, alors se leva sur sa couche,
Fit un geste de haine à son époux farouche,
Et l'ardeur d'autrefois brilla dans ses yeux verts.

«Le voyez-vous, dit-elle, il meurt, ce vieux pervers,
Tous les frimas du monde ont passé par sa bouche,
Attachez son pied tors, éteignez son œil louche,
C'est le dieu des volcans et le roi des hivers!

I know why the volcano opened down there again. … It was because yesterday you had touched it with a nimble foot, and suddenly the horizon was covered with ashes.

Since a Norman duke broke your clay gods, beneath the branches of Virgil's laurel, the pale hydrangea is still joined to the green myrtle!

Horus

Trembling the god Kneph shook the universe: then Isis, the mother, raised herself on her couch, made a gesture of hatred towards her savage husband, and the passion of former days shone in her green eyes.

'Do you see him?' she said; 'he is dying, the old lecher; all the hoar-frosts of the world have passed through his mouth; bind his crooked foot, put out his squinting eye, he is the god of volcanoes and the king of winters!

«L'aigle a déjà passé, l'esprit nouveau m'appelle,
J'ai revêtu pour lui la robe de Cybèle …
C'est l'enfant bien-aimé d'Hermès et d'Osiris!»

La déesse avait fui sur sa conque dorée,
La mer nous renvoyait son image adorée,
Et les cieux rayonnaient sous l'écharpe d'Iris.

Antéros

Tu demandes pourquoi j'ai tant de rage au cœur
Et sur un col flexible une tête indomptée;
C'est que je suis issu de la race d'Antée,
Je retourne les dards contre le dieu vainqueur.

Oui, je suis de ceux-là qu'inspire le Vengeur,
Il m'a marqué le front de sa lèvre irritée,
Sous la pâleur d'Abel, hèlas! ensanglantée,
J'ai parfois de Caïn l'implacable rougeur!

'Already the eagle has passed by, the new spirit calls me, for him I have put on the dress of Cybele. … He is the beloved child of Hermes and Osiris!'

The goddess had fled on her golden shell, the sea sent us back her sweet image, and the skies shone beneath Iris's scarf.

Anteros

You ask why I have so much anger in my heart and an undaunted head on a neck that inclines; it is because I am sprung from the race of Antaeus; I turn back the arrows against the conquering god.

Yes, I am of those whom the Avenger inspires; he marked me on the brow with his angry lip; sometimes I have the implacable crimson of Cain beneath Abel's pallor, covered in blood, alas!

Jéhovah! le dernier, vaincu par ton génie,
Qui du fond des enfers, criait: «O tyrannie!»
C'est mon aïeul Bélus ou mon père Dagon. ...

Ils m'ont plongé trois fois dans les eaux du Cocyte,
Et, protégeant tout seul ma mère Amalécyte,
Je ressème à ses pieds les dents du vieux dragon.

Delfica

LA connais-tu, Dafné, cette ancienne romance,
Au pied du sycomore, ou sous les lauriers blancs,
Sous l'olivier, le myrte, ou les saules tremblants,
Cette chanson d'amour qui toujours recommence? ...

Reconnais-tu le TEMPLE au péristyle immense,
Et les citrons amers où s'imprimaient tes dents,
Et la grotte, fatale aux hôtes imprudents,
Où du dragon vaincu dort l'antique semence? ...

Jehovah! the last to be conquered by your genius, who from the depth of hell cried: 'O tyranny!', was my grandfather Belus or my father Dagon. ...

They dipped me three times in the waters of Cocytus, and, while alone protecting my Amalekite mother, I sow the old dragon's teeth again at her feet.

Delfica

DAPHNE, do you know this old ballad, at the sycamore's foot or beneath the white laurels, beneath the olive tree, the myrtle or the trembling willows, this love song which always begins anew? ...

Do you recognize the TEMPLE with the vast peristyle, and the bitter lemons which were marked by your teeth, and the cave, fatal to rash guests, where sleeps the old seed of the defeated dragon? ...

Ils reviendront, ces Dieux que tu pleures toujours!
Le temps va ramener l'ordre des anciens jours;
La terre a tressailli d'un souffle prophétique. ...

Cependant la sibylle au visage latin
Est endormie encor sous l'arc de Constantin
– Et rien n'a dérangé le sévère portique.

Artémis

LA Treizième revient. ... C'est encor la première;
Et c'est toujours la seule, – ou c'est le seul moment;
Car es-tu reine, ô toi! la première ou dernière?
Es-tu roi, toi le seul ou le dernier amant? ...

Aimez qui vous aima du berceau dans la bière;
Celle que j'aimai seul m'aime encore tendrement:
C'est la mort – ou la morte. ... O délice! o tourment!
La rose qu'elle tient, c'est la *Rose trémière.*

They will return, those Gods for which you still weep! Time will lead back the order of ancient days; the earth has shuddered at a prophetic breath. ...

Yet the sibyl with the Latin face is still asleep beneath the arch of Constantine – and nothing has disturbed the severe porch.

Artemis

THE thirteenth woman returns. ... Still she is the first; and still the only one – or it is the only moment; for are you queen, O you who are the first or last woman? Are you king, you who are the sole or last lover?

Love him who loved you from the cradle to the grave; she whom I loved alone still loves me tenderly; she is death – or the dead. ... O delight! O torment! The rose she holds is the *Hollyhock.* *

---

* The contrast between *rose* and *rose trémière* is lost in the English *rose* and *hollyhock*, but I thought it better to stick to the literal translation.

Sainte napolitaine aux mains pleines de feux,
Rose au cœur violet, fleur de sainte Gudule:
As-tu trouvé ta croix dans le désert des cieux?

Roses blanches, tombez! vous insultez nos dieux,
Tombez, fantômes blancs, de votre ciel qui brûle:
– La sainte de l'abîme est plus sainte à mes yeux!

Le Christ aux oliviers

> *Dieu est mort! le ciel est vide …*
> *Pleurez! enfants, vous n'avez plus*
> *de père!*
>
> JEAN-PAUL.

I

QUAND le Seigneur, levant au ciel ses maigres bras,
Sous les arbres sacrés, comme font les poètes,
Se fut longtemps perdu dans ses douleurs muettes,
Et se jugea trahi par des amis ingrats;

Neapolitan saint with your hands full of fires, rose with the violet heart, Saint Gudula's flower: did you find your cross in the desert of the skies?

White roses, fall! You insult our gods, fall, white spectres, from your burning heaven: – the saint from the abyss is more holy in my eyes!

Christ in the Olive Grove

> *God is dead! the sky is empty. …*
> *Weep! children, you have no more*
> *father!*
>
> JEAN-PAUL RICHTER.

I

WHEN the Lord, raising his lean arms to the sky, beneath the holy trees as poets do, had been lost for a long time in his dumb griefs and thought himself betrayed by ungrateful friends;

Il se tourna vers ceux qui l'attendaient en bas
Rêvant d'être des rois, des sages, des prophètes ...
Mais engourdis, perdus dans le sommeil des bêtes,
Et se prit à crier: «Non, Dieu n'existe pas!»

Ils dormaient. «Mes amis, savez-vous *la nouvelle*?
J'ai touché de mon front à la voûte éternelle;
Je suis sanglant, brisé, souffrant pour bien des jours!

«Frères, je vous trompais: Abîme! abîme! abîme!
Le dieu manque à l'autel où je suis la victime ...
Dieu n'est pas! Dieu n'est plus!» Mais ils dormaient
    toujours! ...

2

Il reprit: «Tout est mort! J'ai parcouru les mondes;
Et j'ai perdu mon vol dans leurs chemins lactés,
Aussi loin que la vie, en ses veines fécondes,
Répand des sables d'or et des flots argentés:

He turned towards those who awaited him below, dreaming of
being kings, sages, and prophets ... but grown dull, lost in bestial
slumber, and began to cry: 'No, God does not exist!'
    They slept. 'My friends, do you know *the news*? I have touched
the eternal vault with my brow; I am bleeding, broken, sick for
many days!
    'Brothers, I deceived you: abyss! abyss! abyss! The god is miss-
ing from the altar where I am the sacrifice. ... There is no God!
there is no God any more!' But still they slept! ...

2

He began again: 'Everything is dead! I passed through the worlds
and lost my flight among their milky ways, as far as life, in its fertile veins, spreads golden sands and silvery waves:

«Partout le sol désert côtoyé par des ondes,
Des tourbillons confus d'océans agités …
Un souffle vague émeut les sphères vagabondes,
Mais nul esprit existe en ces immensités.

«En cherchant l'œil de Dieu, je n'ai vu qu'une orbite
Vaste, noire et sans fond, d'où la nuit qui l'habite
Rayonne sur le monde et s'épaissit toujours;

«Un arc-en-ciel étrange entoure ce puits sombre,
Seuil de l'ancien chaos dont le néant est l'ombre,
Spirale engloutissant les Mondes et les Jours!»

3

«Immobile Destin, muette sentinelle,
Froide Nécessité! … Hasard qui, t'avançant
Parmi les mondes morts sous la neige éternelle,
Refroidis, par dégrés, l'univers pâlissant,

'Everywhere the desert soil bordered by the waves, by the confused eddies of rough oceans … An uncertain breath moves the wandering spheres, but no spirit exists in those vast spaces.

'Seeking the eye of God, I only saw a huge black bottomless socket, whence the night that dwells in it radiates over the world and becomes ever more dense;

'A strange rainbow surrounds this dark pit, threshold of old chaos whose shadow is nothingness, a vortex swallowing up the Worlds and Days!

3

'Motionless Destiny, dumb sentinel, cold Necessity! … Chance, that, advancing among dead worlds beneath everlasting snow, gradually chills the whitening universe,

«Sais-tu ce que tu fais, puissance originelle,
De tes soleils éteints, l'un l'autre se froissant ...
Es-tu sûr de transmettre une haleine immortelle,
Entre un monde qui meurt et l'autre renaissant? ...

«Ô mon père! est-ce toi que je sens en moi-même?
As-tu pouvoir de vivre et de vaincre la mort?
Aurais-tu succombé sous un dernier effort

«De cet ange des nuits que frappa l'anathème? ...
Car je me sens tout seul à pleurer et souffrir,
Hélas! et, si je meurs, c'est que tout va mourir!»

4

Nul n'entendait gémir l'éternelle victime,
Livrant au monde en vain tout son cœur épanché;
Mais prêt à défaillir et sans force penché,
Il appela le *seul* – éveillé dans Solyme:

'Do you know what you are doing, original power, with your
burnt-out suns, the one dashing against the other? ... Are you certain of passing on an immortal breath between a world that is dying
and another born again? ...
    'O my father! is it you I feel in myself? Have you the power to
live and conquer death? Have you perhaps succumbed to a last
effort
    'Of that angel of night whom the anathema struck? ... For I feel
myself quite alone in weeping and suffering, alas! and, if I die,
everything will die!'

4

No one heard the groans of the eternal sacrifice vainly giving to the
world all his overflowing heart; but ready to faint and stooping
without strength, he called the *only one* – awake in Jerusalem:

«Judas! lui cria-t-il, tu sais ce qu'on m'estime,
Hâte-toi de me vendre, et finis ce marché:
Je suis souffrant, ami! sur la terre couché …
Viens! ô toi qui, du moins, as la force du crime!»

Mais Judas s'en allait, mécontent et pensif,
Se trouvant mal payé, plein d'un remords si vif
Qu'il lisait ses noirceurs sur tous les murs écrites. …

Enfin Pilate seul, qui veillait pour César,
Sentant quelque pitié, se tourna par hasard:
«Allez chercher ce fou!» dit il aux satellites.

5

C'était bien lui, ce fou, cet insensé sublime …
Cet Icare oublié qui remontait les cieux,
Ce Phaéton perdu sous la foudre des dieux,
Ce bel Atys meurtri que Cybèle ranime!

'Judas!' he cried 'to him, you know what they value me at, hurry
to sell me, and end this bargaining: I am sick, friend! lying on the
ground. … Come! O you who at least have the strength of crime!'

But Judas went away, discontented and thoughtful, thinking
himself badly paid, full of so keen a remorse that he read his base-
ness written on all the walls. …

At last Pilate alone who watched for Caesar, feeling some pity,
chanced to turn round: 'Go seek this madman!' he said to his
officers.

5

Indeed it was he, this madman, this sublime fool. … This forgotten
Icarus reascending the skies, this Phaeton destroyed beneath the
thunder of the gods, this lovely mangled Atys brought to life again
by Cybele!

L'augure interrogeait le flanc de la victime,
La terre s'enivrait de ce sang précieux …
L'univers étourdi penchait sur ses essieux,
Et l'Olympe un instant chancela vers l'abîme.

«Réponds! criait César à Jupiter Ammon,
Quel est ce nouveau dieu qu'on impose à la terre?
Et si ce n'est un dieu, c'est au moins un démon …»

Mais l'oracle invoqué pour jamais dut se taire;
Un seul pouvait au monde expliquer ce mystère:
– Celui qui donna l'âme aux enfants du limon.

Vers dorés

Eh quoi! tout est sensible!
PYTHAGORE

Homme, libre penseur! te crois-tu seul pensant
Dans ce monde où la vie éclate en toute chose?
Des forces que tu tiens ta liberté dispose,
Mais de tous tes conseils l'univers est absent.

The augurer questioned the entrails of the sacrifice, the earth was drunk with this precious blood. … The dizzy universe tottered on its axes, and Olympus for a moment reeled towards the abyss.

'Answer!' cried Caesar to Jupiter Ammon, 'who is this new god forced upon the earth? And if it is no god, at least it is a demon. …'

But the oracle he called upon was to be silent for ever; one alone could explain this mystery to the world. – He who gave souls to the children of clay.

Golden Verses

What! Everything is sentient!
PYTHAGORAS

Man, free thinker! do you believe that you alone think in this world where life bursts forth in everything? Your freedom has power to use the strength you possess, but the universe is absent from all your councils.

Respecte dans la bête un esprit agissant:
Chaque fleur est une âme à la Nature éclose;
Un mystère d'amour dans le métal repose;
«Tout est sensible!» Et tout sur ton être est puissant.

Crains, dans le mur aveugle, un regard qui t'épie:
A la matière même un verbe est attaché ...
Ne la fais pas servir à quelque usage impie!

Souvent dans l'être obscur habite un Dieu caché;
Et comme un œil naissant couvert par ses paupières,
Un pur esprit s'accroît sous l'écorce des pierres!

Chanson Gothique

BELLE épousée
J'aime tes pleurs!
C'est la rosée
Qui sied aux fleurs.

Les belles choses
N'ont qu'un printemps,
Semons de roses
Les pas du Temps!

In the beast respect an active soul: every flower is a soul unfolded to Nature; in metal sleeps a mystery of love; 'Everything is sentient!' And everything has power over your being.

Fear a glance watching you in the blind wall: a Word is connected even with matter. ... Do not make it serve some impious purpose!

Often in the dark being dwells a hidden God; and, like an eye born covered by its lids, a pure spirit grows beneath the surface of stones!

Gothic Song

FAIR wife, I love your tears! It is the dew which is becoming for flowers.

Beautiful things have only one Spring, let us sow the footprints of Time with roses!

Soit brune ou blonde
Faut-il choisir?
Le Dieu du monde,
C'est le Plaisir.

ALFRED DE MUSSET

A Julie

O n me demande, par les rues,
Pourquoi je vais bayant aux grues,
Fumant mon cigare au soleil,
A quoi se passe ma jeunesse,
Et depuis trois ans de paresse
Ce qu'ont fait mes nuits sans sommeil.

Donne-moi tes lèvres, Julie;
Les folles nuits qui t'ont pâlie
Ont séché leur corail luisant.
Parfume-les de ton haleine;
Donne-les-moi, mon Africaine,
Tes belles lèvres de pur sang.

Whether brunette or blonde, must we choose? The God of the
world is Pleasure.

To Julia

In the streets they ask me why I go gaping at the tarts, smoking
my cigar in the sun, how my youth is passed, and what my sleep-
less nights have produced during three years of idleness.

Give me your lips, Julia; the wild nights that made you pale have
dried their shining coral. Perfume them with your breath; give them
me, my Barbary, your lovely lips of pure blood-stock.

Mon imprimeur crie à tue-tête
Que sa machine est toujours prête,
Et que la mienne n'en peut mais.
D'honnêtes gens, qu'un club admire,
N'ont pas dédaigné de prédire
Que je n'en reviendrai jamais.

Julie, as-tu du vin d'Espagne?
Hier, nous battions la campagne;
Va donc voir s'il en reste encor.
Ta bouche est brûlante, Julie;
Inventons donc quelque folie
Qui nous perde l'âme et le corps.

On dit que ma gourme me rentre,
Que je n'ai plus rien dans le ventre,
Que je suis vide à faire peur;
Je crois, si j'en valais la peine,
Qu'on m'enverrait à Sainte-Hélène,
Avec un cancer dans le cœur.

My printer cries with all his might that his machine is always
ready and that mine can do nothing any more. Honest folk, whom
clubs admire, have not disdained to say that I shall never recover
from it.

Julia, have you Spanish wine? Yesterday we were roving; go
then and see if there is any left. Your mouth is burning, Julia; let us
find out some madness to destroy us body and soul.

They say I am reaping my wild oats, that I have nothing more in
my belly, that I am frightfully hollow; I think, if I were worth it,
they would send me to Saint Helena with a cancer in my heart.

Allons, Julie, il faut t'attendre
A me voir quelque jour en cendre,
Comme Hercule sur son rocher.
Puisque c'est par toi que j'expire,
Ouvre ta robe, Déjanire,
Que je monte sur mon bûcher.

Chanson: à Saint-Blaise, à la Zuecca ...

A SAINT-BLAISE, à la Zuecca,
Vous étiez, vous étiez bien aise
A Saint-Blaise.
A Saint-Blaise, à la Zuecca,
Nous étions bien là.

Mais de vous en souvenir
Prendrez-vous la peine?
Mais de vous en souvenir
Et d'y revenir,

A Saint-Blaise, à la Zuecca,
Dans les prés fleuris cueillir la verveine,
A Saint-Blaise, à la Zuecca,
Vivre et mourir là!

Come, Julia, you must be prepared to see me in ashes some day like Hercules on his rock. Since it is through you I die, open your dress, Dejanira, let me climb upon my pyre.

Song: at Saint Blaise, at the Zuecca. ...

AT Saint Blaise, at the Zuecca, you were, you were well at ease at Saint Blaise. At Saint Blaise, at the Zuecca, we were happy there.
But will you take the trouble to remember it? But to remember it and to return there,
To Saint Blaise, to the Zuecca, in the flowery meadows to gather the verbena, to Saint Blaise, to the Zuecca, to live and die there!

Lettre à M. de Lamartine

LORSQUE le grand Byron allait quitter Ravenne
Et chercher sur les mers quelque plage lointaine
Où finir en héros son immortel ennui,
Comme il était assis aux pieds de sa maîtresse,
Pâle, et déjà tourné du côté de la Grèce,
Celle qu'il appelait alors sa Guiccioli
Ouvrit un soir un livre où l'on parlait de lui.

Avez-vous de ce temps conservé la mémoire,
Lamartine, et ces vers au prince des proscrits,
Vous souvient-il encor qui les avait écrits?
Vous étiez jeune alors, vous, notre chère gloire.
Vous veniez d'essayer pour la première fois
Ce beau luth éploré qui vibre sous vos doigts.
La Muse que le ciel vous avait fiancée
Sur votre front rêveur cherchait votre pensée,
Vierge craintive encore, amante des lauriers.
Vous ne connaissiez pas, noble fils de la France,
Vous ne connaissiez pas, sinon par sa souffrance,
Ce sublime orgueilleux à qui vous écriviez.

Letter to Monsieur de Lamartine

WHEN the great Byron was about to leave Ravenna and seek out some distant shore across the seas where he might end heroically his immortal tedium; as he was seated at his mistress's feet, pale and already turned towards Greece, she, whom he then called his Guiccioli, one evening opened a book which spoke of him.

Have you kept the memory of that time, Lamartine, and do you recall who wrote those lines to the prince of the banished? Then you were young, you who are our special glory. You had just tried out for the first time that beautiful desolate lute which throbs beneath your fingers. The Muse whom heaven had betrothed to you, a timid maiden still and lover of the bays, sought your thought upon your dreamy brow.

You did not know, O noble son of France, you did not know, except by his suffering, the sublime pride of the man to whom you

De quel droit osiez-vous l'aborder et le plaindre?
Quel aigle, Ganymède, à ce dieu vous portait?
Pressentiez-vous qu'un jour vous le pourriez atteindre,
Celui qui de si haut alors vous écoutait?
Non, vous aviez vingt ans, et le cœur vous battait.
Vous aviez lu *Lara, Manfred* et *le Corsaire*,
Et vous aviez écrit sans essuyer vos pleurs;
Le souffle de Byron vous soulevait de terre,
Et vous alliez à lui, porté par ses douleurs.
Vous appeliez de loin cette âme désolée;
Pour grand qu'il vous parût, vous le sentiez ami,
Et, comme le torrent dans la verte vallée,
L'écho de son génie en vous avait gémi.

Et lui, lui dont l'Europe, encore tout armée,
Écoutait en tremblant les sauvages concerts;
Lui qui depuis dix ans fuyait sa renommée
Et de sa solitude emplissait l'univers;
Lui, le grand inspiré de la Mélancolie,
Qui, las d'être envié, se changeait en martyr;
Lui, le dernier amant de la pauvre Italie,
Pour son dernier exil s'apprêtant à partir;

wrote. By what right did you dare to approach and pity him?
Ganymede, what eagle carried you to this god? Did you guess that
one day you might reach him who listened to you then from such a
height. No, you were twenty years old, and your heart was beating.
You had read *Lara, Manfred,* and *The Corsair,* and you had written
without wiping away your tears; Byron's breath raised you up from
earth, and you went to him carried upon his grief. You called from
afar that desolate soul; however great he seemed to you, you felt
him as a friend, and, like the stream in the green valley, the echo of
his genius had murmured in you.

And he, he, whose wild strains Europe, still in arms, heard trembling; he who for ten years had fled his own fame and filled
the universe with his solitude; he, the poet whom Melancholy inspired above all, who, tired of being envied, transformed himself
into a martyr; he, the last lover of poor Italy, getting ready to leave

Lui qui, rassasié de la grandeur humaine,
Comme un cygne, à son chant sentant sa mort prochaine,
Sur terre autour de lui cherchait pour qui mourir ...
Il écouta ces vers que lisait sa maîtresse,
Ce doux salut lointain d'un jeune homme inconnu.
Je ne sais si du style il comprit la richesse;
Il laissa dans ses yeux sourire sa tristesse:
Ce qui venait du cœur lui fut le bienvenu.

Poète, maintenant que ta muse fidèle,
Par ton unique amour sûre d'être immortelle,
De la verveine en fleur t'a couronné le front,
A ton tour, reçois-moi comme le grand Byron.
De t'égaler jamais je n'ai pas l'espérance;
Ce que tu tiens du ciel, nul ne me l'a promis,
Mais de ton sort au mien plus grande est la distance,
Meilleur en sera Dieu qui peut nous rendre amis.
Je ne t'adresse pas d'inutiles louanges,
Et je ne songe point que tu me répondras;
Pour être proposés, ces illustres échanges
Veulent être signés d'un nom que je n'ai pas.

for his final exile; he who, glutted with human grandeur, like a swan feeling its death approaching at its own song, sought on the earth around him someone for whom to die. ... He listened to those lines that his mistress read, that sweet, distant greeting from an unknown young man. I do not know if he understood the richness of the style; he allowed his sorrow to smile in his eyes; what came from the heart was welcome to him.

Poet, now that your faithful muse, sure of immortality through your only love, has crowned your brow with flowering verbena, in your turn receive me like the great Byron. I have no hope of ever equalling you; no one has promised me what you hold from heaven, but the greater the distance from your fate to mine, the better it will be for God who can make us friends. I send you no useless praises, and I do not dream that you will answer me; to be offered, these famous exchanges must be signed with a name I do not possess. I

J'ai cru pendant longtemps que j'étais las du monde;
J'ai dit que je niais, croyant avoir douté,
Et j'ai pris, devant moi, pour une nuit profonde
Mon ombre qui passait pleine de vanité.
Poète, je t'écris pour te dire que j'aime,
Qu'un rayon de soleil est tombé jusqu'à moi,
Et qu'en un jour de deuil et de douleur suprême,
Les pleurs que je versais m'ont fait penser à toi.

Qui de nous, Lamartine, et de notre jeunesse,
Ne sait par cœur ce chant, des amants adoré,
Qu'un soir, au bord d'un lac, tu nous as soupiré?
Qui n'a lu mille fois, qui ne relit sans cesse
Ces vers mystérieux où parle ta maîtresse,
Et qui n'a sangloté sur ces divins sanglots,
Profonds comme le ciel et purs comme les flots?
Hélas! ces longs regrets des amours mensongères,
Ces ruines du temps qu'on trouve à chaque pas,
Ces sillons infinis de lueurs éphémères,
Qui peut se dire un homme, et ne les connaît pas?
Quiconque aima jamais porte une cicatrice;
Chacun l'a dans le sein, toujours prête à s'ouvrir;

thought for a long time I was tired of the world; I said I denied,
believing I doubted, and I took for deep night before me my passing
shadow full of vanity. Poet, I write to tell you that I am in love, that
a beam of sunlight came down to me, and that on a day of mourning
and supreme grief, the tears I shed made me think of you.

Which of us, Lamartine, and of our youth, does not know by
heart that song, adored by lovers, which you sighed to us one evening beside a lake? Who has not read a thousand times, who does not
constantly re-read those mysterious lines where your mistress
speaks, and who has not sobbed over those divine tears, deep as the
sky and pure as the waves? Alas! those long regrets for deceitful
loves, those ruins of time that we find at every step, those infinite
trails of fleeting lights, who can call himself a man and does not
know them? Whoever loved carries a scar; everyone has it in their
breast always ready to open; everyone keeps it within himself, a

Chacun la garde en soi, cher et secret supplice,
Et mieux il est frappé, moins il en veut guérir.
Te le dirai-je, à toi, chantre de la souffrance,
Que ton glorieux mal, je l'ai souffert aussi?
Qu'un instant, comme toi, devant ce ciel immense,
J'ai serré dans mes bras la vie et l'espérance,
Et qu'ainsi que le tien, mon rêve s'est enfui?
Te dirai-je qu'un soir, dans la brise embaumée,
Endormi, comme toi, dans la paix du bonheur,
Aux célestes accents d'une voix bien-aimée,
J'ai cru sentir le temps s'arrêter dans mon cœur?
Te dirai-je qu'un soir, resté seul sur la terre,
Dévoré, comme toi, d'un affreux souvenir,
Je me suis étonné de ma propre misère,
Et de ce qu'un enfant peut souffrir sans mourir?
Ah! ce que j'ai senti dans cet instant terrible,
Oserai-je m'en plaindre et te le raconter?
Comment exprimerai-je une peine indicible?
Après toi, devant toi, puis-je encor le tenter?

dear and secret torment, and the deeper he is struck, the less he
wishes to be cured. Shall I tell you, bard of suffering, that I too have
suffered from your proud sickness? That for a moment, like you,
before this vast sky, I pressed life and hope within my arms, and
that, like yours, my dream has fled away? Shall I tell you that one
evening, in the scented breeze, sleeping like you in the peace of
happiness, to the heavenly notes of a beloved voice, I thought I felt
time stop in my heart? Shall I tell you that one evening, left alone
on earth, eaten up, like you, by a frightful memory, I was surprised
at my own wretchedness and at what a child can suffer without
dying? Ah! shall I dare to complain and tell you of what I felt at
that awful moment? How shall I express unspeakable anguish?
Beside you, in face of you, can I still attempt it? Yes, I want to tell

Oui, de ce jour fatal, plein d'horreur et de charmes,
Je veux fidèlement te faire le récit;
Ce ne sont pas des chants, ce ne sont que des larmes,
Et je ne te dirai que ce que Dieu m'a dit.

Lorsque le laboureur, regagnant sa chaumière,
Trouve le soir son champ rasé par le tonnerre,
Il croit d'abord qu'un rêve a fasciné ses yeux,
Et, doutant de lui-même, interroge les cieux.
Partout la nuit est sombre, et la terre enflammée.
Il cherche autour de lui la place accoutumée
Où sa femme l'attend sur le seuil entr'ouvert;
Il voit un peu de cendre au milieu d'un désert.
Ses enfants demi-nus sortent de la bruyère,
Et viennent lui conter comme leur pauvre mère
Est morte sous le chaume avec des cris affreux;
Mais maintenant au loin tout est silencieux.
Le misérable écoute et comprend sa ruine.
Il serre, désolé, ses fils sur sa poitrine;
Il ne lui reste plus, s'il ne tend pas la main,
Que la faim pour ce soir et la mort pour demain.

you faithfully the story of that fatal day full of horror and charm; these are not songs, they are but tears, and I will only tell you what God has told me.

When the labourer, returning to his cottage in the evening, finds his field razed by thunder, he thinks at first that a dream has bewitched his eyes, and, doubting himself, questions the heavens. Everywhere the night is dark, and the earth glowing. He seeks around him the usual place where his wife awaits him on the half-open threshold; he sees a little ash in the midst of a desert. His half-naked children come out of the heath to tell him how their poor mother died beneath the thatch with dreadful cries; but now far off everything is quiet. The wretch listens and understands his loss. Grief-stricken, he presses his sons to his bosom; nothing remains for him if he does not beg, but hunger for this evening and death

Pas un sanglot ne sort de sa gorge oppressée;
Muet et chancelant, sans force et sans pensée,
Il s'assoit à l'écart, les yeux sur l'horizon,
Et, regardant s'enfuir sa moisson consumée,
Dans les noirs tourbillons de l'épaisse fumée
L'ivresse du malheur emporte sa raison.

Tel, lorsque abandonné d'une infidèle amante,
Pour la première fois j'ai connu la douleur,
Transpercé tout à coup d'une flèche sanglante,
Seul, je me suis assis dans la nuit de mon cœur.
Ce n'était pas au bord d'un lac au flot limpide,
Ni sur l'herbe fleurie au penchant des coteaux;
Mes yeux noyés de pleurs ne voyaient que le vide,
Mes sanglots étouffés n'éveillaient point d'échos.
C'était dans une rue obscure et tortueuse
De cet immense égout qu'on appelle Paris;
Autour de moi criait cette foule railleuse
Qui des infortunés n'entend jamais les cris.
Sur le pavé noirci les blafardes lanternes
Versaient un jour douteux plus triste que la nuit,
Et, suivant au hasard ces feux vagues et ternes,
L'homme passait dans l'ombre, allant où va le bruit.

for to-morrow. Not a sob issues from his constricted throat; dumb and staggering, without strength and without thought, he sits himself apart, his eyes on the horizon and, watching his burnt crop disappear in black spirals of thick smoke, the frenzy of misfortune carries away his reason.

So when, abandoned by a faithless love, I knew grief for the first time, transfixed all at once by a cruel arrow, I sat down alone in the night of my heart. It was not on the shore of a lake with clear waves nor on the flowery grass of hillside slopes; my eyes, drowned with tears, saw only the void, my stifled sobbing woke no echoes. It was in a dark and winding street of this huge sewer they call Paris; around me shrieked the jeering crowd that never hears the cries of the unfortunate. On the blackened pavement the dim street-lamps threw a doubtful daylight sadder than night, and, following at random those hazy, dull beacons, men passed in the shadow going with

Partout retentissait comme une joie étrange;
C'était en février, au temps du carnaval.
Les masques avinés, se croisant dans la fange,
S'accostaient d'une injure ou d'un refrain banal.
Dans un carosse ouvert une troupe entassée
Paraissait par moments sous le ciel pluvieux,
Puis se perdait au loin dans la ville insensée,
Hurlant un hymne impur sous la résine en feux.
Cependant des vieillards, des enfants et des femmes
Se barbouillaient de lie au fond des cabarets,
Tandis que de la nuit les prêtresses infâmes
Promenaient çà et là leurs spectres inquiets.
On eût dit un portrait de la débauche antique,
Un de ces soirs fameux chers au peuple romain,
Où des temples secrets la Vénus impudique
Sortait échevelée, une torche à la main.
Dieu juste! pleurer seul par une nuit pareille!
Ô mon unique amour! que vous avais-je fait?
Vous m'aviez pu quitter, vous qui juriez la veille
Que vous étiez ma vie et que Dieu le savait?

the noise. Everywhere resounded a sort of strange joy; it was in
February, in the time of the carnival. The tipsy masks, passing in
the dirt, accosted one another with an oath or a banal song. A band
crammed in an open carriage appeared from time to time beneath
the rainy sky, then were lost far off in the frenzied town, howling a
lewd anthem beneath the burning resin of the lamps. Meanwhile,
old men, children, and women smeared themselves with lees in the
depth of the taverns, while the infamous priestesses of the night
paraded their restless phantoms here and there. One would have
said a picture of a debauch of antiquity, one of those famous evenings dear to the Roman people, when shameless Venus came forth
from secret temples, her hair streaming and a torch in her hand.

Just God! to weep alone on such a night! O my only love! What
had I done to you? You could leave me when you swore the night
before that you were my life and that God knew it? Ah! cold and

Ah! toi, le savais-tu, froide et cruelle amie,
Qu'à travers cette honte et cette obscurité,
J'étais là, regardant de ta lampe chérie,
Comme une étoile au ciel, la tremblante clarté?
Non, tu n'en savais rien, je n'ai pas vu ton ombre;
Ta main n'est pas venue entr'ouvrir ton rideau.
Tu n'as pas regardé si le ciel était sombre;
Tu ne m'as pas cherché dans cet affreux tombeau!

Lamartine, c'est là, dans cette rue obscure,
Assis sur une borne, au fond d'un carrefour,
Les deux mains sur mon cœur, et serrant ma blessure,
Et sentant y saigner un invincible amour;
C'est là, dans cette nuit d'horreur et de détresse,
Au milieu des transports d'un peuple furieux
Qui semblait en passant crier à ma jeunesse:
«Toi qui pleures ce soir, n'as-tu pas ri comme eux?»
C'est là, devant ce mur, où j'ai frappé ma tête,
Où j'ai posé deux fois le fer sur mon sein nu;
C'est là, le croiras-tu? chaste et noble poète,
Que de tes chants divins je me suis souvenu.

cruel love, did you know that, through this shame and darkness, I was there watching the trembling light of your beloved lamp like a star in the sky? No, you knew nothing of it, I did not see your shadow; your hand did not come to half-open your curtain. You did not look to see if the sky was dark; you did not seek me out in that frightful tomb!

Lamartine, it was there, in that dark street, seated on a milestone, by a crossroad, both hands on my heart, pressing my wound, while feeling unconquerable love bleed there; it was there in that night of horror and distress, in the midst of the raptures of a mad crowd that, passing by, seemed to cry to my youth: 'You who weep to-night, have you not laughed like them?' It was there, in front of this wall where I struck my head, where twice I placed the steel on my naked breast; it was there, will you believe it? chaste and noble poet, that I remembered your divine songs.

Ô toi qui sais aimer, réponds, amant d'Elvire,
Comprends-tu que l'on parte et qu'on se dise adieu?
Comprends-tu que ce mot, la main puisse l'écrire,
Et le cœur le signer, et les lèvres le dire,
Les lèvres, qu'un baiser vient d'unir devant Dieu!
Comprends-tu qu'un lien qui, dans l'âme immortelle,
Chaque jour plus profond se forme à notre insu;
Qui déracine en nous la volonté rebelle,
Et nous attache au cœur son merveilleux tissu;
Un lien tout-puissant dont les nœuds et la trame
Sont plus durs que la roche et que les diamants;
Qui ne craint ni le temps, ni le fer, ni la flamme,
Ni la mort elle-même, et qui fait des amants
Jusque dans le tombeau s'aimer les ossements;
Comprends-tu que dix ans ce lien nous enlace,
Qu'il ne fasse dix ans qu'un seul être de deux,
Puis tout à coup se brise, et, perdu dans l'espace,
Nous laisse épouvantés d'avoir cru vivre heureux?

O you who know how to love, answer, Elvira's lover, do you understand how one can part and say good-bye? Do you understand how the hand can write that word, and the heart sign it, and the lips say it, the lips which a kiss has just joined before God! Do you understand how a bond which, in the immortal soul, unknown to us, is formed more deeply every day; which uproots the rebel will within us and binds its wonderful web upon our heart; an all-powerful bond whose knots and woof are harder than rock and diamonds; which fears neither time nor steel nor flame nor death itself, and which makes lovers' bones love each other even in the tomb; do you understand how for ten years this bond can entwine us, can make for ten years a single being of two, then all at once can break and, lost in space, leave us frightened at having thought we could live happily?

Ô poète! il est dur que la nature humaine,
Qui marche à pas comptés vers une fin certaine,
Doive encor s'y traîner en portant une croix,
Et qu'il faille ici-bas mourir plus d'une fois.
Car de quel autre nom peut s'appeler sur terre
Cette nécessité de changer de misère,
Qui nous fait, jour et nuit, tout prendre et tout quitter,
Si bien que notre temps se passe à convoiter?
Ne sont-ce pas des morts, et des morts effroyables,
Que tant de changements d'êtres si variables,
Qui se disent toujours fatigués d'espérer,
Et qui sont toujours prêts à se transfigurer?
Quel tombeau que le cœur, et quelle solitude!
Comment la passion devient-elle habitude,
Et comment se fait-il que, sans y trébucher,
Sur ses propres débris l'homme puisse marcher?
Il y marche pourtant; c'est Dieu qui l'y convie.
Il va semant partout et prodiguant sa vie:
Désir, crainte, colère, inquiétude, ennui,
Tout passe et disparaît, tout est fantôme en lui.
Son misérable cœur est fait de telle sorte,
Qu'il faut incessament qu'une ruine en sorte;

O poet! it is hard that human nature, which marches with mea-
sured steps towards a certain end, must always drag itself carrying
a cross, and that down here on earth we must die more than once.
For by what other name on earth can this necessity of changing
wretchedness be called, which makes us, day and night, take and
leave everything, so that our time is passed in desire? Are not these
deaths and terrible deaths; so many changes of such variable beings,
always saying that they are tired of hoping and always ready to be
transformed? What a tomb is the heart and what a solitude! How
does passion become habit, and how is it that man can walk on his
own ruins without stumbling? Yet he walks there; it is God who
summons him to it. He goes scattering seed everywhere and
squandering his life: desire, fear, wrath, care, and boredom, everything passes by and disappears; everything is a spectre within him.
His wretched heart is made in such a way that disaster must con-

Que la mort soit son terme, il ne l'ignore pas,
Et, marchant à la mort, il meurt à chaque pas.
Il meurt dans ses amis, dans son fils, dans son père;
Il meurt dans ce qu'il pleure et dans ce qu'il espère;
Et, sans parler des corps qu'il faut ensevelir,
Qu'est-ce donc qu'oublier, si ce n'est pas mourir?
Ah! c'est plus que mourir; c'est survivre à soi-même.
L'âme remonte au ciel quand on perd ce qu'on aime.
Il ne reste de nous qu'un cadavre vivant;
Le désespoir l'habite, et le néant l'attend.

Eh bien! bon ou mauvais, inflexible ou fragile,
Humble ou fier, triste ou gai, mais toujours gémissant,
Cet homme, tel qu'il est, cet être fait d'argile,
Tu l'as vu, Lamartine, et son sang est ton sang.
Son bonheur est le tien; sa douleur est la tienne;
Et des maux qu'ici-bas il lui faut endurer,
Pas un qui ne te touche et qui ne t'appartienne;
Puisque tu sais chanter, ami, tu sais pleurer.

stantly issue from it; he is not unaware that death is his goal and, marching towards death, he dies at every step. He dies in his friends, in his son, in his father; he dies in what he weeps and in what he hopes; and, without speaking of bodies which must be buried, what is forgetting if it is not death? Ah! it is more than death; it is outliving oneself. The soul ascends again to heaven when we lose what we love. There only remains of us a living corpse; despair inhabits it and annihilation awaits it.

Well! good or bad, unbending or brittle, humble or proud, sad or gay, but always lamenting, this man such as he is, this being made of clay, you saw him, Lamartine, and his blood is your blood. His happiness is yours; his grief is yours; and there is not one of the ills he has to endure down here on earth which does not touch you and belong to you; since you know how to sing, friend, you know how

Dis-moi, qu'en penses-tu dans tes jours de tristesse?
Que t'a dit le malheur, quand tu l'as consulté?
Trompé par tes amis, trahi par ta maîtresse,
Du ciel et de toi-même as-tu jamais douté?

Non, Alphonse, jamais. La triste expérience
Nous apporte la cendre, et n'éteint pas le feu.
Tu respectes le mal fait par la Providence,
Tu le laisses passer et tu crois à ton Dieu.
Quel qu'il soit, c'est le mien; il n'est pas deux croyances.
Je ne sais pas son nom, j'ai regardé les cieux.
Je sais qu'ils sont à lui, je sais qu'ils sont immenses,
Et que l'immensité ne peut être à deux.
J'ai connu, jeune encor, de sévères souffrances;
J'ai vu verdir les bois, et j'ai tenté d'aimer.
Je sais ce que la terre engloutit d'espérances,
Et, pour y recueillir, ce qu'il faut y semer.
Mais ce que j'ai senti, ce que je veux t'écrire,
C'est ce que m'ont appris les anges de douleur;
Je le sais mieux encore et puis mieux te le dire,
Car leur glaive, en entrant, l'a gravé dans mon cœur:

to weep. Tell me, what do you think of it in your days of sadness?
What did misfortune tell you, when you consulted it? Deceived by
your friends, betrayed by your mistress, did you ever doubt heaven
and yourself?

No, Alphonse, never. Sad experience brings us the ash and does
not put out the fire. You respect the evil done by Providence, you
let it go by and you believe in your God. Whoever he is, he is mine;
there are no two beliefs. I do not know his name. I have gazed at the
skies. I know they belong to him, I know they are vast, and that
immensity cannot belong to two masters. I knew harsh suffering
when still young. I saw the woods grow green and I tried to love.
I know what hopes the earth swallows up, and what must be sown
there in order to reap. But what I felt, what I want to write to you,
is what the angels of suffering taught me; I know it still better and
can tell it you better, for their sword, piercing me, has engraved
it in my heart:

Créature d'un jour qui t'agites une heure,
De quoi viens-tu te plaindre et qui te fait gémir?
Ton âme t'inquiète, et tu crois qu'elle pleure:
Ton âme est immortelle, et tes pleurs vont tarir.

Tu te sens le cœur pris d'un caprice de femme,
Et tu dis qu'il se brise à force de souffrir.
Tu demandes à Dieu de soulager ton âme:
Ton âme est immortelle, et ton cœur va guérir.

Le regret d'un instant te trouble et te dévore;
Tu dis que le passé te voile l'avenir.
Ne te plains pas d'hier; laisse venir l'aurore:
Ton âme est immortelle, et le temps va s'enfuir.

Ton corps est abattu du mal de ta pensée;
Tu sens ton front peser et tes genoux fléchir.
Tombe, agenouille-toi, créature insensée:
Ton âme est immortelle, et la mort va venir.

Tes os dans le cercueil vont tomber en poussière,
Ta mémoire, ton nom, ta gloire vont périr,
Mais non pas ton amour, si ton amour t'est chère:
Ton âme est immortelle, et va s'en souvenir.

Creature of a day who are busy for an hour, of what do you complain and who makes you murmur? Your soul disturbs you, and you think it is weeping: your soul is immortal and your tears will be dried.

You feel your heart taken with a woman's whim, and you say it is breaking because of its suffering. You ask God to give your soul relief: your soul is immortal, and your heart will be cured.

A moment's regret troubles and consumes you; you say that the past veils the future for you. Do not complain of yesterday; let the dawn come: your soul is immortal, and time will disappear.

Your body is cast down by the sickness of your thoughts; you feel your brow weighed down and your knees bending. Fall down, kneel, foolish creature: your soul is immortal, and death will come.

Your bones will fall to dust in the coffin, your memory, your name, your fame will perish; but not your love, if your love is dear to you: your soul is immortal and will remember it.

Chanson de Barberine

Beau chevalier qui partez pour la guerre,
          Qu'allez-vous faire
          Si loin d'ici?
Voyez-vous pas que la nuit est profonde,
          Et que le monde
          N'est que souci?

Vous qui croyez qu'une amour délaissée
          De la pensée
          S'enfuit ainsi,
Hélas! hélas! chercheurs de renommée,
          Votre fumée
          S'envole aussi.

Beau chevalier qui partez pour la guerre,
          Qu'allez-vous faire
          Si loin de nous?
J'en vais pleurer, moi qui me laissais dire
          Que mon sourire
          Était si doux.

Barbarina's Song

Handsome knight going to the war, what will you do so far from here? Do you not see that the night is deep and that the world brings only trouble?

You who think that an abandoned love disappears from the mind so, alas! alas! seekers of fame, your smoke too flies away.

Handsome knight going to the war, what will you do so far from us? I shall weep for it, I who let myself be told that my smile was so sweet.

Une Soirée perdue

J'ÉTAIS seul, l'autre soir, au Théâtre Français,
Ou presque seul; l'auteur n'avait pas grand succès.
Ce n'était que Molière, et nous savons de reste
Que ce grand maladroit, qui fit un jour *Alceste*,
Ignora le bel art de chatouiller l'esprit
Et de servir à point un dénoûement bien cuit.
Grâce à Dieu, nos auteurs ont changé de méthode,
Et nous aimons bien mieux quelque drame à la mode
Où l'intrigue, enlacée et roulée en feston,
Tourne comme un rébus autour d'un mirliton.

J'écoutais cependant cette simple harmonie,
Et comme le bon sens fait parler le génie.
J'admirais quel amour pour l'âpre vérité
Eut cet homme si fier en sa naïveté,
Quel grand et vrai savoir des choses de ce monde,
Quelle mâle gaieté, si triste et si profonde
Que, lorsqu'on vient d'en rire, on devrait en pleurer!
Et je me demandais: Est-ce assez d'admirer?

A Wasted Evening

I WAS alone the other evening at the *Comédie Française*, or almost alone; the author had not much success. It was only Molière, and, moreover, we know that this great bungler, who created *Alceste* one day, was not aware of the fine art of tickling the mind and of serving medium done a well-cooked conclusion. Thank God, our authors have changed their methods, and we far prefer some fashionable drama where the intrigue, twined and rolled in festoons, is twisted like a pun round a doggerel verse.

Yet I listened to this simple harmony, and how common sense makes genius speak. I marvelled at the love this man, so proud in his simplicity, had for the harsh truth, what great and true knowledge of the things of this world, what virile gaiety, so sad and so deep that, when one has just been laughing at it, one should be weeping! And I asked myself: Is it enough to marvel? Is it enough

Est-ce assez de venir, un soir, par aventure,
D'entendre au fond de l'âme un cri de la nature,
D'essuyer une larme, et de partir ainsi,
Quoi qu'on fasse d'ailleurs, sans en prendre souci?
Enfoncé que j'étais dans cette rêverie,
Çà et là, toutefois, lorgnant la galerie,
Je vis que, devant moi, se balançait gaiement
Sous une tresse noire un cou svelte et charmant;
Et, voyant cet ébène enchâssé dans l'ivoire,
Un vers d'André Chénier chanta dans ma mémoire,
Un vers presque inconnu, refrain inachevé,
Frais comme le hasard, moins écrit que rêvé.
J'osai m'en souvenir, même devant Molière;
Sa grande ombre, à coup sûr, ne s'en offensa pas;
Et, tout en écoutant, je murmurais tout bas,
Regardant cette enfant, qui ne s'en doutait guère:
«Sous votre aimable tête, un cou blanc, délicat,
Se plie, et de la neige effacerait l'éclat.»

Puis je songeais encore (ainsi va la pensée)
Que l'antique franchise, à ce point délaissée,
Avec notre finesse et notre esprit moqueur,
Ferait croire, après tout, que nous manquons de cœur;

to come one evening by chance to hear nature's cry in the depth of
the soul, to wipe away a tear and to depart so, without taking heed,
whatever one does besides? Immersed as I was in this meditation,
yet glancing here and there at the gallery, I saw gaily poised in
front of me a slim and charming neck beneath a black plait; and, seeing this ebony set in the ivory, a line from André Chénier sung in
my memory, an almost unknown line, an unfinished song, fresh as
chance, less written than dreamed. I dared to recall it even before
Molière; most certainly his great shade was not offended; and, while
still listening, I whispered softly, glancing at that child, who hardly
suspected it: 'Beneath your fair head, a white delicate neck inclines
and would outshine the brightness of snow.'

Then I thought again (so thought goes) that the old frankness
being abandoned thus far, together with our subtlety and mocking
wit, would make one believe, after all, that we lack heart; that this

Que c'était une triste et honteuse misère
Que cette solitude à l'entour de Molière,
Et qu'il est *pourtant temps*, comme dit la chanson,
De sortir de ce siècle ou d'en avoir raison;
Car à quoi comparer cette scène embourbée,
Et l'effroyable honte où la muse est tombée?
La lâcheté nous bride, et les sots vont disant
Que, sous ce vieux soleil, tout est fait à présent;
Comme si les travers de la famille humaine
Ne rajeunissaient pas chaque an, chaque semaine.
Notre siècle a ses mœurs, partant, sa vérité;
Celui qui l'ose dire est toujours écouté.

Ah! j'oserais parler, si je croyais bien dire,
J'oserais ramasser le fouet de la satire,
Et l'habiller de noir, cet homme aux rubans verts,
Qui se fâchait jadis pour quelques mauvais vers.
S'il rentrait aujourd'hui dans Paris, la grand'ville,
Il y trouverait mieux pour émouvoir sa bile
Qu'une méchante femme et qu'un méchant sonnet;
Nous avons autre chose à mettre au cabinet.
Ô notre maître à tous, si ta tombe est fermée,
Laisse-moi dans ta cendre, un instant ranimée,

solitude around Molière was a sad and shameful disgrace, and that it is *time indeed*, as the song says, to quit this age or get the better of it; for what are we to compare this muddy stage and the frightful shame into which the muse has fallen? Cowardice reins us in, and fools say that everything has now been done beneath this aged sun; as if the human family's whims were not renewed every year, every week. Our age has its manners, consequently its truth; he who dares tell it is always listened to.

Ah! I would dare to speak if I thought I could speak well, I would dare to take up satire's whip and dress in black that man in green ribbons who once was angered by some bad lines of verse. If he came back today to Paris, the great town, he would find more to move him to anger than a bad woman and a bad sonnet; we have other things to put down the drain. O master of us all, if your tomb is closed, let me find a spark in your ashes, brought to

Trouver une étincelle, et je vais t'imiter!
Apprends-moi de quel ton, dans ta bouche hardie,
Parlait la vérité, ta seule passion,
Et, pour me faire entendre, à défaut du génie,
J'en aurai le courage et l'indignation!

Ainsi je caressais une folle chimère.
Devant moi cependant, à côté de sa mère,
L'enfant restait toujours, et le cou svelte et blanc
Sous les longs cheveux noirs se berçait mollement.
Le spectacle fini, la charmante inconnue
Se leva. Le beau cou, l'épaule à demi nue,
Se voilèrent; la main glissa dans le manchon;
Et, lorsque je la vis au seuil de sa maison
S'enfuir, je m'aperçus que je l'avais suivie.
Hélas! mon cher ami, c'est là toute ma vie.
Pendant que mon esprit cherchait sa volonté,
Mon corps avait la sienne et suivait la beauté;
Et, quand je m'éveillai de cette rêverie,
Il ne m'en restait plus que l'image chérie:
«Sous votre aimable tête, un cou blanc, délicat,
Se plie, et de la neige effacerait l'éclat.»

life again for a moment, and I shall follow your example! Teach me in what strain your only passion, truth, spoke in your bold mouth, and, to make myself heard, for want of genius, I shall have its courage and indignation!

So I indulged a foolish fancy. Meanwhile in front of me, beside her mother, the child still remained, and her slim white neck swayed gently beneath the long black hair. The play finished, the charming stranger rose. The lovely neck, the half-naked shoulder were veiled; the hand slipped into the muff; and, when I saw her disappear on the threshold of her home, I realized that I had followed her. Alas! my dear friend, there is my whole life. While my soul sought its will, my body had its own, and followed beauty; and, when I awoke from this dream, there only remained to me the sweet image: 'Beneath your fair head, a white delicate neck inclines and would outshine the brightness of snow.'

Sur une morte

ELLE était belle, si la Nuit
Qui dort dans la sombre chapelle
Où Michel-Ange a fait son lit,
Immobile peut être belle.

Elle était bonne, s'il suffit
Qu'en passant la main s'ouvre et donne,
Sans que Dieu n'ait rien vu, rien dit,
Si l'or sans pitié fait l'aumône.

Elle pensait, si le vain bruit
D'une voix douce et cadencée,
Comme le ruisseau qui gémit
Peut faire croire à la pensée.

Elle priait, si deux beaux yeux,
Tantôt s'attachant à la terre,
Tantôt se levant vers les cieux,
Peuvent s'appeler la Prière.

Elle aurait souri, si la fleur
Qui ne s'est point épanouie
Pouvait s'ouvrir à la fraîcheur
Du vent qui passe et qui l'oublie.

On a Dead Lady

SHE was fair, if Night that sleeps motionless in the dark chapel, where Michelangelo made her bed, can be fair.

She was generous, if it is enough for the hand to open and give while passing by, without God seeing or saying anything, if gold without pity is charity.

She thought, if the empty noise of a sweetly modulated voice, like the murmuring stream, can make one believe in the existence of thought.

She prayed, if two fair eyes, sometimes fixed on earth, sometimes raised towards heaven, can be called Prayer.

She would have smiled, if the flower, which has not bloomed, could open to the coolness of the passing, forgetful wind.

Elle aurait pleuré si sa main,
Sur son cœur froidement posée,
Eût jamais, dans l'argile humain,
Senti la céleste rosée.

Elle aurait aimé, si l'orgueil
Pareil à la lampe inutile
Qu'on allume près d'un cercueil,
N'eût veillé sur son cœur stérile.

Elle est morte, et n'a point vécu.
Elle faisait semblant de vivre.
De ses mains est tombé le livre
Dans lequel elle n'a rien lu.

THÉOPHILE GAUTIER

A une robe rose

QUE tu me plais dans cette robe
Qui te déshabille si bien,
Faisant jaillir ta gorge en globe,
Montrant tout nu ton bras païen!

She would have wept, if her hand coldly placed upon her heart
had ever felt the heavenly dew in human clay.

She would have loved, if pride, like the useless lamp lighted beside a coffin, had not watched over her barren heart.

She is dead and has not lived. She made a pretence of living.
From her hands the book has fallen in which she read nothing.

To a Pink Dress

How I like you in that dress that undresses you so well, making
your round bosom jut, showing your pagan arm quite naked!

Frêle comme une aile d'abeille,
Frais comme un cœur de rose-thé,
Son tissu, caresse vermeille,
Voltige autour de ta beauté.

De l'épiderme sur la soie
Glissent des frissons argentés,
Et l'étoffe à la chair renvoie
Ses éclairs roses reflétés.

D'où te vient cette robe étrange
Qui semble faite de ta chair,
Trame vivante qui mélange
Avec ta peau son rose clair?

Est-ce à la rougeur de l'aurore,
A la coquille de Vénus,
Au bouton de sein près d'éclore,
Que sont pris ces tons inconnus?

Ou bien l'étoffe est-elle teinte
Dans les roses de ta pudeur?
Non; vingt fois modelée et peinte,
Ta forme connaît sa splendeur.

As delicate as a bee's wing, cool as the heart of a tea-rose, its material hovers around your beauty like a rosy caress.

Silvery rustlings glide from the skin to the silk, and the cloth sends back its reflected pink lights to the flesh.

Whence comes to you this strange dress that seems to be made from your flesh, a living woof that mingles its bright pink with your skin?

Are these secret hues taken from the crimson of the dawn, from Venus's shell, or from the breast's nipple about to burst forth?

Or else is the cloth dyed in the roses of your modesty? No; after being modelled and painted twenty times, your figure knows its own splendour.

Jetant le voile qui te pèse,
Réalité que l'art rêva,
Comme la princesse Borghèse
Tu poserais pour Canova.

Et ces plis roses sont les lèvres
De mes désirs inapaisés,
Mettant au corps dont tu les sèvres
Une tunique de baisers.

La Mansarde

Sur les tuiles où se hasarde
Le chat guettant l'oiseau qui boit,
De mon balcon une mansarde
Entre deux tuyaux s'aperçoit.

Pour la parer d'un faux bien-être,
Si je mentais comme un auteur,
Je pourrais faire à sa fenêtre
Un cadre de pois de senteur,

Throwing off the veil that oppresses you, you would be the
reality dreamt of by art, and, like the Princess Borghese, you would
pose for Canova.

And these pink folds are the lips of my unsatisfied desires, dress-
ing the body, from which you hold them apart, with a tunic of
kisses.

The Garret

On the tiles where the cat risks his life to watch the bird drinking,
from my balcony I can see a garret between two drain-pipes.

To adorn it with a false comfort, if I were to lie like an author,
I could put a box of sweet peas at its window.

Et vous y montrer Rigolette
Riant à son petit miroir,
Dont le tain rayé ne reflète
Que la moitié de son œil noir;

Ou, la robe encor sans agrafe,
Gorge et cheveux au vent, Margot
Arrosant avec sa carafe
Son jardin planté dans un pot;

Ou bien quelque jeune poète
Qui scande ses vers sibyllins,
En contemplant la silhouette
De Montmartre et de ses moulins.

Par malheur, ma mansarde est vraie;
Il n'y grimpe aucun liseron,
Et la vitre y fait voir sa taie
Sous l'ais verdi d'un vieux chevron.

Pour la grisette et pour l'artiste,
Pour le veuf et pour le garçon,
Une mansarde est toujours triste:
Le grenier n'est beau qu'en chanson.

And show you Rigolette laughing in her little mirror, whose streaky quick-silver only reflects half of her black eye;

Or Margot, her dress still not hooked up, bosom and hair in the wind, watering with her jug her garden planted in a pot;

Or else some young poet scanning his sibylline lines, while gazing at the silhouette of Montmartre and its windmills.

Unfortunately my garret is real; no convolvulus climbs there, and the window shows its frosted glass beneath the green rotting timber of an old rafter.

For the girl of easy virtue and for the artist, for the widower and for the bachelor, a garret is always dismal: the attic is only pleasant in songs.

Jadis, sous le comble dont l'angle
Penchait les fronts pour le baiser,
L'amour, content d'un lit de sangle,
Avec Suzon venait causer;

Mais pour ouater notre joie,
Il faut des murs capitonnés,
Des flots de dentelle et de soie,
Des lits par Monbro festonnés.

Un soir, n'étant pas revenue,
Margot s'attarde au mont Bréda,
Et Rigolette entretenue
N'arrose plus son réséda.

Voilà longtemps que le poète,
Las de prendre la rime au vol,
S'est fait *reporter* de gazette,
Quittant le ciel pour l'entresol.

Et l'on ne voit contre la vitre
Qu'une vieille au maigre profil,
Devant Minet, qu'elle chapitre,
Tirant sans cesse un bout de fil.

In former times, beneath the roof whose angle bent brows together for the kiss, love, contented with a camp bed, came to chat
with Suzon.

But, to cosset our joy, there must be quilted walls, floods of lace
and silk, beds festooned by Monbro.

Not having returned one evening, Margot delays at the Mount
Breda, and Rigolette waters her mignonette no more since she is a
kept woman.

The poet a long time ago, tired of catching rhyme in its flight
has become a *reporter* on a paper, leaving the sky for the mezzanine.

And against the window one only sees an old woman with a lean
profile, ceaselessly pulling a piece of thread in front of pussy, while
she scolds him.

L'Art

Oui, l'œuvre sort plus belle
D'une forme au travail
    Rebelle,
Vers, marbre, onyx, émail.

Point de contraintes fausses!
Mais que pour marcher droit
    Tu chausses,
Muse, un cothurne étroit.

Fi du rhythme commode,
Comme un soulier trop grand,
    Du mode
Que tout pied quitte et prend!

Statuaire, repousse
L'argile que pétrit
    Le pouce
Quand flotte ailleurs l'esprit;

Lutte avec le carrare,
Avec le paros dur
    Et rare,
Gardiens du contour pur;

Art

Yes, the work of art emerges more beautiful from a form that resists working, verse, marble, onyx, enamel.

No false hindrances! But to march straight, put on, O Muse, a narrow buskin.

Shame on the easy rhythm, like a shoe that is too large, of the kind that every foot takes off and puts on!

Sculptor, reject clay moulded by the thumb when the mind hovers elsewhere;

Struggle with Carrara marble, with the hard, rare Parian, keepers of the pure outline;

Emprunte à Syracuse
Son bronze où fermement
    S'accuse
Le trait fier et charmant;

D'une main délicate
Poursuis dans un filon
    D'agate
Le profil d'Apollon.

Peintre, fuis l'aquarelle,
Et fixe la couleur
    Trop frêle
Au four de l'émailleur;

Fais les sirènes bleues,
Tordant de cent façons
    Leurs queues,
Les monstres des blasons;

Dans son nimbe trilobe
La Vierge et son Jésus,
    Le globe
Avec la croix dessus.

Tout passe. – L'art robuste
Seul a l'éternité:
    Le buste
Survit à la cité.

Borrow from Syracuse its bronze where the proud enchanting stroke is firmly marked;

With a delicate hand hunt the profile of Apollo in a vein of agate.

Painter, flee the water-colour, and fix too delicate a tint in the enameller's oven.

Create blue sirens, writhing their tails in a hundred ways, create the monsters of heraldry,

Create the Virgin and her Jesus in their three-lobed halo, create the globe with the cross above it.

Everything passes. – Only strong art possesses eternity. The bust outlives the city.

Et la médaille austère
Que trouve un laboureur
    Sous terre
Révèle un empereur.

Les dieux eux-mêmes meurent.
Mais les vers souverains
    Demeurent
Plus forts que les airains.

Sculpte, lime, cisèle;
Que ton rêve flottant
    Se scelle
Dans le bloc résistant!

LECONTE DE LISLE

Midi

MIDI, roi des étés, épandu sur la plaine,
Tombe en nappes d'argent des hauteurs du ciel bleu.
Tout se tait. L'air flamboie et brûle sans haleine;
La terre est assoupie en sa robe de feu.

And the austere medal found by a labourer beneath the earth reveals an emperor.

The gods themselves die. But sovereign lines of verse remain stronger than brass.

Carve, file, and chisel; let your hazy dream be sealed in the hard block!

Noon

NOON, king of summers, spread over the plain, falls in silver sheets from the heights of the blue sky. Everything is quiet. Breathlessly the air flames and burns; earth drowses in its fiery dress.

L'étendue est immense, et les champs n'ont point d'ombre,
Et la source est tarie où buvaient les troupeaux;
La lointaine forêt, dont la lisière est sombre,
Dort là-bas, immobile, en un pesant repos.

Seuls, les grands blés mûris, tels qu'une mer dorée,
Se déroulent au loin, dédaigneux du sommeil;
Pacifiques enfants de la terre sacrée,
Ils épuisent sans peur la coupe du soleil.

Parfois, comme un soupir de leur âme brûlante,
Du sein des épis lourds qui murmurent entre eux,
Une ondulation majestueuse et lente
S'éveille, et va mourir à l'horizon poudreux.

Non loin, quelques bœufs blancs, couchés parmi les
        herbes,
Bavent avec lenteur sur leurs fanons épais,
Et suivent de leurs yeux languissants et superbes
Le songe intérieur qu'ils n'achèvent jamais.

The expanse is vast, the fields have no shade, and the spring
where the flocks used to drink is dried up; the distant forest, whose
edge is dark, motionlessly slumbers over there in a heavy sleep.

Only the great ripe cornfields, like a golden sea, roll far away dis-
daining sleep; as peaceful children of the sacred earth, fearlessly they
drain the sun's cup.

Sometimes, like a sigh from their burning soul, from the bosom
of the heavy ears, murmuring among themselves, a majestically
slow undulation awakens and goes to die on the dusty horizon.

Not far away some white oxen lying in the grass dribble slowly
on their heavy dewlaps and follow with their proud, languid eyes
the inner dream they never finish.

Homme, si, le cœur plein de joie ou d'amertume,
Tu passais vers midi dans les champs radieux,
Fuis! la nature est vide et le soleil consume:
Rien n'est vivant ici, rien n'est triste ou joyeux.

Mais si, désabusé des larmes et du rire,
Altéré de l'oubli de ce monde agité,
Tu veux, ne sachant plus pardonner ou maudire,
Goûter une suprême et morne volupté,

Viens! Le soleil te parle en paroles sublimes;
Dans sa flamme implacable absorbe-toi sans fin;
Et retourne à pas lents vers les cités infimes,
Le cœur trempé sept fois dans le néant divin.

Les Taureaux

LES plaines de la mer, immobiles et nues,
Coupent d'un long trait d'or la profondeur des nues.
Seul, un rose brouillard, attardé dans les cieux,
Se tord languissamment comme un grêle reptile
Au faîte dentelé des monts silencieux.

Man, if towards noon you passed into the blazing fields with your heart full of joy or bitterness, flee! nature is empty and the sun devours: nothing is living here, nothing is sad or joyful.

But if, disillusioned with tears or laughter, parched for forgetfulness of this busy world, no longer knowing how to pardon or to curse, you wish to taste a last desolate pleasure,

Come! The sun speaks to you in sublime words; be endlessly absorbed in its relentless flame; and return with slow steps towards the abject cities, your heart seven times bathed in the divine void.

The Bulls

THE sea plains, motionless and bare, cut the depth of the clouds with a long streak of gold. Only a pink mist, dawdling in the sky, twists languidly like a slender snake on the jagged crest of the silent

Un souffle lent, chargé d'une ivresse subtile,
Nage sur la savane et les versants moussus
Où les taureaux aux poils lustrés, aux cornes hautes,
A l'œil cave et sanglant, musculeux et bossus,
Paissent l'herbe salée et rampante des côtes.
Deux nègres d'Antongil, maigres, les reins courbés,
Les coudes aux genoux, les paumes aux mâchoires,
Dans l'abêtissement d'un long rêve absorbés,
Assis sur les jarrets, fument leurs pipes noires.
Mais, sentant venir l'ombre et l'heure de l'enclos,
Le chef accoutumé de la bande farouche,
Une bave d'argent aux deux coins de la bouche,
Tend son mufle camus, et beugle sur les flots.

Le Rêve du Jaguar

Sous les noirs acajous, les lianes en fleur,
Dans l'air lourd, immobile et saturé de mouches,
Pendent, et, s'enroulant en bas parmi les souches,
Bercent le perroquet splendide et querelleur,

mountains. A slow breath filled with subtle intoxication floats over
the savannah and the mossy slopes where muscular, hump-backed
bulls with glossy coats, long horns, and hollow, bloodshot eyes are
grazing upon the short salty grass of the coasts. Two lean Antongil
negroes, loins bent, elbows on knees, palms beneath their chins,
squatting on their hams, smoke their black pipes absorbed in the
stupidity of a long dream. But the usual head of the savage herd,
feeling the shadow coming and the hour for the corral, with silver
foam at both corners of his mouth, stretches out his flat muzzle and
bellows over the waves.

The Jaguar's Dream

BENEATH the black mahogany trees the flowering creepers hang in
the heavy, motionless air which is filled with flies; and, twining
downwards among the tree-stumps, they cradle the brilliant,

L'araignée au dos jaune et les singes farouches.
C'est là que le tueur de bœufs et de chevaux,
Le long des vieux troncs morts à l'écorce moussue,
Sinistre et fatigué, revient à pas égaux.
Il va, frottant ses reins musculeux qu'il bossue;
Et, du mufle béant par la soif alourdi,
Un souffle rauque et bref, d'une brusque secousse,
Trouble les grands lézards, chauds des feux de midi,
Dont la fuite étincelle à travers l'herbe rousse.
En un creux du bois sombre interdit au soleil
Il s'affaisse, allongé sur quelque roche plate;
D'un large coup de langue il se lustre la patte;
Il cligne ses yeux d'or hébétés de sommeil;
Et, dans l'illusion de ses forces inertes,
Faisant mouvoir sa queue et frissonner ses flancs,
Il rêve qu'au milieu des plantations vertes,
Il enfonce d'un bond ses ongles ruisselants
Dans la chair des taureaux effarés et beuglants.

quarrelsome parrot, the spider with the yellow back and the wild
monkeys. It is there that the tired, sinister killer of oxen and horses
returns with regular steps along old, dead, mossy-barked tree-
trunks. He goes rubbing and humping his muscular loins; and from
his gaping muzzle heavy with thirst a short harsh breath with a sudden shock disturbs the great lizards warm from noon's fires, whose
flight sparkles through the tawny grass. In a hollow of the dark
wood concealed from the sun he sinks down, stretched out on some
flat rock; with a broad stroke of his tongue he polishes his paw; he
blinks his golden eyes dulled by sleep; and in the illusion of his
passive strength, making his tail move and his sides quiver, he
dreams that in the middle of green plantations with one bound he is
plunging his dripping claws into the flesh of frightened, bellowing
bulls.

Le Cœur de Hialmar

UNE nuit claire, un vent glacé. La neige est rouge.
Mille braves sont là qui dorment sans tombeaux,
L'épée au poing, les yeux hagards. Pas un ne bouge.
Au-dessus tourne et crie un vol de noirs corbeaux.

La lune froide verse au loin sa pâle flamme.
Hialmar se soulève entre les morts sanglants,
Appuyé des deux mains au tronçon de sa lame.
La pourpre du combat ruisselle de ses flancs.

– Holà! Quelqu'un a-t-il encore un peu d'haleine,
Parmi tant de joyeux et robustes garçons
Qui, ce matin, riaient et chantaient à voix pleine
Comme des merles dans l'épaisseur des buissons?

Tous sont muets. Mon casque est rompu, mon armure
Est trouée, et la hache a fait sauter ses clous.
Mes yeux saignent. J'entends un immense murmure
Pareil aux hurlements de la mer ou des loups.

The Heart of Hialmar

A CLEAR night, an icy wind. The snow is red. A thousand brave
men are there sleeping without graves, sword in hand, their eyes
sunken. Not one moves. Above a flight of black crows circles and
cries.

The cold moon pours its pale flame afar. Hialmar raises himself
from among the bleeding dead, leaning with both hands on the
stump of his sword. The crimson of battle drips from his sides.

– Halloo! Has anyone still a little breath among so many joyful,
healthy lads who this morning laughed and sang at the top of their
voices, like blackbirds in the depth of the bushes?

All are dumb. My helmet is broken, my armour pierced, and its
nails burst by the axe. My eyes are bleeding. I hear a vast murmuring like the howl of the sea or of wolves.

Viens par ici, Corbeau, mon brave mangeur d'hommes
Ouvre-moi la poitrine avec ton bec de fer.
Tu nous retrouveras demain tels que nous sommes.
Porte mon cœur tout chaud à la fille d'Ylmer.

Dans Upsal, où les Jarls boivent la bonne bière,
Et chantent, en heurtant les cruches d'or, en chœur,
A tire-d'aile vole, ô rôdeur de bruyère!
Cherche ma fiancée et porte lui mon cœur.

Au sommet de la tour que hantent les corneilles
Tu la verras debout, blanche, aux longs cheveux noirs.
Deux anneaux d'argent fin lui pendent aux oreilles,
Et ses yeux sont plus clairs que l'astre des beaux soirs.

Va, sombre messager, dis-lui bien que je l'aime,
Et que voici mon cœur. Elle reconnaîtra
Qu'il est rouge et solide et non tremblant et blême;
Et la fille d'Ylmer, Corbeau, te sourira!

Come here, Crow, my fine eater of men, open my bosom with
your iron beak. To-morrow you will find us again as we are now.
Carry my warm heart to the daughter of Ylmer.

In Upsala, where the Jarls drink good beer, and sing in chorus,
clinking the golden pitchers, fly as fast as your wings can carry you,
O prowler in the heather! Seek out my fiancée and carry her my
heart.

At the top of the rook-haunted tower you will see her standing,
white with long black hair. Two rings of fine silver hang from her
ears, and her eyes are brighter than the clear evening star.

Go, dark messenger, tell her I love her well and that here is my
heart. She will recognize that it is red and firm and not trembling
and pale; and the daughter of Ylmer, Crow, will smile on you!

Moi, je meurs. Mon esprit coule par vingt blessures.
J'ai fait mon temps. Buvez, ô loups, mon sang vermeil.
Jeune, brave, riant, libre et san flétrissures,
Je vais m'asseoir parmi les Dieux, dans le soleil!

CHARLES BAUDELAIRE

A une Dame créole

Au pays parfumé que le soleil caresse,
J'ai connu, sous un dais d'arbres tout empourprés
Et de palmiers d'où pleut sur les yeux la paresse,
Une dame créole aux charmes ignorés.

Son teint est pâle et chaud; la brune enchanteresse
A dans le cou des airs noblement maniérés;
Grande et svelte en marchant comme une chasseresse,
Son sourire est tranquille et ses yeux assurés.

Si vous alliez, Madame, au vrai pays de gloire,
Sur les bords de la Seine ou de la verte Loire,
Belle digne d'orner les antiques manoirs,

Myself, I am dying. My spirit flows forth from twenty wounds. I have had my time. Drink my crimson blood, O wolves. Young, brave, laughing, free, and without reproach, I go to sit among the Gods in the sun!

To a Creole Lady

In the scented land caressed by the sun, beneath a canopy of trees tinged with crimson and palms whence idleness rains down upon the eyes, I knew a Creole lady of unknown charms.

Her complexion is pale and warm; the dark sorceress has a nobly affected air about the poise of her neck; tall and slim, walking like a huntress, her smile is calm and her eyes are assured.

Madame, if you went to the true land of fame, on the banks of the Seine or of the green Loire, O beauty worthy to adorn old manor-houses,

Vous feriez à l'abri des ombreuses retraites,
Germer mille sonnets dans le cœur des poètes,
Que vos grands yeux rendraient plus soumis que vos
   noirs.

Le Crépuscule du soir

Voici le soir charmant, ami du criminel;
Il vient comme un complice, à pas de loup; le ciel
Se ferme lentement comme une grande alcôve,
Et l'homme impatient se change en bête fauve.

Ô soir, aimable soir, désiré par celui
Dont les bras, sans mentir, peuvent dire: Aujourd'hui
Nous avons travaillé! – C'est le soir qui soulage
Les esprits que dévore une douleur sauvage,
Le savant obstiné dont le front s'alourdit,
Et l'ouvrier courbé qui regagne son lit.
Cependant des démons malsains dans l'atmosphère
S'éveillent lourdement, comme des gens d'affaire,
Et cognent en volant les volets et l'auvent.

In the shelter of shady retreats you would make a thousand sonnets spring in the hearts of poets, whom your great eyes would
render more obedient than your black slaves.

Evening Twilight

HERE is pleasant evening, the criminal's friend; it comes stealthily
like an accomplice with a wolf's tread; the sky closes slowly like a
huge alcove, and impatient man is changed to a wild beast.
   O evening, sweet evening, longed for by the man whose arms
can say without deceit: To-day we have worked! – It is evening
that relieves minds consumed by savage grief, the scholar whose
brow grows heavy and the bent workman returning to his bed.
Meanwhile foul demons in the atmosphere awaken heavily like
business men and, flying, knock against the shutters and the porch.

A travers les lueurs que tourmente le vent
La Prostitution s'allume dans les rues;
Comme une fourmilière elle ouvre ses issues;
Partout elle se fraye un occulte chemin,
Ainsi que l'ennemi qui tente un coup de main;
Elle remue au sein de la cité de fange
Comme un ver qui dérobe à l'Homme ce qu'il mange.
On entend çà et là les cuisines siffler,
Les théâtres glapir, les orchestres ronfler;
Les tables d'hôte, dont le jeu fait les délices,
S'emplissent de catins et d'escrocs, leurs complices,
Et les voleurs, qui n'ont ni trêve ni merci,
Vont bientôt commencer leur travail, eux aussi,
Et forcer doucement les portes et les caisses
Pour vivre quelques jours et vêtir leurs maîtresses.

Recueille-toi, mon âme, en ce grave moment,
Et ferme ton oreille à ce rugissement.
C'est l'heure où les douleurs des malades s'aigrissent!
La sombre Nuit les prend à la gorge; ils finissent
Leur destinée et vont vers le gouffre commun;
L'hôpital se remplit de leurs soupirs. – Plus d'un

Through the lights flickering in the wind Prostitution begins to flare in the streets; like an ant-heap it opens its doors; everywhere it traces a secret path like an enemy attempting a surprise; it moves in the bosom of the filthy city like a worm stealing man's food. Here and there you can hear kitchens hiss, theatres yelp and orchestras snore; the cheap eating-houses, whose delight is gambling, are filled with whores and sharks, their accomplices, and the robbers, who know neither truce nor mercy, they too are soon going to begin their work, and gently force open doors and coffers to live a few days and clothe their mistresses.

Recollect yourself, my soul, at this solemn moment, and shut your ear to the roar. It is the hour when the pains of the sick grow worse! Dark Night takes them by the throat; they end their life and go towards the common abyss; the hospital is filled with their sighs.

Ne viendra plus chercher la soupe parfumée,
Au coin du feu, le soir, auprès d'une âme aimée.

Encore la plupart n'ont-ils jamais connu
La douceur du foyer et n'ont jamais vécu!

L'Albatros

SOUVENT, pour s'amuser, les hommes d'équipage
Prennent des albatros, vastes oiseaux des mers,
Qui suivent, indolents compagnons de voyage,
Le navire glissant sur les gouffres amers.

A peine les ont-ils déposés sur les planches,
Que ces rois de l'azur, maladroits et honteux,
Laissent piteusement leurs grandes ailes blanches
Comme des avirons traîner à côté d'eux.

Ce voyageur ailé, comme il est gauche et veule!
Lui, naguère si beau, qu'il est comique et laid!
L'un agace son bec avec un brûle-gueule,
L'autre mime, en boitant, l'infirme qui volait!

– More than one will come no more to seek his fragrant soup, in the evening, by the fireside beside a soul he loves.

Moreover, most of them have never known home's sweetness and have never lived!

The Albatross

OFTEN to amuse themselves the men of the crew trap albatrosses, the great sea-birds, that follow the ship slipping over the bitter deeps, like idle travelling companions.

Hardly have they put them down on the planks than these kings of the blue sky, clumsy and shamefaced, let their broad white wings trail beside them pitifully like oars.

How clumsy and feeble this winged traveller is! How grotesque and ugly he who was lately so beautiful! One man teases his beak with a pipe, another limping mimics the cripple who once flew!

Le Poète est semblable au prince des nuées
Qui hante la tempête et se rit de l'archer;
Exilé sur le sol au milieu des huées,
Ses ailes de géant l'empêchent de marcher.

Harmonie du soir

Voici venir les temps où vibrant sur sa tige
Chaque fleur s'évapore ainsi qu'un encensoir;
Les sons et les parfums tournent dans l'air du soir;
Valse mélancolique et langoureux vertige!

Chaque fleur s'évapore ainsi qu'un encensoir;
Le violon frémit comme un cœur qu'on afflige;
Valse mélancolique et langoureux vertige!
Le ciel est triste et beau comme un grand reposoir.

Le violon frémit comme un cœur qu'on afflige,
Un cœur tendre, qui hait le néant vaste et noir!
Le ciel est triste et beau comme un grand reposoir;
Le soleil s'est noyé dans son sang qui se fige.

The Poet is like the prince of the clouds, haunting the storm and laughing at archers; exiled on earth in the midst of cat-calls his giant's wings prevent him from walking.

Evening Harmony

HERE comes the time when, vibrating on its stem, every flower fumes like a censer; noises and perfumes circle in the evening air; O melancholy waltz and languid vertigo!

Every flower fumes like a censer; the violin shudders like an afflicted heart; O melancholy waltz and languid vertigo! The sky is sad and beautiful like a vast station of the Cross.

The violin shudders like an afflicted heart, a tender heart that hates the great dark void! The sky is sad and beautiful like a vast station of the Cross; the sun is drowned in its own congealing blood.

Un cœur tendre, qui hait le néant vaste et noir,
Du passé lumineux recueille tout vestige!
Le soleil s'est noyé dans son sang qui se fige ...
Ton souvenir en moi luit comme un ostensoir!

Sed non satiata

BIZARRE déité, brune comme les nuits,
Au parfum mélangé de musc et de havane,
Œuvre de quelque obi, le Faust de la savane,
Sorcière au flanc d'ébène, enfant des noirs minuits,

Je préfère au constance, à l'opium, au nuits,
L'élixir de ta bouche où l'amour se pavane;
Quand vers toi mes désirs partent en caravane,
Tes yeux sont la citerne où boivent mes ennuis.

Par ces deux grands yeux noirs, soupiraux de ton âme,
Ô démon sans pitié! verse-moi moins de flamme;
Je ne suis pas le Styx pour t'embrasser neuf fois,

A tender heart that hates the great dark void gathers up every
remnant of the bright past! The sun is drowned in its own congealing blood. ... Your memory shines within me like a monstrance!

Sed non satiata

STRANGE deity, dark as night, with the mingled scent of musk and
Havana tobacco, the work of some witch-doctor, the Faust of the
savannah, witch with the ebony thigh, child of black midnights,
  I prefer the elixir of your mouth, where love sits in state, to the wine
of Constance, opium, or Burgundy; when my desires take the caravan
towards you, your eyes are the cistern where my troubles drink.
  Through those two great black eyes, the vents of your soul, O
pitiless demon! pour me less flame; I am not the Styx to clasp you
nine times,

Hélas! et je ne puis, Mégère libertine,
Pour briser ton courage et te mettre aux abois,
Dans l'enfer de ton lit devenir Proserpine!

Je t'adore à l'égal de la voûte nocturne ...

JE t'adore à l'égal de la voûte nocturne,
Ô vase de tristesse, ô grande taciturne,
Et t'aime d'autant plus, belle, que tu me fuis,
Et que tu me parais, ornement de mes nuits,
Plus ironiquement accumuler les lieues
Qui séparent mes bras des immensités bleues.

Je m'avance à l'attaque, et je grimpe aux assauts,
Comme après un cadavre un chœur de vermisseaux,
Et je chéris, ô bête implacable et cruelle!
Jusqu'à cette froideur par où tu m'es plus belle!

Alas! and, dissolute Megaera, I cannot become Proserpine in the
hell of your bed to break your courage and reduce you to despera-
tion!

I adore you as much as the vault of night ...

I ADORE you as much as the vault of night, O vessel of sorrow,
O tall, silent woman, and I love you the more, my beauty, the more
you flee me, and seem, O ornament of my nights, to pile up ironically the leagues that separate my arms from the blue spaces.

I advance to the attack and I climb to the assault like a band of
worms on a corpse, and I hold dear, O mercilessly cruel beast!, even
that coldness through which you appear more beautiful to me!

La Chevelure

Ô TOISON, moutonnant jusque sur l'encolure!
Ô boucles! Ô parfum chargé de nonchaloir!
Extase! Pour peupler ce soir l'alcôve obscure
Des souvenirs dormant dans cette chevelure,
Je la veux agiter dans l'air comme un mouchoir!

La langoureuse Asie et la brûlante Afrique,
Tout un monde lointain, absent, presque défunt,
Vit dans tes profondeurs, forêt aromatique!
Comme d'autres esprits voguent sur la musique,
Le mien, ô mon amour! nage sur ton parfum.

J'irai là-bas où l'arbre et l'homme, pleins de sève,
Se pâment longuement sous l'ardeur des climats;
Fortes tresses, soyez la houle qui m'enlève!
Tu contiens, mer d'ebène, un éblouissant rêve
De voiles, de rameurs, de flammes et de mâts:

Un port retentissant où mon âme peut boire
A grands flots le parfum, le son et la couleur;

The Hair

O FLEECE curling right down on the neck! O ringlets! O perfume laden with indifference! Ecstasy! This evening to people the dark alcove with the memories sleeping in this hair, I want to wave it in the air like a handkerchief!

Languorous Asia and burning Africa, the whole of a distant world, far away, almost extinct, lives in your depths, aromatic forest! As other spirits drift upon music, mine, O my love! floats upon your perfume.

I shall go to the land where trees and men, full of sap, slowly swoon beneath the passionate heat of the climate; strong locks, be the swell that carries me away! O ebony sea, you hold a dazzling dream of sails, rowers, pennants, and masts:

An echoing harbour where my soul can drink scent, sound, and

Où les vaisseaux, glissant dans l'or et dans la moire,
Ouvrent leurs vastes bras pour embrasser la gloire
D'un ciel pur où frémit l'éternelle chaleur.

Je plongerai ma tête amoureuse d'ivresse
Dans ce noir océan où l'autre est enfermé;
Et mon esprit subtil que le roulis caresse
Saura vous retrouver, ô féconde paresse!
Infinis bercements du loisir embaumé!

Cheveux bleus, pavillon de ténèbres tendues,
Vous me rendez l'azur du ciel immense et rond;
Sur les bords duvetés de vos mèches tordues
Je m'enivre ardemment des senteurs confondues
De l'huile de coco, du musc et du goudron.

Longtemps! toujours! ma main dans ta crinière lourde
Sèmera le rubis, la perle et le saphir,
Afin qu'à mon désir tu ne sois jamais sourde!
N'es-tu pas l'oasis où je rêve, et la gourde
Où je hume à longs traits le vin du souvenir?

colour in great waves; where the ships, slipping through the gold and watered silk, open their huge arms to clasp the glory of a pure sky trembling with eternal heat.

I shall plunge my head, which loves intoxication, into this dark ocean where the other ocean is enclosed; and my keen spirit caressed by the swell will know how to seek you out, O fertile idleness! Infinite rocking of scented leisure!

Blue hair, tent of stretched shadows, you give me back the blue of the vast round sky; on the downy verges of your twisted locks passionately I drink the intoxication of the mingled scents of coconut oil, musk, and tar.

For many a day! For ever! My hand will sow the ruby, pearl, and sapphire in your heavy mane so that you may never be deaf to my desire! Are you not the oasis where I dream and the gourd where I drink memory's wine in long draughts?

Correspondances

LA Nature est un temple où de vivants piliers
Laissent parfois sortir de confuses paroles;
L'homme y passe à travers des forêts de symboles
Qui l'observent avec des regards familiers.

Comme de longs échos qui de loin se confondent
Dans une ténébreuse et profonde unité,
Vaste comme la nuit et comme la clarté,
Les parfums, les couleurs et les sons se répondent.

Il est des parfums frais comme des chairs d'enfants,
Doux comme les hautbois, verts comme les prairies,
— Et d'autres, corrompus, riches et triomphants,

Ayant l'expansion des choses infinies,
Comme l'ambre, le musc, le benjoin et l'encens,
Qui chantent les transports de l'esprit et des sens.

Correspondences

NATURE is a temple where living pillars sometimes allow confused words to escape; man passes there through forests of symbols that watch him with familiar glances.

Like long-drawn-out echoes mingled far away into a deep and shadowy unity, vast as darkness and light, scents, colours, and sounds answer one another.

There are some scents cool as the flesh of children, sweet as oboes and green as meadows, — and others corrupt, rich, and triumphant,

Having the expansion of things infinite, like amber, musk, benzoin, and incense, singing the raptures of the mind and senses.

Un Voyage à Cythère

MON cœur, comme un oiseau, voltigeait tout joyeux
Et planait librement à l'entour des cordages;
Le navire roulait sous un ciel sans nuages,
Comme un ange enivré d'un soleil radieux.

Quelle est cette île triste et noire? – C'est Cythère,
Nous dit-on, un pays fameux dans les chansons,
Eldorado banal de tous les vieux garçons.
Regardez, après tout, c'est une pauvre terre.

– Île des doux secrets et des fêtes du cœur!
De l'antique Vénus le superbe fantôme
Au-dessus de tes mers plane comme un arôme,
Et charge les esprits d'amour et de langueur.

Belle île aux myrtes verts, pleine de fleurs écloses,
Vénérée à jamais par toute nation,
Où les soupirs des cœurs en adoration
Roulent comme l'encens sur un jardin de roses

A Journey to Cytherea

MY heart like a bird floated joyously and hovered in freedom around the rigging; the ship rolled on beneath a cloudless sky, like an angel intoxicated by the radiant sun.

What is this dark sad island? – It is Cytherea, they tell us, a country well known in song, the banal Eldorado of all old rakes. Look, after all, what a poor land it is.

– Island of sweet secrets and of the heart's feasts! The proud ghost of ancient Venus hovers above your seas like a perfume, filling souls with love and langour.

Fair island of green myrtles, full of flowers in bloom, for ever reverenced by all peoples, where the sighs of adoring hearts roll like incense over a rose-garden

Ou le roucoulement éternel d'un ramier!
– Cythère n'était plus qu'un terrain des plus maigres,
Un désert rocailleux troublé par des cris aigres.
J'entrevoyais pourtant un objet singulier!

Ce n'était pas un temple aux ombres bocagères,
Où la jeune prêtresse, amoureuse des fleurs,
Allait, le corps brûlé de secrètes chaleurs,
Entre-bâillant sa robe aux brises passagères;

Mais voilà qu'en rasant la côte d'assez près
Pour troubler les oiseaux avec nos voiles blanches,
Nous vîmes que c'était un gibet à trois branches,
Du ciel se détachant en noir, comme un cyprès.

De féroces oiseaux perchés sur leur pâture
Détruisaient avec rage un pendu déjà mûr,
Chacun plantant, comme un outil, son bec impur
Dans tous les coins saignants de cette pourriture;

Les yeux étaient deux trous, et du ventre effondré
Les intestins pesants lui coulaient sur les cuisses,
Et ses bourreaux, gorgés de hideuses délices,
L'avaient à coups de bec absolument châtré.

Or the perpetual cooing of a dove! – Cytherea was only the lean-est of lands, a stony desert disturbed by shrill lamentations. Yet, I glimpsed a strange object!

It was no temple with shady groves, where the young priestess, in love with the flowers, walked, her body burned by secret heats, half-opening her dress to the passing breezes;

But, keeping close enough to the coast to disturb the birds with our white sails, we saw it was a three-branched gallows, profiled against the sky in black, like a cypress.

Fierce birds perched on their prey furiously tore at a man hanging there and already decayed, each one planting his filthy beak like an instrument in all the bloody corners of this carrion;

The eyes were two holes, and from the opened stomach his heavy bowels flowed down his thighs, and his executioners crammed with hideous dainties had completely castrated him with blows of their beaks.

Sous les pieds, un troupeau de jaloux quadrupèdes,
Le museau relevé, tournoyait et rôdait;
Une plus grande bête au milieu s'agitait
Comme un exécuteur entouré de ses aides.

Habitant de Cythère, enfant d'un ciel si beau,
Silencieusement tu souffrais ces insultes
En expiation de tes infâmes cultes
Et des péchés qui t'ont interdit le tombeau.

Ridicule pendu, tes douleurs sont les miennes!
Je sentis, à l'aspect de tes membres flottants,
Comme un vomissement, remonter vers mes dents
Le long fleuve de fiel des douleurs anciennes;

Devant toi, pauvre diable au souvenir si cher,
J'ai senti tous les becs et toutes les mâchoires
Des corbeaux lancinants et des panthères noires
Qui jadis aimaient tant à triturer ma chair.

– Le ciel était charmant, la mer était unie;
Pour moi tout était noir et sanglant désormais,
Hélas! et j'avais, comme en un suaire épais,
Le cœur enseveli dans cette allégorie.

Beneath his feet a band of jealous beasts circled and prowled,
their muzzles raised; a larger animal moved in the middle like a
hangman surrounded by his assistants.

Inhabitant of Cytherea, child of so fair a sky, you suffered these
insults silently to atone for your infamous worship and for the sins
which denied you the grave.

Ridiculous hanged man, your sufferings are mine! At the sight of
your dangling limbs I felt the long, bitter river of old griefs rise towards my teeth like vomit;

In face of you, poor devil of such dear memory, I felt all the
beaks and all the jaws of the piercing crows and the black panthers
who lately so loved to chew my flesh.

– The sky was beautiful, the sea was calm; for me henceforward
everything was dark and bloody, alas! and I had my heart buried in
this allegory as in a thick shroud.

Dans ton île, ô Vénus! je n'ai trouvé debout
Qu'un gibet symbolique où pendait mon image ...
– Ah! Seigneur! donnez-moi la force et le courage
De contempler mon cœur et mon corps sans dégoût!

Moesta et errabunda

Dis-moi, ton cœur, parfois, s'envole-t-il, Agathe,
Loin du noir océan de l'immonde cité,
Vers un autre océan où la splendeur éclate,
Bleu, clair, profond, ainsi que la virginité?
Dis-moi, ton cœur, parfois, s'envole-t-il, Agathe?

La mer, la vaste mer, console nos labeurs!
Quel démon a doté la mer, rauque chanteuse
Qu'accompagne l'immense orgue des vents grondeurs,
De cette fonction sublime de berceuse?
La mer, la vaste mer, console nos labeurs!

In your island, O Venus! I found standing only a symbolic gallows where my image hung. ... Ah! Lord! give me strength and courage to look upon my heart and body without disgust!

Moesta et errabunda

Tell me, does your heart sometimes fly away, Agatha, far from the dark ocean of the filthy city, towards another ocean where splendour blazes, an ocean blue, clear, and deep as virginity? Tell me, does your heart sometimes fly away, Agatha?

The sea, the great sea, comforts our toil! What demon has given the sea, that hoarse singer accompanied by the vast organ of the complaining winds, this sublime office of lullaby? The sea, the great sea, comforts our toil!

Emporte-moi, wagon! enlève-moi, frégate!
Loin! loin! ici la boue est faite de nos pleurs!
– Est-il vrai que parfois le triste cœur d'Agathe
Dise: Loin des remords, des crimes, des douleurs,
Emporte-moi, wagon, enlève-moi, frégate?

Comme vous êtes loin, paradis parfumé,
Où sous un clair azur tout n'est qu'amour et joie,
Où tout ce que l'on aime est digne d'être aimé!
Où dans la volupté pure le cœur se noie!
Comme vous êtes loin, paradis parfumé!

Mais le vert paradis des amours enfantines,
Les courses, les chansons, les baisers, les bouquets,
Les violons vibrant derrière les collines,
Avec les brocs de vin, le soir, dans les bosquets,
– Mais le vert paradis des amours enfantines,

L'innocent paradis, plein de plaisirs furtifs,
Est-il déjà plus loin que l'Inde et que la Chine?
Peut-on le rappeler avec des cris plaintifs,
Et l'animer encor d'une voix argentine,
L'innocent paradis plein de plaisirs furtifs?

Coach, carry me off! Frigate, take me away! Far away! far away!
here the mud is made from our tears! – Is it true that sometimes
Agatha's sad heart says: far from remorse, from crime, from grief,
coach, carry me off, frigate, take me away?

How distant you are, scented paradise, where beneath a clear blue
sky there is only love and joy, where everything we love is worthy
to be loved! Where the heart is drowned in pure pleasure! How distant you are, scented paradise!

But the green paradise of childish loves, the races, the songs, the
kisses, the bouquets, the violins throbbing behind the hills, with the
jugs of wine in the evening in the groves – but the green paradise of
childish loves,

The innocent paradise, full of secret pleasures; is it already
further away than India or China? Can we call it back with plaintive
crys, and give it life again with a silvery voice, the innocent paradise
full of secret pleasures?

Spleen

Je suis comme le roi d'un pays pluvieux,
Riche, mais impuissant, jeune et pourtant très-vieux,
Qui, de ses précepteurs méprisant les courbettes,
S'ennuie avec ses chiens comme avec d'autres bêtes.
Rien ne peut l'égayer, ni gibier, ni faucon,
Ni son peuple mourant en face du balcon.
Du bouffon favori la grotesque ballade
Ne distrait plus le front de ce cruel malade;
Son lit fleurdelisé se transforme en tombeau,
Et les dames d'atour, pour qui tout prince est beau,
Ne savent plus trouver d'impudique toilette
Pour tirer un souris de ce jeune squelette,
Le savant qui lui fait de l'or n'a jamais pu
De son être extirper l'élément corrompu,
Et dans ces bains de sang qui des Romains nous viennent
Et dont sur leurs vieux jours les puissants se souviennent,
Il n'a su réchauffer ce cadavre hébété
Où coule au lieu de sang l'eau verte du Léthé.

Spleen

I am like the king of a rainy country, rich but impotent, young and
yet aged, who, scorning his tutors' obeisances, passes his time in
boredom with his dogs as with other beasts. Nothing can cheer him,
neither game nor falcon nor his people dying opposite his balcony.
The comical ballad of his favourite fool no longer distracts the brow
of this cruel invalid; his bed with the fleur-de-lys is changed to a
tomb, and the ladies of the bedchamber, for whom any prince is
beautiful, can no longer find a shameless dress to draw a smile from
the young skeleton. The scholar who makes gold for him has never
been able to drive out the corrupt element from his being, and could
not heat this dull corpse, where, instead of blood, flows the green
water of Lethe, in those baths of blood which come to us from the
Romans and which the powerful recall in the days of their old age.

Les Bijoux

La très-chère était nue, et, connaissant mon cœur,
Elle n'avait gardé que ses bijoux sonores,
Dont le riche attirail lui donnait l'air vainqueur
Qu'ont dans leurs jours heureux les esclaves des Mores.

Quand il jette en dansant son bruit vif et moqueur,
Ce monde rayonnant de métal et de pierre
Me ravit en extase, et j'aime à la fureur
Les choses où le son se mêle à la lumière.

Elle était donc couchée et se laissait aimer,
Et du haut du divan elle souriait d'aise
A mon amour profond et doux comme la mer,
Qui vers elle montait comme vers sa falaise.

Les yeux fixés sur moi, comme un tigre dompté,
D'un air vague et rêveur elle essayait des poses,
Et la candeur unie à la lubricité
Donnait un charme neuf à ses métamorphoses;

The Jewels

The darling was naked, and, knowing my heart, she had only kept on her sonorous jewels, whose rich accoutrement gave her the conquering air that Moorish slaves have in their happy days.

When dancing it throws off its bright, mocking noise, this shining world of metal and stone transports me into ecstasy, and I love to distraction things where sound is mingled with light.

She was lying down and let herself be loved, and from the divan's height she smiled for pleasure at my passion, deep and gentle as the sea rising towards her as towards its cliff.

Her eyes fixed on me, like a tame tiger, with a vague dreamy air she tried various positions, and ingenuousness joined to lubricity gave a new charm to her metamorphoses;

Et son bras et sa jambe, et sa cuisse et ses reins,
Polis comme de l'huile, onduleux comme un cygne,
Passaient devant mes yeux clairvoyants et sereins;
Et son ventre et ses seins, ces grappes de ma vigne,

S'avançaient, plus câlins que les Anges du mal,
Pour troubler le repos où mon âme était mise,
Et pour la déranger du rocher de cristal
Où, calme et solitaire, elle s'était assise.

Je croyais voir unis par un nouveau dessin
Les hanches de l'Antiope au buste d'un imberbe,
Tant sa taille faisait ressortir son bassin.
Sur ce teint fauve et brun le fard était superbe!

— Et la lampe s'étant résignée à mourir,
Comme le foyer seul illuminait la chambre,
Chaque fois qu'il poussait un flamboyant soupir,
Il inondait de sang cette peau couleur d'ambre!

And her arm and her leg and her thigh and her loins, polished as oil, sinuous as a swan, passed before my calm, clear-sighted eyes; and her belly and breasts, those clusters of my vine,

Advanced more coaxing than evil Angels to disturb the quiet in which my soul was stationed, and to displace it from the crystal rock where, calm and solitary, it had taken up its seat.

Her waist set off her hips so well that I thought I saw the haunches of the Antiope joined to the bust of a young boy in a new drawing. On that dark tawny complexion the rouge was magnificent!

— And the lamp having decided to die, as the fire alone lighted the room, each time it uttered a sigh of flame, it flooded with blood that amber-coloured skin!

Les Sept Vieillards

A Victor Hugo

FOURMILLANTE cité, cité pleine de rêves,
Où le spectre en plein jour raccroche le passant!
Les mystères partout coulent comme des sèves
Dans les canaux étroits du colosse puissant.

Un matin, cependant que dans la triste rue
Les maisons, dont la brume allongeait la hauteur,
Simulaient les deux quais d'une rivière accrue,
Et que, décor semblable à l'âme de l'acteur,

Un brouillard sale et jaune inondait tout l'espace,
Je suivais, roidissant mes nerfs comme un héros
Et discutant avec mon âme déjà lasse,
Le faubourg secoué par les lourds tombereaux.

Tout à coup, un vieillard dont les guenilles jaunes
Imitaient la couleur de ce ciel pluvieux,
Et dont l'aspect aurait fait pleuvoir les aumônes,
Sans la méchanceté qui luisait dans ses yeux,

The Seven Old Men

To Victor Hugo

SWARMING city, city full of dreams, where in full light of day ghosts catch at the passer-by! Everywhere mysteries flow like sap in the narrow channels of the mighty giant.

One morning, while in the dismal street the houses, whose height was lengthened by the mist, resembled the two banks of a river in flood, and while, creating a scene like the actor's soul,

A dirty yellow fog flooded the whole space, I followed the street, which was shaken by heavy carts, bracing my nerves like a hero and arguing with my weary soul.

All at once an old man, whose yellow rags imitated the colour of the rainy sky, and whose appearance would have made alms rain upon him but for the wickedness shining in his eyes,

M'apparut. On eût dit sa prunelle trempée
Dans le fiel; son regard aiguisait les frimas,
Et sa barbe à longs poils, roide comme une épée,
Se projetait, pareille à celle de Judas.

Il n'était pas voûté, mais cassé, son échine
Faisant avec sa jambe un parfait angle droit,
Si bien que son bâton, parachevant sa mine,
Lui donnait la tournure et le pas maladroit

D'un quadrupède infirme ou d'un juif à trois pattes.
Dans la neige et la boue il allait s'empêtrant,
Comme s'il écrasait des morts sous ses savates,
Hostile à l'univers plutôt qu'indifférent.

Son pareil le suivait: barbe, œil, dos, baton, loques,
Nul trait ne distinguait, du même enfer venu,
Ce jumeau centenaire, et ces spectres baroques
Marchaient du même pas vers un but inconnu.

Appeared before me. One would have said his pupil was soaked in gall; his glance put an edge to the hoarfrost, and his beard of long hairs, stiff as a sword, stuck out like that of Judas.

He was not bent, but broken, his spine making a perfect right-angle with his leg, so that his stick, finishing off his appearance, gave him the clumsy shape and step

Of a crippled quadruped or a three-legged Jew. He walked paddling in the snow and mud, as if he were crushing dead men beneath his old shoes; he was hostile rather than indifferent to the universe.

His fellow followed him: beard, eye, back, stick, rags, no feature distinguished this hundred-year-old twin come from the same pit, and these baroque ghosts marched with the same step towards an unknown end.

A quel complot infâme étais-je donc en butte,
Ou quel méchant hasard ainsi m'humiliait?
Car je comptai sept fois, de minute en minute,
Ce sinistre vieillard qui se multipliait!

Que celui-là qui rit de mon inquiétude,
Et qui n'est pas saisi d'un frisson fraternel,
Songe bien que malgré tant de décrépitude
Ces sept monstres hideux avaient l'air éternel!

Aurais-je, sans mourir, contemplé le huitième,
Sosie inexorable, ironique et fatal,
Dégoûtant Phénix, fils et père de lui-même?
– Mais je tournai le dos au cortège infernal.

Exaspéré comme un ivrogne qui voit double,
Je rentrai, je fermai ma porte, épouvanté,
Malade et morfondu, l'esprit fiévreux et trouble,
Blessé par le mystère et par l'absurdité!

Vainement ma raison voulait prendre la barre;
La tempête en jouant déroutait ses efforts,
Et mon âme dansait, dansait, vieille gabarre
Sans mâts, sur une mer monstrueuse et sans bords!

What sordid plot was aimed at me or what evil chance so humiliated me? For, from minute to minute, I counted this sinister multiple old man seven times!

Let him who laughs at my anxiety and is not seized by a fraternal shudder consider that, in spite of being so decrepit, these seven hideous monsters had the air of eternity!

Would I have looked upon the eighth without dying, this unrelenting, fatally ironic double, this disgusting Phoenix, his own son and father? – But I turned my back on the hellish procession.

Exasperated, like a drunkard seeing double, I went home and shut my door, frightened, sick, and chilled, my mind feverish and confused, wounded by the mystery and the absurdity!

In vain my reason tried to take the helm; the storm blowing baffled all its efforts, and my soul danced, danced like an old barge without masts on a monstrous and shoreless sea!

Le Voyage

A Maxime du Camp

I

POUR l'enfant, amoureux de cartes et d'estampes,
L'univers est égal à son vaste appétit.
Ah! que le monde est grand à la clarté des lampes!
Aux yeux du souvenir que le monde est petit!

Un matin nous partons, le cerveau plein de flamme,
Le cœur gros de rancune et de désirs amers,
Et nous allons, suivant le rhythme de la lame,
Berçant notre infini sur le fini des mers:

Les uns, joyeux de fuir une patrie infâme;
D'autres, l'horreur de leurs berceaux, et quelques-uns,
Astrologues noyés dans les yeux d'une femme,
La Circé tyrannique aux dangereux parfums.

Pour n'être pas changés en bêtes, ils s'enivrent
D'espace et de lumière et de cieux embrasés;
La glace qui les mord, les soleils qui les cuivrent,
Effacent lentement la marque des baisers.

The Voyage

To Maxime du Camp

I

FOR the child fond of maps and prints the universe equals his huge appetite. Ah, how large the world is by lamplight! How small in the eyes of memory!

One morning we depart, our brains full of flame, hearts swollen with rancour and bitter desires, and we travel following the rhythm of the waves and rocking our infinity on the finite sea:

Some, glad to leave an infamous country; others, the horror of their cradles, and some, astrologers drowned in a woman's eyes, the tyrant Circe with the dangerous perfume.

Not to be changed into beasts, they drink the intoxication of space and light and glowing skies; the ice that gnaws them, the suns that bronze them slowly blot out the mark of the kisses.

Mais les vrais voyageurs sont ceux-là seuls qui partent
Pour partir; cœurs légers, semblables aux ballons,
De leur fatalité jamais ils ne s'écartent,
Et, sans savoir pourquoi, disent toujours: Allons!

Ceux-là dont les désirs ont la forme des nues,
Et qui rêvent, ainsi qu'un conscrit le canon,
De vastes voluptés, changeantes, inconnues,
Et dont l'esprit humain n'a jamais su le nom!

2

Nous imitons, horreur! la toupie et la boule
Dans leur valse et leurs bonds; même dans nos sommeils
La Curiosité nous tourmente et nous roule,
Comme un Ange cruel qui fouette des soleils.

Singulière fortune où le but se déplace,
Et, n'étant nulle part, peut être n'importe où!
Où l'Homme, dont jamais l'espérance n'est lasse,
Pour trouver le repos court toujours comme un fou!

But the true travellers are only those who depart for the sake of departing; with hearts light as balloons, they never avoid their destiny and always say: Let us go! without knowing why.

Those whose desires have the shape of clouds, and who dream, as a conscript dreams of cannon, of vast, secretly shifting pleasures, whose name the human mind has never known!

2

O horror! We follow the top and the ball in their waltzing and bouncing; even in our sleep curiosity torments and rolls us along like a cruel angel whipping on the suns.

What a curious destiny where the goal is always moved and, being nowhere, can be anywhere! Where Man, whose capacity for hope is tireless, ever runs like a madman to find rest!

Notre âme est un trois-mâts cherchant son Icarie;
Une voix retentit sur le pont: «Ouvre l'œil!»
Une voix de la hune, ardente et folle, crie:
«Amour … gloire … bonheur!» Enfer! c'est un écueil!

Chaque îlot signalé par l'homme de vigie
Est un Eldorado promis par le Destin;
L'Imagination qui dresse son orgie
Ne trouve qu'un récif aux clartés du matin.

Ô le pauvre amoureux des pays chimériques!
Faut-il le mettre aux fers, le jeter à la mer,
Ce matelot ivrogne, inventeur d'Amériques
Dont le mirage rend le gouffre plus amer?

Tel le vieux vagabond, piétinant dans la boue,
Rêve, le nez en l'air, de brillants paradis;
Son œil ensorcelé découvre une Capoue
Partout où la chandelle illumine un taudis.

Our soul is a three-master seeking its Icaria; a voice resounds on the bridge: 'Alert!' A wild, passionate voice from the crow's nest cries: 'Love … fame … happiness!' Hell! It is a rock!

Every islet pointed out by the look-out is fate's promised Eldorado; Imagination preparing her orgy only finds a reef in the morning light.

O the poor lover of mythical countries! Should we put him in irons or throw him in the sea, this drunken sailor, the inventor of Americas, whose mirage makes the gulf more bitter?

As the old tramp paddling in the mud with his nose in the air dreams of shining Paradises; his bewitched eye discovers a Capua wherever a candle lights up a slum.

3

Étonnants voyageurs! quelles nobles histoires
Nous lisons dans vos yeux profonds comme les mers!
Montrez-nous les écrins de vos riches mémoires,
Ces bijoux merveilleux, faits d'astres et d'éthers.

Nous voulons voyager sans vapeur et sans voile!
Faites, pour égayer l'ennui de nos prisons,
Passer sur nos esprits, tendus comme une toile,
Vos souvenirs avec leurs cadres d'horizons.

Dites, qu'avez-vous vu?

4

«Nous avons vu des astres
Et des flots; nous avons vu des sables aussi;
Et, malgré bien des chocs et d'imprévus désastres,
Nous nous sommes souvent ennuyés, comme ici.

La gloire du soleil sur la mer violette,
La gloire des cités dans le soleil couchant,
Allumaient dans nos cœurs une ardeur inquiète
De plonger dans un ciel au reflet alléchant.

3

Surprising travellers! What noble tales we read in your eyes, deep as the seas! Show us the coffers of your rich memories, those marvellous jewels made out of stars and ether.

We wish to travel without steam or sail! To cheer the boredom of our prison let your memories framed by the horizon pass over our spirits set for them like a sail.

Say, what have you seen?

4

'We saw stars and waves; we saw sand dunes as well; and, in spite of many shocks and unforeseen catastrophes, we were often bored as we are here.

'The glory of the sun on the purple sea, the glory of cities in the setting sun lighted in our hearts a restless longing to plunge into a sky, whose reflection was so alluring.

Les plus riches cités, les plus grands paysages,
Jamais ne contenaient l'attrait mystérieux
De ceux que le hasard fait avec les nuages.
Et toujours le désir nous rendait soucieux!

– La jouissance ajoute au désir de la force.
Désir, vieil arbre à qui le plaisir sert d'engrais,
Cependant que grossit et durcit ton écorce,
Tes branches veulent voir le soleil de plus près!

Grandiras-tu toujours, grand arbre plus vivace
Que le cyprès? – Pourtant, nous avons, avec soin,
Cueilli quelques croquis pour votre album vorace,
Frères qui trouvez beau tout ce qui vient de loin!

Nous avons salué des idoles à trompe;
Des trônes constellés de joyaux lumineux;
Des palais ouvragés dont la féerique pompe
Serait pour vos banquiers un rêve ruineux;

Des costumes qui sont pour les yeux une ivresse;
Des femmes dont les dents et les ongles sont teints,
Et des jongleurs savants que le serpent caresse.»

'The richest cities, the widest landscapes never held the mysterious attraction of those that chance constructs with the clouds. And
desire always made us anxious!
'– Enjoyment adds strength to desire. Desire, old tree that pleasure serves to fertilize, as your bark thickens and hardens, your
branches wish to see the sun nearer to!
'Will you always grow, great tree, longer-lived than the cypress?
– Yet with care we gathered some sketches for your greedy album,
brothers who find everything beautiful that comes from afar!
'We have hailed idols with elephants' trunks; thrones studded
with shining gems; carved palaces whose fairy pomp would be a
ruinous dream for your bankers;
'Clothes that are an intoxication for the eyes; women, whose
teeth and nails are dyed, and skilful jugglers fondled by snakes.'

5

Et puis, et puis encore?

6

«Ô cerveaux enfantins!

Pour ne pas oublier la chose capitale,
Nous avons vu partout, et sans l'avoir cherché,
Du haut jusques en bas de l'échelle fatale,
Le spectacle ennuyeux de l'immortel péché:

La femme, esclave vile, orgueilleuse et stupide,
Sans rire s'adorant et s'aimant sans dégoût;
L'homme, tyran goulu, paillard, dur et cupide,
Esclave de l'esclave et ruisseau dans l'égout;

Le bourreau qui jouit, le martyr qui sanglote;
La fête qu'assaisonne et parfume le sang;
Le poison du pouvoir énervant le despote,
Et le peuple amoureux du fouet abrutissant;

5

And then, and then again?

6

'O childish minds!
   'Not to forget the main thing, without having searched we saw everywhere, from top to bottom of the fatal ladder, the tedious spectacle of immortal sin:
   'Woman, a base slave, arrogant and stupid, worshipping herself without laughter and loving herself without disgust; man, a gluttonous, lecherous tyrant, hard and avaricious, slave of a slave and gutter pouring into a sewer;
   'The happy torturer, the sobbing martyr; the feast flavoured and scented with blood; power's poison enfeebling the despot and the people loving the brutalizing whip;

Plusieurs religions semblables à la nôtre,
Toutes escaladant le ciel; la Sainteté,
Comme en un lit de plume un délicat se vautre,
Dans les clous et le crin cherchant la volupté;

L'Humanité bavarde, ivre de son génie,
Et, folle maintenant comme elle était jadis,
Criant à Dieu, dans sa furibonde agonie:
«Ô mon semblable, ô mon maître, je te maudis!»

Et les moins sots, hardis amants de la Démence,
Fuyant le grand troupeau parqué par le Destin,
Et se réfugiant dans l'opium immense!
– Tel est du globe entier l'éternel bulletin.»

7

Amer savoir, celui qu'on tire du voyage!
Le monde, monotone et petit, aujourd'hui,
Hier, demain, toujours, nous fait voir notre image:
Une oasis d'horreur dans un désert d'ennui!

'Several religions like ours, all storming heaven; Sanctity seeking pleasure in nails and hair-shirts, like a sybarite wallowing in a feather-bed;
'Loquacious humanity drunk with its own genius and, mad now as it was before, crying to God in its wild agony: "O my fellow, O my master, I curse you!"
'And the less foolish, bold lovers of Lunacy, shunning the great herd corralled by fate and taking refuge in the immensity of opium! – Such is the perpetual news of the whole globe.'

7

What bitter knowledge one gets from travelling! The monotonously small world to-day, yesterday, to-morrow, always, makes us see our own likeness: an oasis of horror in a desert of boredom!

Faut-il partir? rester? Si tu peux rester, reste;
Pars, s'il le faut. L'un court, et l'autre se tapit
Pour tromper l'ennemi vigilant et funeste;
Le Temps! Il est, hélas! des coureurs sans répit,

Comme le Juif errant et comme les apôtres,
A qui rien ne suffit, ni wagon ni vaisseau,
Pour fuir ce rétiaire infâme; il en est d'autres
Qui savent le tuer sans quitter leur berceau.

Lorsque enfin il mettra le pied sur notre échine,
Nous pourrons espérer et crier: En avant!
De même qu'autrefois nous partions pour la Chine,
Les yeux fixés au large et les cheveux au vent,

Nous nous embarquerons sur la mer des Ténèbres
Avec le cœur joyeux d'un jeune passager.
Entendez-vous ces voix, charmantes et funèbres,
Qui chantent: «Par ici! vous qui voulez manger

Le Lotus parfumé: c'est ici qu'on vendange
Les fruits miraculeux dont votre cœur a faim;
Venez vous enivrer de la douceur étrange
De cette aprés-midi qui n'a jamais de fin!»

Must we depart? Or stay? If you can stay, stay; depart if you must. One man runs and another crouches to trick the sinister watchful enemy: Time! Alas! there are some runners who can take no rest,

Like the Wandering Jew and like the apostles, for whom nothing, neither coach nor ship, suffices to flee this infamous retiary; there are others who can kill him without leaving their cradle.

When at last he places his foot upon our spine, we can take hope and cry: Forward! In the same way as before we left for China, our eyes on the horizon and our hair in the wind,

We shall embark upon the sea of shadows with the joyful heart of a young voyager. Do you hear those charming funereal voices singing: 'This way! You who would eat

'The scented Lotus! Here is the harvest gathered of the wondrous fruits for which your heart hungers; come and get drunk on the strange sweetness of this unending afternoon!'

A l'accent familier nous devinons le spectre;
Nos Pylades là-bas tendent leurs bras vers nous.
«Pour rafraîchir ton cœur nage vers ton Électre!»
Dit celle dont jadis nous baisions les genoux.

8

Ô Mort, vieux capitaine, il est temps! levons l'ancre!
Ce pays nous ennuie, ô Mort! Appareillons!
Si le ciel et la mer sont noirs comme de l'encre,
Nos cœurs que tu connais sont remplis de rayons!

Verse-nous ton poison pour qu'il nous réconforte!
Nous voulons, tant ce feu nous brûle le cerveau,
Plonger au fond du gouffre, Enfer ou Ciel, qu'importe?
Au fond de l'Inconnu pour trouver du *nouveau*!

La Chambre double

UNE chambre qui ressemble à une rêverie, une chambre
véritablement *spirituelle*, où l'atmosphère stagnante est
légèrement teintée de rose et de bleu.

At the familiar voice we guess who the ghost is; there our Pylades
stretch their arms towards us. 'To cool your heart swim towards
your Electra!' says she whose knees we once kissed.

8

O Death, old captain, it is time! Raise anchor! This country bores
us, Death! make ready! If the sky and sea are black as ink, our
hearts, which you know, are filled with sunbeams!

Pour us your poison to comfort us! This fire burns our brains
so, that we want to plunge to the bottom of the gulf, Hell or
Heaven, what does it matter? To find something *new* in the depth
of the Unknown!

The Double Room

A ROOM resembling a dream, a really *spiritual* room, where the
stagnant atmosphere is lightly tinted with pink and blue.

L'âme y prend un bain de paresse, aromatisé par le regret et le désir. – C'est quelque chose de crépusculaire, de bleuâtre et de rosâtre; un rêve de volupté pendant une éclipse.

Les meubles ont des formes allongées, prostrées, alanguies. Les meubles ont l'air de rêver; on les dirait doués d'une vie somnambulique, comme le végétal et le minéral. Les étoffes parlent une langue muette, comme les fleurs, comme les ciels, comme les soleils couchants.

Sur les murs nulle abomination artistique. Relativement au rêve pur, à l'impression non analysée, l'art défini, l'art positif est un blasphème. Ici, tout a la suffisante clarté et la délicieuse obscurité de l'harmonie.

Une senteur infinitésimale du choix le plus exquis, à laquelle se mêle une très-légère humidité, nage dans cette atmosphère, où l'esprit sommeillant est bercé par des sensations de serre chaude.

La mousseline pleut abondamment devant les fenêtres et devant le lit; elle s'épanche en cascades neigeuses. Sur ce lit est couchée l'Idole, la souveraine des rêves. Mais

The soul takes a bath of idleness there, a bath perfumed by regret and desire. – It is something like the twilight, something bluish and pinkish; a dream of pleasure during an eclipse.

The pieces of furniture have shapes stretched out, prostrate, languid. The pieces of furniture have the air of dreaming; one would say they were endowed with a sleep-walker's life, like the vegetable and the mineral. The materials speak a dumb language like flowers, skies, and setting suns.

No artistic abomination on the walls. Relative to the pure dream, to the unanalysed impression, defined art, positive art is a blasphemy. Here everything has the sufficient light and the delectable darkness of harmony.

The faintest fragrance of most exquisite choice to which a very slight humidity is mingled floats in this atmosphere where the slumbering mind is cradled by sensations like those caused by a hothouse.

Muslin rains abundantly in front of the windows and the bed; it pours forth in snowy cascades. On this bed lies the Idol, the sover-

comment est-elle ici? Qui l'a amenée? quel pouvoir magique l'a installée sur ce trône de rêverie et de volupté? Qu'importe? là voilà! je la reconnais.

Voilà bien ces yeux dont la flamme traverse le crépuscule: ces subtiles et terribles *mirettes*, que je reconnais à leur effrayante malice! Elles attirent, elles subjuguent, elles dévorent le regard de l'imprudent qui les contemple. Je les ai souvent étudiées, ces étoiles noires qui commandent la curiosité et l'admiration.

A quel demon bienveillant dois-je d'être ainsi entouré de mystère, de silence, de paix et de parfums? O béatitude! ce que nous nommons généralement la vie, même dans son expansion la plus heureuse, n'a rien de commun avec cette vie suprême dont j'ai maintenant connaissance et que je savoure minute par minute, seconde par seconde!

Non! il n'est plus de minutes, il n'est plus de secondes! Le temps a disparu; c'est l'Éternité qui règne, une éternité de délices!

eign of dreams. But how is she here? Who brought her? What magic power placed her on this throne of dreams and pleasure? What does it matter? there she is! I recognize her.

There indeed are those eyes whose flame pierces the twilight; those subtle and terrible *optics* that I recognize by their terrifying malice! They attract, they subdue, they consume the glance of the rash man who gazes upon them. I have often studied these black stars which command curiosity and wonder.

To what kindly demon do I owe thus being surrounded by mystery, silence, peace, and perfumes? O beatitude! what we generally call life has nothing in common, even in its happiest expansion, with this supreme life that I know now and which I taste minute by minute, second by second!

No! there are no more minutes, there are no more seconds! Time has disappeared; it is Eternity which reigns, an eternity of delights!

Mais un coup terrible, lourd, a retenti à la porte, et, comme dans les rêves infernaux, il m'a semblé que je recevais un coup de pioche dans l'estomac.

Et puis un Spectre est entré. C'est un huissier qui vient me torturer au nom de la loi; une infâme concubine qui vient crier misère et ajouter les trivialités de sa vie aux douleurs de la mienne; ou bien le saute-ruisseau d'un directeur de journal qui réclame la suite du manuscrit.

La chambre paradisiaque, l'idole, la souveraine des rêves, la *Sylphide*, comme disait le grand René, toute cette magie a disparu au coup brutal frappé par le Spectre.

Horreur! je me souviens! je me souviens! Oui! ce taudis, ce séjour de l'éternel ennui, est bien le mien. Voici les meubles sots, poudreux, écornés: la cheminée sans flamme et sans braise, souillée de crachats; les tristes fenêtres où la pluie a tracé des sillons dans la poussière; les manuscrits, raturés ou incomplets; l'almanach où le crayon a marqué les dates sinistres!

But a terrible heavy knock resounded at the door, and, as in infernal dreams, it seemed to me as if I received a blow from a pick in the stomach.

And then a Ghost entered. It is a sheriff's officer coming to torment me in the name of the law; an infamous concubine coming to cry woe and add the trivialities of her life to the sufferings of mine; or else the messenger of a newspaper editor wanting the next instalment of a manuscript.

The paradisiacal room, the idol, the sovereign of dreams, the *Sylphide*, as the great René said – all this magic disappeared at the brutal knocking of the Ghost.

O horror! I remember! I remember! Yes! this slum, this dwelling of perpetual vexation is indeed mine. Here are the idiotic, dusty, broken-down pieces of furniture: the hearth without flame or embers, soiled with gobs of spit; the melancholy windows where the rain has made furrows in the dust; the manuscripts crossed out or not completed; the almanac where the pencil has marked the unlucky days!

Et ce parfum d'un autre monde, dont je m'enivrais avec une sensibilité perfectionnée, hélas! il est remplacé par une fétide odeur de tabac mêlée à je ne sais quelle nauséabonde moisissure. On respire ici maintenant le ranci de la désolation.

Dans ce monde étroit, mais si plein de dégoût, un seul objet connu me sourit: la fiole de laudanum; une vieille et terrible amie; comme toutes les amies, hélas! féconde en caresses et en traîtrises.

Oh! oui! le Temps a reparu; le Temps règne en souverain maintenant, et avec le hideux vieillard est revenu tout son démoniaque cortège de Souvenirs, de Regrets, de Spasmes, de Peurs, d'Angoisses, de Cauchemars, de Colères et de Névroses.

Je vous assure que les secondes maintenant sont fortement et solennellement accentuées, et chacune, en jaillissant de la pendule, dit: – «Je suis la Vie, l'insupportable, l'implacable Vie!»

Il n'y a qu'une Seconde dans la vie humaine qui ait mission d'annoncer une bonne nouvelle, la *bonne nouvelle* qui cause à chacun une inexplicable peur.

And this perfume from another world on which I grew drunk with refined sensibility, alas! it is replaced by a fetid smell of tobacco mixed with I know not what loathsome mould. Here we now breathe the rankness of desolation.

In this narrow world so full of disgust one well-known object alone smiles on me: the phial of laudanum; an old and terrible mistress; like all mistresses, alas! fertile in caresses and in treachery.

Oh, yes! Time has reappeared; Time reigns sovereign now, and with the hideous old man has returned all his diabolical train of Memories, Regrets, Spasms, Fears, Anguishes, Nightmares, Angers, and Neuroses.

I assure you that now the seconds are strongly and solemnly stressed, and each one, spouting from the clock, says: 'I am Life, unbearable, unrelenting Life!'

There is only one Second in human life whose mission it is to announce good news, *the good news* that causes everyone inexplicable fear.

Oui! le Temps règne; il a repris sa brutale dictature. Et il me pousse, comme si j'étais un bœuf, avec son double aiguillon. – «Et hue donc! bourrique! Sue donc, esclave! Vis donc, damné!»

Enivrez-vous

Il faut être toujours ivre. Tout est là: c'est l'unique question. Pour ne pas sentir l'horrible fardeau du Temps qui brise vos épaules et vous penche vers la terre, il faut vous enivrer sans trêve.

Mais de quoi? De vin, de poésie, ou de vertu, à votre guise. Mais enivrez-vous.

Et si quelquefois, sur les marches d'un palais, sur l'herbe verte d'un fossé, dans la solitude morne de votre chambre, vous vous réveillez, l'ivresse déjà diminuée ou disparue, demandez au vent, à la vague, à l'étoile, à l'oiseau, à l'horloge, à tout ce qui fuit, à tout ce qui gémit, à tout ce qui roule, à tout ce qui chante, à tout ce qui parle, demandez quelle heure il est; et le vent, la vague, l'étoile, l'oiseau, l'horloge, vous répondront: «Il est l'heure de

Yes, Time reigns; he has begun his brutal dictatorship again. And he urges me, as if I were an ox, with his double goad. – 'Gee up! donkey! Sweat for it, slave! Live, damned soul!'

Get Drunk

You must always be drunk. Everything is there: it is the only question. Not to feel the horrible burden of Time breaking your shoulders and bowing you towards the ground, you must get drunk without stopping.

But on what? On wine, on poetry, or on virtue, after your fashion. But get drunk.

And if sometimes, on the steps of a palace, in the green grass of a ditch, in the dreary solitude of your own room, you wake up, with your drunkenness already lessened or gone, ask wind, wave, star, bird, clock, everything that flees, murmurs, rolls, sings, speaks, ask what time it is; and wind, wave, star, bird, clock will answer you:

s'enivrer! Pour n'être pas les esclaves martyrisés du
Temps, enivrez-vous sans cesse! De vin, de poésie ou de
vertu, à votre guise.»

JOSÉ-MARIA DE HÉRÉDIA

L'Oubli

LE temple est en ruine au haut du promontoire.
Et la Mort a mêlé, dans ce fauve terrain,
Les Déesses de marbre et les Héros d'airain
Dont l'herbe solitaire ensevelit la gloire.

Seul, parfois, un bouvier menant ses buffles boire,
De sa conque où soupire un antique refrain
Emplissant le ciel calme et l'horizon marin,
Sur l'azur infini dresse sa forme noire.

La Terre maternelle et douce aux anciens Dieux
Fait à chaque printemps, vainement éloquente,
Au chapiteau brisé verdir une autre acanthe;

'It is time to get drunk! Not to be the tormented slaves of Time, get
drunk without stopping! On wine, on poetry, or on virtue, after
your fashion.'

Forgetfulness

ON the top of the headland the temple is in ruins. And death has
mingled in this tawny earth marble Goddesses and brazen Heroes,
whose fame is buried by the deserted grass.

Only sometimes a drover, leading his buffaloes to drink, profiles
his dark shape against the blue infinity, filling the calm sky and the
sea horizon with his horn, in which an ancient tune sighs.

The earth, gentle mother of the old Gods, every Spring with
vain eloquence makes another acanthus grow green on the broken
capital;

Mais l'Homme indifférent au rêve des aïeux
Écoute sans frémir, du fond des nuits sereines,
La Mer qui se lamente en pleurant les Sirènes.

Villula

Oui, c'est au vieux Gallus qu'appartient l'héritage
Que tu vois au penchant du coteau cisalpin;
La maison tout entière est à l'abri d'un pin
Et le chaume du toit couvre à peine un étage.

Il suffit pour qu'un hôte avec lui le partage.
Il a sa vigne, un four à cuire plus d'un pain.
Et dans son potager foisonne le lupin.
C'est peu? Gallus n'a pas désiré davantage.

Son bois donne un fagot ou deux tous les hivers,
Et de l'ombre, l'été, sous les feuillages verts;
A l'automne on y prend quelque grive au passage.

But Man, indifferent to the dream of his ancestors, hears without trembling from the depth of serene nights the Sea lamenting and weeping for the Sirens.

Villula

Yes, it is to old Gallus that the inheritance belongs which you see on the slope of the Cisalpine hill; the whole house is in the shade of a pine, and the roof's thatch hardly covers one story.

It is enough for a guest to share it with him. He has his vine, an oven to cook more than one loaf, and in his kitchen garden the lupin abounds. It is little? Gallus did not wish for more.

His wood gives a bundle or two every winter, and shade beneath the green leaves in the summer; in the autumn one can trap some journeying thrush there.

C'est là que, satisfait de son destin borné,
Gallus finit de vivre où jadis il est né.
Va, tu sais à présent que Gallus est un sage.

La Trebbia

L'aube d'un jour sinistre a blanchi les hauteurs.
Le camp s'éveille. En bas roule et gronde le fleuve
Où l'escadron léger des Numides s'abreuve.
Partout sonne l'appel clair des buccinateurs.

Car malgré Scipion, les augures menteurs,
La Trebbia débordée, et qu'il vente et qu'il pleuve,
Sempronius Consul, fier de sa gloire neuve,
A fait lever la hache et marcher les licteurs.

Rougissant le ciel noir de flamboîments lugubres,
A l'horizon, brûlaient les villages Insubres;
On entendait au loin barrir un éléphant.

It is there that, satisfied with his narrow lot, Gallus is ending his
life where formerly he was born. Go, now you know that Gallus is
a sage.

The Trebbia

The dawn of an ominous day whitened the heights. The camp
awakens. Below rolls and murmurs the river, where the light squad-
ron of Numidians is watering its horses. Everywhere sounds the
clear call of the trumpeters.

For in spite of Scipio, the lying augurs, the Trebbia in flood, and
the wind and the rain, the Consul Sempronius, proud of his new
glory, has raised the axe and made the lictors advance.

Reddening the dark sky with a melancholy blaze, the Insubri villages burned on the horizon; far off the trumpeting of an elephant
was heard.

Et là-bas, sous le pont, adossé contre une arche,
Hannibal écoutait, pensif et triomphant,
Le piétinement sourd des légions en marche.

Antoine et Cléopâtre

Tous deux ils regardaient, de la haute terrasse,
L'Égypte s'endormir sous un ciel étouffant
Et le Fleuve, à travers le Delta noir qu'il fend,
Vers Bubaste ou Saïs rouler son onde grasse.

Et le Romain sentait sous la lourde cuirasse,
Soldat captif berçant le sommeil d'un enfant,
Ployer et défaillir sur son cœur triomphant
Le corps voluptueux que son étreinte embrasse.

Tournant sa tête pâle entre ses cheveux bruns
Vers celui qu'enivraient d'invincibles parfums,
Elle tendit sa bouche et ses prunelles claires;

Et sur elle courbé, l'ardent Imperator
Vit dans ses larges yeux étoilés de points d'or
Toute une mer immense où fuyaient des galères.

And down there beneath the bridge, with his back against an arch, triumphant and thoughtful, Hannibal listened to the dull tramp of the marching legions.

Antony and Cleopatra

From the high terrace they both watched Egypt sleeping beneath a stifling sky and the river rolling its oily waves towards Bubastis or Sais through the black delta that it divides.

And beneath his heavy armour, the Roman, a captive soldier cradling a child's slumber, felt the voluptuous body grasped in his embrace yielding and fainting on his triumphant heart.

Turning her head, pale amid her dark hair, towards him who was maddened by irresistible perfumes, she offered her mouth and her clear eyes;

And bent over her the passionate Imperator saw in her wide eyes starred with golden specks a whole vast sea where galleys were in flight.

Floridum Mare

LA moisson débordant le plateau diapré
Roule, ondule et déferle au vent frais qui la berce;
Et le profil, au ciel lointain, de quelque herse
Semble un bateau qui tangue et lève un noir beaupré.

Et sous mes pieds, la mer, jusqu'au couchant pourpré,
Céruléenne ou rose ou violette ou perse
Ou blanche de moutons que le reflux disperse,
Verdoie à l'infini comme un immense pré.

Aussi les goëlands qui suivent la marée,
Vers les blés murs que gonfle une houle dorée,
Avec des cris joyeux, volaient en tourbillons;

Tandis que, de la terre, une brise emmiellée
Éparpillait au gré de leur ivresse ailée
Sur l'Océan fleuri des vols de papillons.

Floridum Mare

THE harvest overflowing the multi-coloured plain rolls, undulates, and unfurls in the cool wind cradling it; and the profile of some harrow on the distant sky seems like a ship pitching and raising a dark bowsprit.

And beneath my feet the sea, right to the purple west, sky-blue or pink or violet or ultramarine or the white horses scattered by the ebb, becomes infinitely green, like a huge meadow.

The gulls, too, following the flood, flew in whirlwinds with joyful cries towards the ripe corn swollen by a golden tide;

While from the land a honeyed breeze spread flights of butterflies over the flowery ocean after the desire of their winged ecstasy.

La Mort de l'aigle

QUAND l'aigle a dépassé les neiges éternelles,
A sa vaste envergure il veut chercher plus d'air
Et le soleil plus proche en un azur plus clair
Pour échauffer l'éclat de ses mornes prunelles.

Il s'enlève. Il aspire un torrent d'étincelles.
Toujours plus haut, enflant son vol tranquille et fier,
Il monte vers l'orage où l'attire l'éclair;
Mais la foudre d'un coup a rompu ses deux ailes.

Avec un cri sinistre, il tournoie, emporté
Par la trombe, et, crispé, buvant d'un trait sublime
La flamme éparse, il plonge au fulgurant abîme.

Heureux qui pour la Gloire ou pour la Liberté,
Dans l'orgueil de la force et l'ivresse du rêve,
Meurt ainsi d'une mort éblouissante et brève!

The Death of the Eagle

WHEN the eagle has passed beyond the everlasting snows, he desires to seek more air for his vast spread of wing and a nearer sun in a clearer blue to rouse the brightness of his dull eyes.

He soars. He breathes a stream of sparks. Ever higher, raising his calm, proud flight, he climbs towards the storm allured by the lightning; but the thunder has broken both his wings with a single blow.

With a dismal cry, he whirls round and round, carried away by the whirlwind, and, shrivelled, drinking the scattered flame at one sublime draught, he dives into the abyss of lightnings.

Happy he who, for Fame or Freedom, in the pride of his strength and the intoxication of a dream, dies so dazzling and swift a death!

STÉPHANE MALLARMÉ

Le Pitre châtié

Yᴇᴜx, lacs avec ma simple ivresse de renaître
Autre que l'histrion qui du geste évoquais
Comme plume la suie ignoble des quinquets,
J'ai troué dans le mur de toile une fenêtre.

De ma jambe et des bras limpide nageur traître,
A bonds multipliés, reniant le mauvais
Hamlet! c'est comme si dans l'onde j'innovais
Mille sépulcres pour y vierge disparaître.

Hilare or de cymbale à des poings irrité,
Tout à coup le soleil frappe la nudité
Qui pure s'exhala de ma fraîcheur de nacre,

Rance nuit de la peau quand sur moi vous passiez,
Ne sachant pas, ingrat! que c'était tout mon sacre,
Ce fard noyé dans l'eau perfide des glaciers.

The Clown Punished

Eyᴇs, lakes with my simple intoxication to be reborn other than the actor, who, with his gestures as with a pen, evoked the disgusting soot of the lamps, I have pierced a window in the wall of cloth.

Limpid, treacherous swimmer with my leg and arms in many a bound renouncing the evil Hamlet! it is as if I began a thousand tombs in the waves to disappear into them virgin.

Merry gold of the cymbal beaten with fists, all at once the sun strikes the pure nakedness which was breathed from my cool mother-of-pearl,

When you passed over me, rancid night of the skin, not knowing, ingrate, that it was my whole anointing, this rouge drowned in the deceitful water of glaciers.

Brise Marine

LA chair est triste, hélas! et j'ai lu tous les livres.
Fuir! là-bas fuir! Je sens que des oiseaux sont ivres
D'être parmi l'écume inconnue et les cieux!
Rien, ni les vieux jardins reflétés par les yeux
Ne retiendra ce cœur qui dans la mer se trempe
Ô nuits! ni la clarté déserte de ma lampe
Sur le vide papier que la blancheur défend,
Et ni la jeune femme allaitant son enfant.
Je partirai! Steamer balançant ta mâture,
Lève l'ancre pour une exotique nature!
Un Ennui, désolé par les cruels espoirs,
Croit encore à l'adieu suprême des mouchoirs!
Et, peut-être, les mâts, invitant les orages
Sont-ils de ceux qu'un vent penche sur les naufrages
Perdus, sans mâts, sans mâts, ni fertiles îlots ...
Mais, ô mon cœur, entends le chant des matelots!

Sea Breeze

THE flesh is sad, alas! and I have read all the books. To escape! To escape far away! I feel that birds are drunk to be among unknown foam and the skies! Nothing – not old gardens reflected in the eyes – will keep back this heart soaking itself in the sea, O nights! nor the desolate light of my lamp on the empty paper, defended by its own whiteness, nor the young wife feeding her child. I shall depart! Steamer with swaying masts, raise anchor for exotic landscapes!

A tedium saddened by cruel hopes still believes in the last farewell of handkerchiefs! And perhaps the masts, inviting storms, are among those that a gale bends above shipwrecks lost without masts, without masts or fertile islands. ... But, O my heart, listen to the sailors' song!

Don du poème

Je t'apporte l'enfant d'une nuit d'Idumée!
Noire, à l'aile saignante et pâle, déplumée,
Par le verre brûlé d'aromates et d'or,
Par les carreaux glacés, hélas! mornes encor,
L'aurore se jeta sur la lampe angélique,
Palmes! et quand elle a montré cette relique
A ce père essayant un sourire ennemi,
La solitude bleue et stérile a frémi.
Ô la berceuse, avec ta fille et l'innocence
De vos pieds froids, accueille un horrible naissance:
Et ta voix rappelant viole et clavecin,
Avec le doigt fané presseras-tu le sein
Par qui coule en blancheur sibylline la femme
Pour des lèvres que l'air du vierge azur affame?

Gift of the Poem

I bring you the child of an Idumean night! Dark, with bleeding wing and pale, its feathers plucked, through the glass burned with spices and gold, through the icy panes, still dreary, alas! the dawn threw itself on the angelic lamp, O palms! and when it showed this relic to the father trying out a hostile smile, the blue, sterile solitude shuddered.

O nurse, with your daughter and the innocence of your cold feet, welcome a horrid birth and, your voice recalling viol and harpsichord, with your withered finger will you press the breast whence woman flows in enigmatic whiteness for lips made hungry by the air of the blue, virginal sky?

L'Après-midi d'un faune

Églogue

Le Faune

CES nymphes, je veux les perpétuer.
                              Si clair,
Leur incarnat léger, qu'il voltige dans l'air
Assoupi de sommeils touffus.

                         Aimai-je un rêve?
Mon doute, amas de nuit ancienne, s'achève
En maint rameau subtil, qui, demeuré les vrais
Bois mêmes, prouve, hélas! que bien seul je m'offrais
Pour triomphe la faute idéale de roses.
Réfléchissons. …

                    ou si les femmes dont tu gloses
Figurent un souhait de tes sens fabuleux!
Faune, l'illusion s'échappe des yeux bleus
Et froids, comme une source en pleurs, de la plus chaste:
Mais l'autre, tout soupirs, dis-tu qu'elle contraste

A Faun's Afternoon

Eclogue

The Faun

I DESIRE to perpetuate these nymphs.

So bright their light rosy flesh that it hovers in the air drowsy with tufted slumbers.

Did I love a dream? My doubt, heap of old night, ends in many a subtle branch, which, remaining the true woods themselves, proves, alas! that alone I offered myself the ideal error of roses for triumph. Let us reflect. …

Or if the women that you tell of represent a desire of your fabulous senses! Faun, illusion flows like a weeping spring from the cold blue eyes of the most chaste: but the other, all sighs, do you say that

Comme brise du jour chaude dans ta toison?
Que non! par l'immobile et lasse pâmoison
Suffoquant de chaleurs le matin frais s'il lutte,
Ne murmure point d'eau que ne verse ma flûte
Au bosquet arrosé d'accords; et le seul vent
Hors des deux tuyaux prompt à s'exhaler avant
Qu'il disperse le son dans une pluie aride,
C'est, à l'horizon pas remué d'une ride,
Le visible et serein souffle artificiel
De l'inspiration, qui regagne le ciel.

Ô bords siciliens d'un calme marécage
Qu'à l'envi des soleils ma vanité saccage,
Tacite sous les fleurs d'étincelles, CONTEZ
«Que je coupais ici les creux roseaux domptés
«Par le talent; quand, sur l'or glauque de lointaines
«Verdures dédiant leur vigne à des fontaines,
«Ondoie une blancheur animale au repos:
«Et qu'au prélude lent où naissent les pipeaux
«Ce vol de cygnes, non! de naïades se sauve
«Ou plonge. ...»

she contrasts like the day breeze warm on your fleece? No! Through
the motionless, lazy swoon suffocating with heat the cool morning,
if it struggles, there murmurs no water not poured by my flute on
the thicket sprinkled with melody; and the only wind, quick to
breathe itself forth out of the two pipes, before it scatters the sound
in an arid rain, is, on the horizon unmoved by any wrinkle, the
visible, calm and artificial breath of inspiration returning to the
sky.

O Sicilian shores of a calm pool that my vanity plunders, vying
with the sun, silent beneath flowers of sparkling light, TELL *'That
here I was cutting the hollow reeds subdued by talent; when, on the
green gold of far-off verdures that offer their vine to fountains, ripples
to rest an animal whiteness: and that at the slow prelude in which the
pipes are born this flight of swans, no! of naiads runs away or dives. ...'*

Inerte, tout brûle dans l'heure fauve
Sans marquer par quel art ensemble détala
Trop d'hymen souhaité de qui cherche le *la*:
Alors m'éveillerai-je à la ferveur première,
Droit et seul, sous un flot antique de lumière,
Lys! et l'un de vous tous pour l'ingénuité.

Autre que ce doux rien par leur lèvre ébruité,
Le baiser, qui tout bas des perfides assure,
Mon sein, vierge de preuve, atteste une morsure
Mystérieuse, due à quelque auguste dent;
Mais, bast! arcane tel élut pour confident
Le jonc vaste et jumeau dont sous l'azur on joue:
Qui, détournant à soi le trouble de la joue,
Rêve, dans un solo long, que nous amusions
La beauté d'alentour par des confusions
Fausses entre elle-même et notre chant crédule;
Et de faire aussi haut que l'amour se module
Évanouir du songe ordinaire de dos
Ou de flanc pur suivis avec mes regards clos,
Une sonore, vaine et monotone ligne.

Motionless, everything burns in the tawny hour without remarking by what art there ran off together too much Hymen desired by him who seeks the *natural A*: then shall I awaken to the first fervour, upright and alone, beneath an ancient flood of light, lilies! and one of you both for ingenuousness.

Other than this sweet nothing divulged by their lip, the kiss that softly gives assurance of the treacherous, my breast, virgin of proof, bears witness to a mysterious wound due to some august tooth; but let it pass! A certain secret chose for confidant the great twin reed, on which we play beneath the sky: which, diverting the cheek's emotion to itself, dreams in a long solo that we entertained the beauty of round about by false confusions between itself and our credulous song; and, as high as love is sung, of making a resounding, empty, monotonous line disappear from the habitual dream of back or pure side followed by my half-shut glances.

Tâche donc, instrument des fuites, ô maligne
Syrinx, de refleurir aux lacs où tu m'attends!
Moi, de ma rumeur fier, je vais parler longtemps
Des déesses; et par d'idolâtres peintures,
A leur ombre enlever encore des ceintures:
Ainsi, quand des raisins j'ai sucé la clarté,
Pour bannir un regret par ma feinte écarté,
Rieur, j'élève au ciel d'été la grappe vide
Et, soufflant dans ses peaux lumineuses, avide
D'ivresse, jusqu'au soir je regarde au travers.

O nymphes, regonflons des SOUVENIRS divers.
« *Mon œil, trouant les joncs, dardait chaque encolure*
« *Immortelle, qui noie en l'onde sa brûlure*
« *Avec un cri de rage au ciel de la forêt;*
« *Et le splendide bain de cheveux disparaît*
« *Dans les clartés et les frissons, ô pierreries!*
« *J'accours; quand, à mes pieds, s'entrejoignent (meurtries*
« *De la langueur goûtée à ce mal d'être deux)*
« *Des dormeuses parmi leurs seuls bras hasardeux;*
« *Je les ravis, sans les désenlacer, et vole*
« *A ce massif, haï par l'ombrage frivole,*

Try then, instrument of flights, O malignant Syrinx, to flower once more upon the lakes where you await me! Proud of my murmuring, I shall speak of goddesses for many days; and by idolatrous paintings again remove girdles from their shadow: so, when I have sucked the brightness of grapes, to banish a regret removed by my pretence, laughing I raise the empty cluster to the summer sky and, blowing into its luminous skins, desiring drunkenness, I look through it till the evening.

O nymphs, let us swell various MEMORIES once again. '*My eye, piercing the reeds, touched with its dart each immortal neck that drowns its burning in the wave with a cry of rage to the forest sky; and the splendid bath of hair disappears in light and shuddering, O precious stones! I run up; when at my feet are joined (bruised by the languor tasted in this evil of being two) girls sleeping amid their perilous arms alone; I carry them off, without disentangling them, and fly to this bank, hated by the frivolous shade, of roses drying up every perfume in*

«*De roses tarissant tout parfum au soleil,*
«*Où notre ébat au jour consumé soit pareil.*»
Je t'adore, courroux des vierges, ô délice
Farouche du sacré fardeau nu qui se glisse
Pour fuir ma lèvre en feu buvant, comme un éclair
Tressaille! la frayeur secrète de la chair:
Des pieds de l'inhumaine au cœur de la timide
Que délaisse à la fois une innocence, humide
De larmes folles ou de moins tristes vapeurs.
«*Mon crime, c'est d'avoir, gai de vaincre ces peurs*
«*Traîtresses, divisé la touffe échevelée*
«*De baisers que les dieux gardaient si bien mêlée:*
«*Car, à peine j'allais cacher un rire ardent*
«*Sous les replis heureux d'une seule (gardant*
«*Par un doigt simple, afin que sa candeur de plume*
«*Se teignît à l'émoi de sa sœur qui s'allume,*
«*La petite, naïve et ne rougissant pas:)*
«*Que de mes bras, défaits par de vagues trépas,*
«*Cette proie, à jamais ingrate se délivre*
«*Sans pitié du sanglot dont j'étais encore ivre.*»

*the sun, where our sport may be like to the day consumed.' I adore you,
virgin's wrath, O shy delight of the holy naked burden slipping
away to flee my lip aflame which, like quivering lightning, drinks
the secret terror of the flesh: from the feet of the heartless to the
heart of the timid one, abandoned at the same time by an innocence,
wet with wild tears or less sad vapours. 'Being gay at conquering
these treacherous fears, my crime is to have divided the dishevelled tuft
of kisses that the gods kept so thoroughly mingled; for I scarcely went
to hide passionate laughter beneath the happy sinuosities of a single girl
(holding the little one, who was naive and did not blush, by a mere finger
so that her feathery whiteness might be tinted at her sister's passion
taking fire) than from my arms, untwined by vague deaths, this ever
ungrateful prey frees herself, not pitying the tear with which I still was
drunk.'*

Tant pis! vers le bonheur d'autres m'entraîneront
Par leur tresse nouée aux cornes de mon front:
Tu sais, ma passion, que, pourpre et déjà mûre,
Chaque grenade éclate et d'abeilles murmure;
Et notre sang, épris de qui le va saisir,
Coule pour tout l'essaim éternel du désir.
A l'heure où ce bois d'or et de cendres se teinte,
Une fête s'exalte en la feuillée éteinte:
Etna! c'est parmi toi visité de Vénus
Sur ta lave posant ses talons ingénus,
Quand tonne un somme triste où s'épuise la flamme.
Je tiens la reine!

      Ô sûr châtiment ...
                        Non, mais l'âme
De paroles vacante et ce corps alourdi
Tard succombent au fier silence de midi:
Sans plus il faut dormir en l'oubli du blasphème,
Sur le sable altéré gisant et comme j'aime
Ouvrir ma bouche à l'astre efficace des vins!

Couple, adieu; je vais voir l'ombre que tu devins.

    No matter! Others will lead me towards happiness by their
braids knotted in the horns of my brow: you know, my passion,
that, purple and ripe already, every pomegranate bursts and murmurs with bees; and our blood, enamoured of what shall seize upon
it, flows for all the eternal swarm of desire. At the hour when the
wood is coloured with gold and ashes a feast is exalted in the
dead leaves: Etna! It is upon your slopes visited by Venus, who places
her ingenuous heels upon your lava, when a melancholy slumber
thunders in which the flame dies out. I hold the queen!
    O certain punishment. ...
    No, but the soul empty of words and this heavy body succumb
slowly to the proud silence of noon: with no more ado we must
sleep, forgetting blasphemy, lying on the thirsty sand and as I love
to open my mouth to the effective star of wine!
    Couple, farewell; I go to see the shadow you became.

Quand l'ombre menaça de la fatale loi ...

QUAND l'ombre menaça de la fatale loi
Tel vieux Rêve, désir et mal de mes vertèbres,
Affligé de périr sous les plafonds funèbres
Il a ployé son aile indubitable en moi.

Luxe, ô salle d'ébène où, pour séduire un roi
Se tordent dans leur mort des guirlandes célèbres,
Vous n'êtes qu'un orgueil menti par les ténèbres
Aux yeux du solitaire ébloui de sa foi.

Oui, je sais qu'au lointain de cette nuit, la Terre
Jette d'un grand éclat l'insolite mystère
Sous les siècles hideux qui l'obscurcissent moins.

L'espace à soi pareil qu'il s'accroisse ou se nie
Roule dans cet ennui des feux vils pour témoins
Que s'est d'un astre en fête allumé le génie.

When the Shadow Threatened ...

WHEN the shadow threatened with the fatal law a certain old
Dream, desire and sickness of my spine, afflicted at dying beneath
funereal ceilings it folded its undoubted wing within me.

Pomp, O ebony hall where, to seduce a king, famous garlands
writhe in death, you are only pride, a lie uttered by the shadows to
the eyes of a hermit dazzled by his faith.

Yes, I know that in the distance of this night the Earth throws the
unwonted mystery with vast brilliance beneath the hideous centuries
that darken it the less.

Space, like to itself whether it grows or is denied, revolves in this
tedium base fires for witnesses that there has been kindled the genius
of a festive star.

Le Vierge, le vivace et le bel aujourd'hui …

LE vierge, le vivace et le bel aujourd'hui
Va-t-il nous déchirer avec un coup d'aile ivre
Ce lac dur oublié que hante sous le givre
Le transparent glacier des vols qui n'ont pas fui!

Un cygne d'autrefois se souvient que c'est lui
Magnifique mais qui sans espoir se délivre
Pour n'avoir pas chanté la région où vivre
Quand du stérile hiver a resplendi l'ennui.

Tout son col secouera cette blanche agonie
Par l'espace infligée à l'oiseau qui le nie,
Mais non l'horreur du sol où le plumage est pris.

Fantôme qu'à ce lieu son pur éclat assigne,
Il s'immobilise au songe froid de mépris
Que vêt parmi l'exil inutile le Cygne.

The virginal, living, and beautiful day …

THE virginal, living, and beautiful day, will it tear for us with a
blow of its drunken wing this hard, forgotten lake haunted beneath
the frost by the transparent glacier of flights that have not flown!

A swan of long ago remembers that it is he, magnificent but free-
ing himself without hope, for not having sung the country to live
in, when the tedium of sterile winter shone.

His whole neck will shake off this white agony inflicted by space
on the bird that denies it, but not the horror of the earth where his
feathers are caught.

A phantom condemned to this place by his pure brilliance, he
stays motionless in the cold dream of scorn worn in his useless exile
by the Swan.

Prose

pour des Esseintes

HYPERBOLE! de ma mémoire
Triomphalement ne sais-tu
Te lever, aujourd'hui grimoire
Dans un livre de fer vêtu:

Car j'installe, par la science,
L'hymne des cœurs spirituels
En l'œuvre de ma patience,
Atlas, herbiers et rituels.

Nous promenions notre visage
(Nous fûmes deux, je le maintiens)
Sur maints charmes de paysage,
Ô sœur, y comparant les tiens.

L'ère d'autorité se trouble
Lorsque, sans nul motif, on dit
De ce midi que notre double
Inconscience approfondit

Prose

for des Esseintes *

HYPERBOLE! From my memory can you not triumphantly arise, to-day like an occult language copied into a book bound in iron:

For by my science I install the hymn of spiritual hearts in the work of my patience, atlases, herbals, rituals.

We led our face (I maintain that we were two) over many landscapes' charms, Sister, comparing yours to them.

The era of authority is disturbed when, without any motive, we say of this noon, which our double unconsciousness fathoms,

---

* *Des Esseintes:* a character in Huysman's novel, *A Rebours*, whose determination to live a life of pure art is there described. The sense of this poem is obscure, but it would seem to deal with an attempt to contemplate the eternal Ideas directly and with the poet's inevitable failure to do so (stanzas 9–12).

Que, sol des cent iris, son site,
Ils savent s'il a bien été,
Ne porte pas de nom que cite
L'or de la trompette d'Été.

Oui, dans une île que l'air charge
De vue et non de visions
Toute fleur s'étalait plus large
Sans que nous en devisions.

Telles, immenses, que chacune
Ordinairement se para
D'un lucide contour, lacune
Qui des jardins la sépara.

Gloire du long désir, Idées
Tout en moi s'exaltait de voir
La famille des iridées
Surgir à ce nouveau devoir,

Mais cette sœur sensée et tendre
Ne porta son regard plus loin
Que sourire et, comme à l'entendre
J'occupe mon antique soin.

That its site, the earth of a hundred irises – they know if it has really existed – bears no name quoted by the gold of summer's trumpet.

Yes, in an island that the air loads with sight and not with visions, every flower showed itself to be larger without our discussing it.

Such huge flowers that each one usually was adorned with a lucid contour, a hiatus that separated it from the gardens.

Glory of long desire, Ideas – everything in me was exalted to see the family of irises rise to this new duty,

But this sensible, tender sister carried her glance no further than to smile, and as if to hear her I devote my attention from of old.

Oh! sache l'Esprit de litige,
A cette heure où nous nous taisons,
Que de lis multiples la tige
Grandissait trop pour nos raisons

Et non comme pleure la rive,
Quand son jeu monotone ment
A vouloir que l'ampleur arrive
Parmi mon jeune étonnement

D'ouïr tout le ciel et la carte
Sans fin attestés sur mes pas,
Par le flot même qui s'écarte,
Que ce pays n'exista pas.

L'enfant abdique son extase
Et docte déjà par chemins
Elle dit le mot: Anastase!
Né pour d'éternels parchemins,

Avant qu'un sépulcre ne rie
Sous aucun climat, son aïeul,
De porter ce nom: Pulchérie!
Caché par le trop grand glaïeul.

O let the litigious spirit know, at this hour when we are silent, that the stem of multiple lilies grew too much for our reasons

And not as weeps the shore, when its monotonous game plays false in wishing for abundance to arrive amid my young astonishment,

To hear the whole sky and the map endlessly called upon to bear witness behind my steps, even by the withdrawing wave, that this land did not exist.

The child abdicates from its ecstasy and, learned already on the roads, she says the word: Anastasius! * born for eternal parchments,

Her ancestor, before a tomb laughs beneath any clime to bear this name: Pulcheria! hidden by the too large gladiolus.

---

* *Anastasius:* this proper name means in Greek *arise*. *Pulcheria* means *beauty*.

Feuillet d'album

Tout à coup et comme par jeu
Mademoiselle qui voulûtes
Ouïr se révéler un peu
Le bois de mes diverses flûtes

Il me semble que cet essai
Tenté devant un paysage
A du bon quand je le cessai
Pour vous regarder au visage

Oui ce vain souffle que j'exclus
Jusqu'à la dernière limite
Selon mes quelques doigts perclus
Manque de moyens s'il imite

Votre très naturel et clair
Rire d'enfant qui charme l'air.

Album Leaf

Suddenly, as if in a game, Mademoiselle, who desired to hear display itself a little the wood of my various flutes,

It seems to me that this attempt tried out before a landscape has something good, when I ended it to look you in the face.

Yes, this empty breath, that I excluded up to the furthest limit with my few crippled fingers, lacks the means to imitate

Your very natural clear child's laugh that enchants the air.

Le Tombeau de Charles Baudelaire

LE temple enseveli divulgue par la bouche
Sépulcrale d'égout bavant boue et rubis
Abominablement quelque idole Anubis
Tout le museau flambé comme un aboi farouche

Ou que le gaz récent torde la mèche louche
Essuyeuse on le sait des opprobres subis
Il allume hagard un immortel pubis
Dont le vol selon le réverbère découche

Quel feuillage séché dans les cités sans soir
Votif pourra bénir comme elle se rasseoir
Contre le marbre vainement de Baudelaire

Au voile qui la ceint absente avec frissons
Celle son Ombre même un poison tutélaire
Toujours à respirer si nous en périssons.

The Tomb of Charles Baudelaire

THE buried temple gives forth by the sewer's sepulchral mouth, abominably slobbering mud and rubies, some idol of Anubis, the whole muzzle ablaze like a savage howling,

Or when the recent gas twists the foul wick which, we know, has to wipe away insults suffered, haggard it lights up an immortal pubis, whose flight moves according to the lamp.

What leaves, dried in cities without evening, votive, can bless as she, seating herself in vain against the marble of Baudelaire,

Shudderingly absent from the veil that girdles her, she, his shade herself, a guardian poison, always to be breathed, although we die of it.

Toute l'âme résumée ...

Toute l'âme résumée
Quand lente nous l'expirons
Dans plusieurs ronds de fumée
Abolis en autres ronds

Atteste quelque cigare
Brûlant savamment pour peu
Que la cendre se sépare
De son clair baiser de feu

Ainsi le chœur des romances
A la lèvre vole-t-il
Exclus-en si tu commences
Le réel parce que vil

Le sens trop précis rature
Ta vague littérature.

All the soul summed up ...

ALL the soul summed up, when slowly we breathe it out in several rings of smoke vanishing in other rings,

Bears witness to some cigar burning skilfully as long as the ash is separated from its bright kiss of fire.

So the choir of romances flies to the lip; exclude from it, if you begin, the real because it is base.

Too precise a meaning erases your mysterious literature.

STÉPHANE MALLARMÉ

Tombeau

Anniversaire – Janvier 1897.

Le noir roc courroucé que la bise le roule
Ne s'arrêtera ni sous de pieuses mains
Tâtant sa ressemblance avec les maux humains
Comme pour en bénir quelque funeste moule.

Ici presque toujours si le ramier roucoule
Cet immatériel deuil opprime de maints
Nubiles plis l'astre mûri des lendemains
Dont un scintillement argentera la foule.

Qui cherche, parcourant le solitaire bond
Tantôt extérieur de notre vagabond –
Verlaine? Il est caché parmi l'herbe, Verlaine

A ne surprendre que naïvement d'accord
La lèvre sans y boire ou tarir son haleine
Un peu profond ruisseau calomnié la mort.

Tomb

Anniversary … January 1897.

The black rock, angered that the north wind carries it, will not stop nor under pious hands feeling for its resemblance with human ills as if to bless some fatal mould of them.

Here almost always, if the dove coos, this immaterial grief oppresses with many a nubile fold the ripe star of to-morrows, whose gleam is to colour the crowd silver.

Who seeks, following the solitary leap – exterior now – of our vagabond – Verlaine? He is hidden among the grass, Verlaine

Only to surprise naively in agreement, the lip without drinking from it or drying up its breath, a shallow stream ill-spoken of, death.

Plainte d' Automne

DEPUIS que Maria m'a quitté pour aller dans une autre
étoile – laquelle, Orion, Altaïr, et toi, verte Vénus? – j'ai
toujours chéri la solitude. Que de longues journées j'ai
passées seul avec mon chat. Par *seul*, j'entends sans un
être matériel et mon chat est un compagnon mystique, un
esprit. Je puis donc dire que j'ai passé de longues journées
seul avec mon chat et, seul, avec un des derniers auteurs de
la décadence latine; car depuis que la blanche créature
n'est plus, étrangement et singulièrement j'ai aimé tout ce
qui se résumait en ce mot: chute. Ainsi, dans l'année, ma
saison favorite, ce sont les derniers jours alanguis de
l'été, qui précèdent immédiatement l'automne et, dans la
journée, l'heure où je me promène est quand le soleil se
repose avant de s'évanouir, avec des rayons de cuivre
jaune sur les murs gris et de cuivre rouge sur les carreaux.
De même la littérature à laquelle mon esprit demande une
volupté sera la poésie agonisante des derniers moments de
Rome, tant, cependant, qu'elle ne respire aucunement

Autumn Complaint

SINCE Maria left me to go to another star – which, Orion, Altair,
and you, green Venus? – I have always loved solitude. How many
long days have I passed alone with my cat. By *alone* I mean without
a material being, and my cat is a mystic companion, a spirit. I can
say, therefore, that I have passed long days alone with my cat and
alone with one of the last authors of the Latin decadence; for, since
the white creature is no more, I have loved strangely and singularly
everything which was summed up in this word: fall. Thus, during
the year my favourite season is the last languid days of summer that
immediately precede autumn, and, during the day, the hour when
I go for a walk is when the sun rests before disappearing, with
beams of yellow copper on the grey walls and of red copper on the
tiles. In the same way, the literature, from which my spirit asks
pleasure, will be the dying poetry of the last instants of Rome, as
long, however, as it does not breathe in any way the rejuvenating

l'approche rajeunissante des Barbares et ne bégaie point le latin enfantin des premières proses chrétiennes.

Je lisais donc un de ces chers poèmes (dont les plaques de fard ont plus de charme sur moi que l'incarnat de la jeunesse) et plongeais une main dans la fourrure du pur animal, quand un orgue de Barbarie chanta languissamment et mélancoliquement sous ma fenêtre. Il jouait dans la grande allée des peupliers dont les feuilles me paraissent mornes même au printemps, depuis que Maria a passé là avec des cierges, une dernière fois. L'instrument des tristes, oui, vraiment: le piano scintille, le violon donne aux fibres déchirées la lumière, mais l'orgue de Barbarie, dans le crépuscule de souvenir, m'a fait désespérément rêver. Maintenant qu'il murmurait un air joyeusement vulgaire et qui mit la gaîté au cœur des faubourgs, un air suranné, banal: d'où vient que sa ritournelle m'allait à l'âme et me faisait pleurer comme une ballade romantique? Je la savourai lentement et je ne lançai pas un sou par la fenêtre de peur de me déranger et de m'apercevoir que l'instrument ne chantait pas seul.

approach of the barbarians or stammer the childish Latin of the first Christian proses.

I was reading one of these beloved poems (whose patches of rouge have more charm for me than the rosy flesh of youth) and plunging one hand into the pure animal's fur, when a barrel organ sung with languor and melancholy beneath my window. It was playing in the broad avenue of poplars whose leaves seem dreary to me even in Spring since Maria passed by there with candles for the last time. The instrument of the sorrowful, yes, indeed: the piano sparkles, the violin gives light to the torn fibres, but the barrel organ in the twilight of memory made me dream despairingly. Now that it murmured a joyfully vulgar tune that put gaiety into the heart of the suburbs, a banal, old-fashioned tune: whence comes it that its burden went to my soul and made me weep like a romantic ballad? I tasted it slowly and did not throw a halfpenny through the window for fear of leaving my seat and seeing that the instrument was not alone in its singing.

La Pipe

HIER, j'ai trouvé ma pipe en rêvant une longue soirée de travail, de beau travail d'hiver. Jetées les cigarettes avec toutes les joies enfantines de l'été dans le passé qu'illuminent les feuilles bleues de soleil, les mousselines et reprise ma grave pipe par un homme sérieux qui veut fumer longtemps sans se déranger, afin de mieux travailler: mais je ne m'attendais pas à la surprise que préparait cette délaissée, à peine eus-je tiré la première bouffée, j'oubliai mes grands livres à faire, émerveillé, attendri, je respirai l'hiver dernier qui revenait. Je n'avais pas touché à la fidèle amie depuis ma rentrée en France, et tout Londres, Londres tel que je le vécus en entier à moi seul, il y a un an, est apparu; d'abord les chers brouillards qui emmitouflent nos cervelles et ont, là-bas, une odeur à eux, quand ils pénètrent sous la croisée. Mon tabac sentait une chambre sombre aux meubles de cuir saupoudrés par la poussière du charbon sur lesquels se roulait le maigre chat noir; les grands feux! et la bonne aux bras rouges versant les charbons, et le bruit de ces charbons tombant du seau

The Pipe

YESTERDAY I found my pipe while meditating a long evening's work, fine winter work. The cigarettes thrown away with all the childish joys of summer into the past, lighted up by the leaves, blue with sun, and by the muslins, and my stern pipe taken up again by a serious man who wants to smoke a long time without moving in order to work better: but I did not expect the surprise which this neglected object was preparing; hardly had I taken the first puff than I forgot the big books I had to write; wondering, softened, I breathed in last winter come back again. I had not touched the faithful friend since my return to France, and the whole of London – London as I lived it completely within myself a year ago – appeared: first the dear fogs that muffle our brains and have a smell of their own over there when they creep beneath the sash window. My tobacco smelt of a dark room with leather furniture sprinkled with coal dust, on which the lean black cat used to roll; the big fires! And the red-armed maid putting on the coals, and the noise of

de tôle dans la corbeille de fer, le matin – alors que le facteur frappait le double coup solennel, qui me faisait vivre! J'ai revu par les fenêtres ces arbres malades du square désert – j'ai vu le large, si souvent traversé cet hiver-là, grelottant sur le pont du steamer mouillé de bruine et noirci de fumée – avec ma pauvre bien-aimée errante, en habits de voyageuse, une longue robe terne couleur de la poussière des routes, un manteau qui collait humide à ses épaules froides, un de ces chapeaux de paille sans plume et presque sans rubans, que les riches dames jettent en arrivant, tant ils sont déchiquetés par l'air de la mer et que les pauvres bien-aimées regarnissent pour bien des saisons encore. Autour de son cou s'enroulait le terrible mouchoir qu'on agite en se disant adieu pour toujours.

those coals falling from the sheet-iron bucket into the iron scuttle in the morning – when the postman used to strike the solemn double knock that made me live! Through the windows I saw again those sickly trees of the deserted square – I saw the sea, so often crossed that winter, shivering on the bridge of the steamer wet with spray and blackened by smoke – with my poor, wandering beloved in travelling clothes, a long dull dress, the colour of the dust of the roads, a cloak clinging damply to her cold shoulders, one of those straw hats without a feather and almost without ribbons, which rich ladies throw away on arrival – they are so mangled by the sea air – and which poor beloveds retrim for many seasons to come. Around her neck was rolled the frightful handkerchief we wave when saying good-bye for ever.

CHARLES CROS

Scherzo

SOURIRES, fleurs, baisers, essences,
Après de si fades ennuis,
Après de si ternes absences,
Parfumez le vent de mes nuits!

Illuminez ma fantaisie,
Jonchez mon chemin idéal,
Et versez-moi votre ambroisie,
Longs regards, lys, lèvres, santal!

*

Car j'ignore l'amour caduque
Et le dessillement des yeux,
Puisqu'encor sur ta blanche nuque
L'or flamboie en flocons soyeux.

Et cependant, ma fière amie,
Il-y-a longtemps, n'est-ce pas?
Qu'un matin tu t'es endormie,
Lasse d'amour entre mes bras.

*

Scherzo

SMILES, flowers, kisses, and essences, perfume the wind of my nights after such insipid boredom, after such dreary absences!

Light up my fantasy, strew my ideal path and pour me your ambrosia, lingering glances, lilies, lips, and sandal-wood!

*

For I know nothing of decrepit love and eyes unsealed, since the gold still blazes in silky tufts on your white neck.

And yet, my proud friend, it was a long time ago, wasn't it? that, weary of loving, you went to sleep in my arms one morning.

*

Ce ne sont pas choses charnelles
Qui font ton attrait non pareil,
Qui conservent à tes prunelles
Ces mêmes rayons de soleil.

Car les choses charnelles meurent,
Ou se fanent à l'air réel.
Mais toujours tes beautés demeurent
Dans leur nimbe immatériel.

*

Ce n'est plus l'heure des tendresses
Jalouses, ni des faux serments.
Ne me dis rien de mes maîtresses,
Je ne compte pas tes amants.

*

A toi, comète vagabonde
Souvent attardée en chemin,
Laissant ta chevelure blonde
Flotter dans l'éther surhumain,

It is not carnal things that make your charm unequalled, that keep those same sunbeams in your pupils.

For carnal things die or wither in fresh air. But your beauties always remain within their spiritual halo.

*

It is no longer the time for jealous tenderness nor for false oaths. Tell me nothing of my mistresses; I do not count your lovers.

*

For you, wandering comet, often loitering on your path, letting your fair hair float in the superhuman ether,

Qu'importent quelques astres pâles
Au ciel troublé de ma raison,
Quand tu viens à longs intervalles
Envelopper mon horizon?

*

Je ne veux pas savoir quels pôles
Ta folle orbite a dépassés,
Tends-moi tes seins et tes épaules;
Que je les baise, c'est assez.

PAUL VERLAINE

Nuit du Walpurgis classique

C'est plutôt le sabbat du second Faust que l'autre,
Un rhythmique sabbat, rhythmique, extrêmement
Rhythmique. – Imaginez un jardin de Lenôtre,
    Correct, ridicule et charmant.

What do a few pale stars matter in my reason's troubled sky,
when at long intervals you come to close my horizon round?

*

I do not want to know what poles your mad orbit left behind it;
give me your breasts and shoulders; let me kiss them, and that is
enough.

A Classical Walpurgisnacht

It is rather the sabbath of the second Faust than the other, a rhythmical sabbath, rhythmical, most rhythmical. – Imagine one of Lenôtre's
gardens, correct, ridiculous, and charming.

Des ronds-points; au milieu, des jets d'eau; des allées
Toutes droites; sylvains de marbre; dieux marins
De bronze; çà et là, des Vénus étalées;
    Des quinconces, des boulingrins;

Des châtaigniers; des plants de fleurs formant la dune;
Ici, des rosiers nains qu'un goût docte affila;
Plus loin, des ifs taillés en triangles. La lune
    D'un soir d'été sur tout cela.

Minuit sonne, et réveille au fond du parc aulique
Un air mélancolique, un sourd, lent et doux air
De chasse: tel, doux, lent, sourd et mélancolique,
    L'air de chasse de *Tannhäuser*.

Des chants voilés de cors lointains, où la tendresse
Des sens étreint l'effroi de l'âme en des accords
Harmonieusement dissonants dans l'ivresse;
    Et voici qu'à l'appel des cors

S'entrelacent soudain des formes toutes blanches,
Diaphanes, et que le clair de lune fait
Opalines parmi l'ombre verte des branches,
    – Un Watteau rêvé par Raffet! –

Circuses; in the middle, fountains; straight alleys; marble sylvans;
bronze sea-gods; here and there Venuses displayed; quincunxes and
lawns;

Some chestnut trees; flowering shrubs forming a bank; here,
dwarf rose-trees arranged by a skilful taste; further on, yews cut in
triangles. A summer evening's moon over all that.

Midnight strikes and wakens in the depth of the aulic park a
melancholy tune, a hollow, slow, sweet hunting tune: like the
sweet, slow, hollow, melancholy hunting tune from *Tannhäuser*.

The muffled strains of distant horns, where the senses' tenderness
clasps the soul's terror in notes melodiously discordant in their
intoxication; and now at the call of the horns

Pure white, diaphanous forms, turned opaline by the moonlight
in the green shadow of the branches suddenly entwine – a Watteau
dreamed by Raffet! –

S'entrelacent parmi l'ombre verte des arbres
D'un geste alangui, plein d'un désespoir profond;
Puis, autour des massifs, des bronzes et des marbres,
 Très lentement dansent en rond.

– Ces spectres agités, sont-ce donc la pensée
Du poète ivre, ou son regret ou son remords,
Ces spectres agités en tourbe cadencée,
 Ou bien tout simplement des morts?

Sont-ce donc ton remords, ô rêvasseur qu'invite
L'horreur, ou ton regret, ou ta pensée, – hein? – tous
Ces spectres qu'un vertige irrésistible agite,
 Ou bien des morts qui seraient fous? –

N'importe! ils vont toujours, les fébriles fantômes,
Menant leur ronde vaste et morne et tressautant
Comme dans un rayon de soleil des atomes,
 Et s'évaporant à l'instant

Humide et blême où l'aube éteint l'un après l'autre
Les cors, en sorte qu'il ne reste absolument
Plus rien – absolument – qu'un jardin de Lenôtre,
 Correct, ridicule et charmant.

 Entwine in the green shadow of the trees with a languid gesture full of deep despair; then, around thickets, bronzes, and marbles, very slowly dance in a ring.
 – These moving ghosts, are they then the thoughts of a drunken poet or his regret or his remorse, these ghosts moving in a rhythmic crowd, or else quite simply some of the dead?
 Are they then your remorse, O dreamer, called up by horror or your regrets or your thoughts – say! – all these ghosts moved by an irresistible vertigo, or else some dead who may be mad? –
 No matter! the feverish phantoms still continue leading their vast and dismal ring and leaping like motes in a sunbeam, and turning to mist
 At the damp pale moment when dawn silences the horns one after another, so that there remains absolutely nothing more – absolutely nothing – than one of Lenôtre's gardens, correct, ridiculous, and charming.

Nevermore

SOUVENIR, souvenir, que me veux-tu? L'automne
Faisait voler la grive à travers l'air atone,
Et le soleil dardait un rayon monotone
Sur le bois jaunissant où la bise détone.

Nous étions seul à seule et marchions en rêvant,
Elle et moi, les cheveux et la pensée au vent.
Soudain, tournant vers moi son regard émouvant:
«Quel fut ton plus beau jour?» fit sa voix d'or vivant,

Sa voix douce et sonore, au frais timbre angélique.
Un sourire discret lui donna la réplique,
Et je baisai sa main blanche, dévotement.

– Ah! les premières fleurs, qu'elles sont parfumées!
Et qu'il bruit avec un murmure charmant
Le premier *oui* qui sort de lèvres bien-aimées!

Nevermore

MEMORY, memory, what do you want from me? Autumn made
the thrush fly through the dull air, and the sun darted a monotonous
ray over the yellowing wood where the north wind is loud.

We were by ourselves and walked dreaming, she and I, our hair
and thoughts in the wind. Suddenly, turning her touching gaze
upon me: 'What was your loveliest day?' said her voice of living
gold,

Her gentle, resonant voice with the fresh angelic notes. A discreet
smile gave her her reply, and I kissed her white hand devoutly.

– Ah! how full of perfume the first flowers are! And with what a
charming murmur the first *yes* sounds, coming from beloved lips!

Clair de lune

VOTRE âme est un paysage choisi
Que vont charmant masques et bergamasques,
Jouant du luth, et dansant, et quasi
Tristes sous leurs déguisements fantasques.

Tout en chantant sur le mode mineur
L'amour vainqueur et la vie opportune,
Ils n'ont pas l'air de croire à leur bonheur
Et leur chanson se mêle au clair de lune,

Au calme clair de lune triste et beau,
Qui fait rêver les oiseaux dans les arbres
Et sangloter d'extase les jets d'eau,
Les grands jets d'eau sveltes parmi les marbres.

Colloque sentimental

DANS le vieux parc solitaire et glacé
Deux formes ont tout à l'heure passé.

Moonlight

YOUR soul is a chosen landscape that masks and bergomasks go charming, playing the lute and dancing and almost melancholy beneath their fantastic disguises.

While singing in the minor key of Love the conqueror and the pleasant life, they have the air of not believing in their happiness, and their song is mingled with the moonlight,

With the calm, beautiful, melancholy moonlight that makes the birds in the trees dream and the fountains sob with ecstasy, the tall, slender fountains among the statues.

Sentimental Dialogue

IN the old, solitary, frosty park two shapes passed by just now.

Leurs yeux sont morts et leurs lèvres sont molles,
Et l'on entend à peine leurs paroles.

Dans le vieux parc solitaire et glacé
Deux spectres ont évoqué le passé.

— Te souvient-il de notre extase ancienne?
— Pourquoi voulez-vous donc qu'il m'en souvienne?

— Ton cœur bat-il toujours à mon seul nom?
Toujours vois-tu mon âme en rêve? – Non.

— Ah! les beaux jours de bonheur indicible
Où nous joignions nos bouches! – C'est possible.

— Qu'il était bleu, le ciel, et grand, l'espoir!
— L'espoir a fui, vaincu, vers le ciel noir.

Tels ils marchaient dans les avoines folles,
Et la nuit seule entendit leurs paroles.

Their eyes are dead and their lips are slack, and their words can hardly be heard.

In the old, solitary, frosty park two ghosts recalled the past.

'Do you remember our old ecstasy?' 'Why will you have me remember it?'

'Does your heart still beat at my mere name? Do you still see my soul in dreams?' 'No.'

'Ah! The sweet days of unspeakable happiness when we joined our lips together!' 'It is possible.'

'How blue the sky was and how great our hope!' 'Hope has fled defeated towards the dark sky.'

So they walked in the oat-grass, and night alone heard their words.

Il pleure dans mon cœur ...

Il pleut doucement sur la ville.
ARTHUR RIMBAUD

Il pleure dans mon cœur
Comme il pleut sur la ville.
Quelle est cette langueur
Qui pénètre mon cœur?

Ô bruit doux de la pluie
Par terre et sur les toits!
Pour un cœur qui s'ennuie,
Ô le chant de la pluie!

Il pleure sans raison
Dans ce cœur qui s'écœure.
Quoi! nulle trahison?
Ce deuil est sans raison.

C'est bien la pire peine
De ne savoir pourquoi,
Sans amour et sans haine,
Mon cœur a tant de peine.

There is weeping in my heart ...

It rains gently on the town.
ARTHUR RIMBAUD

THERE is weeping in my heart as it rains on the town. What languor is this that pierces my heart?

O gentle noise of the rain on the ground and the roofs! For a heart that is troubled, O the song of the rain!

There is no cause for weeping in this sickened heart. What! No treason? This sorrow has no cause.

Indeed, it is the worst grief not to know why, without love or hate, my heart has so much grief.

Dans l'interminable ...

DANS l'interminable
Ennui de la plaine
La neige incertaine
Luit comme du sable.

Le ciel est de cuivre
Sans lueur aucune.
On croirait voir vivre
Et mourir la lune.

Comme des nuées
Flottent gris les chênes
Des forêts prochaines
Parmi les buées.

Le ciel est de cuivre
Sans lueur aucune.
On croirait voir vivre
Et mourir la lune.

Corneille poussive
Et vous, les loups maigres,
Par ces bises aigres
Quoi donc vous arrive?

In the interminable ...

IN the interminable tedium of the plain the shifting snow shines like sand.

The sky is of copper without any light. It is as though one were watching the moon living and dying.

Like clouds the oaks of nearby forests float greyly among the vapours.

The sky is of copper without any light. It is as though one were watching the moon living and dying.

Wheezing crow and you, lean wolves, what happens to you in these bitter north winds?

Dans l'interminable
Ennui de la plaine
La neige incertaine
Luit comme du sable.

Bruxelles

Chevaux de Bois.

Par saint-Gille,
Viens-nous-en,
Mon agile
Alezan.

V. HUGO

TOURNEZ, tournez, bons chevaux de bois,
Tournez cent tours, tournez mille tours,
Tournez souvent et tournez toujours,
Tournez, tournez au son des hautbois.

Le gros soldat, la plus grosse bonne
Sont sur vos dos comme dans leur chambre;
Car, en ce jour, au bois de la Cambre,
Les maîtres sont tous deux en personne.

In the interminable tedium of the plain the shifting snow shines like sand.

Brussels

Wooden horses.

By Saint Giles let us come on,
my nimble chestnut.

VICTOR HUGO

TURN, turn, you fine wooden horses, turn a hundred, a thousand times, turn often and turn for ever, turn and turn to the sound of the oboes.

The fat soldier, the fattest maid are at home on your backs, for to-day their masters are both in person in La Cambre park.

I   219

Tournez, tournez, chevaux de leur cœur,
Tandis qu'autour de tous vos tournois
Clignote l'œil du filou sournois,
Tournez au son du piston vainqueur.

C'est ravissant comme ça vous soûle,
D'aller ainsi dans ce cirque bête!
Bien dans le ventre et mal dans la tête,
Du mal en masse et du bien en foule.

Tournez, tournez, sans qu'il soit besoin
D'user jamais de nuls éperons,
Pour commander à vos galops ronds,
Tournez, tournez, sans espoir de foin.

Et dépêchez, chevaux de leur âme:
Déjà, voici que la nuit qui tombe
Va réunir pigeon et colombe,
Loin de la foire et loin de madame.

Tournez, tournez! le ciel en velours
D'astres en or se vêt lentement.
Voici partir l'amante et l'amant.
Tournez au son joyeux des tambours.

Turn, turn, horses that they love, while around all your turnings winks the eye of the cunning pickpocket; turn to the sound of the conquering cornet.

It is delightful how drunk it makes you to go like this in this idiotic ring! Feeling fine in the stomach and bad in the head, lots of trouble, heaps of good things.

Turn and turn without there ever being need to use spurs to command your circular galloping; turn and turn without hope of hay.

And hurry, horses of their soul: already here is night falling to join the pigeon to the dove, far from the fair and far from Madame.

Turn and turn! The velvet sky is slowly decked with golden stars. Behold mistress and lover depart. Turn to the joyful sound of the drums.

A Poor Young Shepherd

J'ai peur d'un baiser
Comme d'une abeille.
Je souffre et je veille
Sans me reposer.
J'ai peur d'un baiser!

Pourtant j'aime Kate
Et ses yeux jolis.
Elle est délicate
Aux longs traits pâlis.
Oh! que j'aime Kate!

C'est Saint-Valentin!
Je dois et je n'ose
Lui dire au matin ...
La terrible chose
Que Saint-Valentin!

Elle m'est promise,
Fort heureusement!
Mais quelle entreprise
Que d'être un amant
Près d'une promise!

A Poor Young Shepherd

I am afraid of a kiss as of a bee. I suffer and watch without resting.
I am afraid of a kiss!

Yet I love Kate and her pretty eyes. She is delicate with long, pale
features. Oh, how I love Kate!

It is Saint Valentine's day! I must and I do not dare tell her in the
morning. ... What a terrible thing Saint Valentine's day is!

Luckily she is betrothed to me! But what an undertaking to be a
lover near his fiancée!

J'ai peur d'un baiser
Comme d'une abeille.
Je souffre et je veille
Sans me reposer:
J'ai peur d'un baiser!

Sagesse d'un Louis Racine, je t'envie! ...

SAGESSE d'un Louis Racine, je t'envie!
Ô n'avoir pas suivi les leçons de Rollin,
N'être pas né dans le grand siècle à son déclin,
Quand le soleil couchant, si beau, dorait la vie,

Quand Maintenon jetait sur la France ravie
L'ombre douce et la paix de ses coiffes de lin,
Et, royale, abritait la veuve et l'orphelin,
Quand l'étude de la prière était suivie,

Quand poète et docteur, simplement, bonnement,
Communiaient avec des ferveurs de novices,
Humbles servaient la Messe et chantaient aux offices,

I am afraid of a kiss as of a bee. I suffer and watch without resting:
I am afraid of a kiss!

Wisdom of a Louis Racine, I envy you! ...

WISDOM of a Louis Racine, I envy you! O not to have followed
Rollin's lectures, not to have been born in the decline of the great
century, when the setting sun gilded life so beautifully,

When Maintenon cast upon enraptured France the gentle shadow
and peace of her linen coifs, and royally sheltered the widow and
orphan, when the study of prayer was observed,

When poet and doctor simply and honestly took communion
with the zeal of novices, humbly serving the Mass and singing in the
offices,

Et, le printemps venu, prenaient un soin charmant
D'aller dans les Auteuils cueillir lilas et roses
En louant Dieu, comme Garo * de toutes choses!

Non. Il fut gallican, ce siècle, et janséniste! ...

NON. Il fut gallican, ce siècle, et janséniste!
C'est vers le moyen âge, énorme et délicat,
Qu'il faudrait que mon cœur en panne naviguât,
Loin de nos jours d'esprit charnel et de chair triste.

Roi, politicien, moine, artisan, chimiste,
Architecte, soldat, médecin, avocat,
Quel temps! Oui, que mon cœur naufragé rembarquât
Pour toute cette force ardente, souple, artiste!

Et là que j'eusse part – quelconque, chez les rois
Ou bien ailleurs, n'importe, – à la chose vitale,
Et que je fusse un saint, actes bons, pensers droits,

And, when Spring came, taking pleasant pains to go out Auteuil
way to gather lilac and roses, like Garo * praising God for all things!

No. That century was Gallican and Jansenist! ...

NO. That century was Gallican and Jansenist! It is towards the
vast, delicate Middle Ages that my becalmed heart must steer, far
from our days of carnal spirit and melancholy flesh.

King, politician, monk, craftsman, chemist, architect, soldier,
doctor, lawyer, what an age! Yes, would that my shipwrecked heart
might re-embark for all this passionately supple, artistic strength!

And would I might have part there – some part or other, with
the kings or elsewhere, no matter – in the thing that is vital, and be
a saint with good actions, upright thoughts,

---

* The character of Garo is to be found in a fable of La Fontaine,
The Acorn and the Pumpkin.

Haute théologie et solide morale,
Guidé par la folie unique de la Croix,
Sur tes ailes de pierre, ô folle Cathédrale!

Art poétique

A Charles Morice

De la musique avant toute chose,
Et pour cela préfère l'Impair
Plus vague et plus soluble dans l'air,
Sans rien en lui qui pèse ou qui pose.

Il faut aussi que tu n'ailles point
Choisir tes mots sans quelque méprise:
Rien de plus cher que la chanson grise
Où l'Indécis au Précis se joint.

C'est des beaux yeux derrière des voiles,
C'est le grand jour tremblant de midi,
C'est, par un ciel d'automne attiédi,
Le bleu fouillis des claires étoiles!

Lofty theology and firm morality, guided by the unique madness of the Cross, on your stone wings, O mad Cathedral!

The Art of Poetry

To Charles Morice

Music before everything, and for that prefer the Uneven hazier and more soluble in the air with nothing in it weighty or fixed.

Also you must not go to choose your words without any obscurity: there is nothing more precious than the grey song where the Undecided is joined to the Precise.

It is lovely eyes behind veils, it is the full shimmering light of noon, it is the blue disorder of clear stars in the sky of a cool autumn!

Car nous voulons la Nuance encor,
Pas la Couleur, rien que la nuance!
Oh! la nuance seule fiance
Le rêve au rêve et la flûte au cor!

Fuis du plus loin la Pointe assassine,
L'Esprit cruel et le Rire impur,
Qui font pleurer les yeux de l'Azur,
Et tout cet ail de basse cuisine!

Prends l'éloquence et tords-lui son cou!
Tu feras bien, en train d'énergie,
De rendre un peu la Rime assagie.
Si l'on n'y veille, elle ira jusqu'où?

Ô qui dira les torts de la Rime?
Quel enfant sourd ou quel nègre fou
Nous a forgé ce bijou d'un sou
Qui sonne creux et faux sous la lime?

De la musique encore et toujours!
Que ton vers soit la chose envolée
Qu'on sent qui fuit d'une âme en allée
Vers d'autres cieux à d'autres amours.

For we still want light and shade, not Colour, nothing but light and shade! Oh, light and shade alone join dream to dream and flute to horn!

Flee as far as possible from the murderous Epigram, cruel Wit, and base Laughter that make the eyes of the blue sky weep, and all that common kitchen garlic!

Take eloquence and wring its neck! You will do well, while you are about it, to make Rhyme a little wiser. If we do not watch, to what lengths will it go?

O who will tell of the wrongs done by Rhyme? What deaf child or mad Negro made us this halfpenny jewel that sounds hollow and false under the file?

Once again and always music! Let your line be the soaring thing which we feel fleeing from a soul going towards other skies and other loves.

Que ton vers soit la bonne aventure
Éparse au vent crispé du matin
Qui va fleurant la menthe et le thym ...
Et tout le reste est littérature.

Parsifal

A Jules Tellier

PARSIFAL a vaincu les Filles, leur gentil
Babil et la luxure amusante – et sa pente
Vers la Chair de garçon vierge que cela tente
D'aimer les seins légers et ce gentil babil;

Il a vaincu la Femme belle, au cœur subtil,
Étalant ses bras frais et sa gorge excitante;
Il a vaincu l'Enfer et rentre sous sa tente
Avec un lourd trophée à son bras puéril,

Avec la lance qui perça le Flanc suprême!
Il a guéri le roi, le voici roi lui-même,
Et prêtre du très saint Trésor essentiel.

Let your line be the lucky chance scattered on the impatient
morning wind that goes breathing mint and thyme. ... And all the
rest is literature.

Parsifal

To Jules Tellier

PARSIFAL has conquered the Girls, their pleasant chatter and
amusing lust – and his virgin boy's bent towards the Flesh which is
tempted to love the light breasts and this gentle chatter;
   He has conquered the fair Woman with the subtle heart, display-
ing her cool arms and provoking bosom; he has conquered Hell and
comes back to his tent with a heavy trophy on his boyish arm,
   With the lance that pierced the supreme Side! He has cured the
king; here he is king himself and priest of the holiest quintessential
Treasure.

En robe d'or il adore, gloire et symbole,
Le vase pur où resplendit le Sang réel,
– Et, ô ces voix d'enfants chantant dans la coupole!

TRISTAN CORBIÈRE

Matelots

Vos marins de quinquets à l'Opéra ... comique,
Sous un frac en bleu-ciel jurent «Mille sabords!»
Et, sur les boulevards, le survivant chronique
Du *Vengeur* vend l'onguent à tuer les rats morts.
Le Jún'homme infligé d'un bras – même en voyage –
Infortuné, chantant par suite de naufrage;
La femme en bain de mer qui tord ses bras au flot;
Et l'amiral ★★★ – Ce n'est pas matelot!
– Matelots – quelle brusque et nerveuse saillie
Fait cette *Race à part* sur la race faillie!

In a golden robe he worships, as glory and symbol, the pure vessel where shines the real Blood – and, O those children's voices singing in the dome!

Sailors *

Your sailors of the Opera footlights – the comic Opera – in sky-blue frock-coats swear: 'A thousand portholes!' and on the boulevard the chronic survivor of the *Avenger* sells ointment to kill dead rats. *The Young man crippled in one arm* – even on a voyage – *by ill luck having to sing as a consequence of being shipwrecked*; the woman in a sea bath brandishing her arms to the waves; and admiral X – these are not sailors!

Sailors – what sudden sinewy effort creates this *race apart* on

---

* This poem contains a good deal of sailor's slang, but no attempt has been made to give the English equivalent, as rendering the slang of one country by that of another is invariably incongruous.

Comme ils vous mettent tous, *terriens*, au même sac!
— *Un curé dans ton lit, un' fill' dans mon hamac!* —
....

— On ne les connaît pas, ces gens à rudes nœuds.
Ils ont le mal de mer sur vos *planchers à bœufs*;
A terre — oiseaux palmés — ils sont gauches et veules.
Ils sont mal culottés comme leurs brûle-gueules.
Quand le roulis leur manque ... ils se sentent rouler:
— *A terre, on a beau boire, on ne peut désoûler!*

— On ne les connaît pas. — Eux: que leur fait la terre? ...
Une relâche, avec l'hôpital militaire,
Des filles, la prison, des horions, du vin.
Le reste: Eh bien, après? — Est-ce que c'est marin? ...

— Eux, ils sont matelots. — A travers les tortures,
Les luttes, les dangers, les larges aventures,
Leur *face-à-coups-de-hache* a pris un tic nerveux
D'insouciant dédain pour ce qui n'est pas Eux ...
C'est qu'ils se sentent bien, ces chiens! Ce sont des mâles!
Eux: l'Océan! — et vous: les plates-bandes sales ...;
Vous êtes des *terriens*, en un mot, des *troupiers*,
— *De la terre de pipe et de la sueur de pieds!* —

feeble humanity! How they put all you *land-lubbers* in the same
box! — *A parson in your bed, a girl in my hammock!*

You do not know them, these harshly knotted folk. They get sea-
sick on your *clod-thumping* floors; on land they are awkward and
ugly, like web-footed birds. They are as ill-breeched as their pipes.
When the rollers are missing ... they feel themselves rolling: *On
land it's all very well drinking, you can't get sober!*

You do not know them. — What does the land mean to them? ...
A stopping place with military hospital, girls, prison, brawls, and
wine. The rest: well, what of it? — Does it belong to the sea? ...

They are sailors. — Through torments, strife, danger, wide adventures, their *hatchet faces* have taken on a nervous twitch of care-
less scorn for everything that is not themselves ... It is because
these dogs feel themselves at ease! They are men! For them: the
Ocean! — and you: the dirty flower-beds ...; you are *land-lubbers*,
in a word *troopers* — *pipe-clay and foot-sweat!*

Eux sont les *vieux-de-cale* et *les frères-la-cote*,
Gens au cœur sur la main, et toujours la main haute;
Des natures en barre! – Et capables de tout ...
– Faites-en donc autant! ... Ils sont de *mauvais goût*.
Peut-être ... Ils ont chez vous des amours tolérées
Par un *grippe-Jésus* accueillant leurs entrées ...
– Eh! faut-il du cœur au ventre quelque part,
Pour entrer en plein jour là – bagne-lupanar,
Qu'ils nomment le «*Cap-Horn*», dans leur langue hâlée:
– Le cap Horn, noir séjour de tempête grêlée –
Et se coller en vrac, sans crampe d'estomac,
De la chair à chiquer – comme un nœud de tabac!
Jetant leur solde avec leur trop-plein de tendresse,
A tout vent; ils vont là comme ils vont à la messe ...
Ces anges mal léchés, ces durs enfants perdus!
– Leur tête a du requin et du petit-Jésus.

Ils aiment à tout crin: Ils aiment plaie et bosse,
La Bonne-Vierge, avec le gendarme qu'on rosse;
Ils font des vœux à tout ... mais leur vœu caressé
A toujours l'habit bleu d'un *Jésus-christ* rossé,

They are *old salts* and *brothers of the coast*: folk with their heart
on their sleeve and their hand always raised; creatures made of oak!
– And capable of anything. ... Then do as much yourselves! ...
They are *ill bred*. Perhaps. ... In your town they have loves licensed
by a *gendarme* who greets them as they enter. ... – Well, you must
have a heart somewhere or other in your stomach to enter there in
daylight – to the brothel they call the '*Cape Horn*' in their sunburnt
lingo: – Cape Horn, the dark home of the hailstorm – and, without
nausea in the stomach, to press flesh pell-mell against them to chew
on – like a quid of tobacco! Throwing their pay to the winds with
their excess of tenderness, they go there as they go to Mass. ...
These half-formed angels, these rough, forlorn children! – Their
head has something of the shark and something of the child Jesus.

They love frenziedly: they love sore and hump, the Holy Virgin
and the gendarme they beat; they offer up prayers to everything ...
but their favourite prayer has always the blue coat of a beaten
gendarme,

— Allez: ce franc cynique a sa grâce native ...
Comme il vous toise un chef, à sa façon naïve!
Comme il connaît son maître. — *Un d'un seul bloc de bois!*
— *Un mauvais chien toujours qu'un bon enfant parfois!*
....

— Allez: à bord, chez eux, ils ont leur poésie!
Ces brutes ont des chants ivres d'âme saisie
Improvisée aux quarts sur le gaillard d'avant ...
— Ils ne s'en doutent pas, eux, poème vivant.

— Ils ont toujours, pour leur *bonne femme de mère,*
Une larme d'enfant, ces héros de misère;
Pour leur *Douce-Jolie,* une larme d'amour! ...
Au pays — loin — ils ont, espérant leur retour,
Ces gens de cuivre rouge, une pâle fiancée
Que, pour la mer jolie, un jour ils ont laissée.
Elle attend vaguement ... comme on attend là-bas.
Eux, ils portent son nom tatoué sur leur bras.
Peut-être elle sera veuve avant d'être épouse ...
— Car la mer est bien grande et la mer est jalouse. —

Come; this open cynic has his original grace. ... How he scans his boss in his simple way! How he knows his master. – *A man made out of a single block of wood! – Always a surly dog, sometimes a good child!*

Come: on board in their home they have their poetry! These brutes have songs of rapture that come from the ravished soul and are made up in the watches on the forecastle. ... They don't suspect it, themselves, a living poem.

For their *good woman of a mother* these heroes of wretchedness always have a child's tear; for their *Sweetheart* a tear of love! ... In their home country – far away – these men of red copper have a pale fiancée hoping for their return, whom they left one day for the fine sea. She waits vaguely ... as folk wait there. They carry her name tattooed on their arm. Perhaps she will be a widow before being a wife. ... – For the sea is vast and the sea is jealous. – But through her

Mais elle sera fière, à travers un sanglot,
De pouvoir dire encore: – Il était matelot!...

– C'est plus qu'un homme aussi devant la mer géante,
Ce matelot entier!...
                                    Piétinant sous la plante
De son pied marin le pont près de crouler:
Tiens bon! Ça le connaît, ça va le désoûler.
Il finit comme ça, simple en sa grande allure,
D'un bloc: – *Un trou dans l'eau, quoi!... pas de fioriture.* –
....

On en voit revenir pourtant: bris de naufrage,
Ramassis de scorbut et hachis d'abordage...
Cassés, défigurés, dépaysés, perclus:
– Un œil en moins. – Et vous, en avez-vous en plus?
– La fièvre-jaune. – Eh bien, et vous, l'avez-vous rose?
– Une balafre. – Ah, c'est signé!... C'est quelquechose!
– Et le bras en pantenne. – Oui, c'est un biscaïen,
Le reste c'est le bel ouvrage au chirurgien.
– Et ce trou dans la joue? – Un ancien coup de pique.
– Cette bosse? – A *tribord?*... excusez: c'est ma chique.

sobbing she will still be proud to be able to say: He was a sailor!...
    Confronted by the giant sea this complete sailor is more than a
man too!... Treading beneath the sole of his sailor's foot the near-
crumbling bridge; hold fast! He knows it all; this will sober him
up. He ends like that, simple in his proud bearing, in one solid
piece: *A hole in the water!... No fancy frills.*
    Yet you see some come back: the flotsam of shipwrecks, remains
of scurvy, remains of collisions. ... Broken, disfigured, uprooted,
and crippled: – Minus an eye. – And are you plus one? – Yellow
fever. – Well, do you have the pink? – A scar. – Ah, I know who
did that!... That is something! – And the arm askew. – Yes, that's
case-shot and the rest's a surgeon's fine work. – And this hole in
your cheek? – An old pike blow. – This lump? – To *starboard?*...

– Ça? – Rien: une *foutaise*, un pruneau dans la main,
Ça sert de baromètre, et vous verrez demain:
Je ne vous dis que ça, sûr! quand je sens ma crampe ...
Allez, on n'en fait plus de coques de ma trempe!
On m'a pendu deux fois ... –

                         Et l'honnête forban
Creuse un bateau de bois pour un petit enfant.

– Ils durent comme ça, reniflant la tempête,
Riches de gloire et de trois cents francs de retraite,
Vieux culots de gargousse, épaves de héros! ...
– Héros? – ils riraient bien! ... – Non, merci: matelots!

– Matelots! – Ce n'est pas vous, jeunes *mateluches*,
Pour qui les femmes ont toujours des coqueluches ...
Ah, les vieux avaient de plus fiers appétits!
En haussant leur épaule ils vous trouvent petits.
A treize ans ils mangeaient de l'Anglais, les corsaires!
Vous, vous n'êtes que des *pelletas* militaires ...
Allez, on n'en fait plus de ces *purs, premier brin!*
Tout s'en va ... tout! La mer ... elle n'est plus *marin!*

Pardon, that's my quid. – That? – Nothing: a *trifle*, a bullet in my
hand; it serves as a barometer and you'll see to-morrow: I tell you
this for sure! When I feel a twinge. ... Come, they don't make hulls
of my sort any more! They hanged me twice. ... – And the honest
rover hollows a wooden boat for a small child.

They last like that, sniffing the storm, rich on fame and three
hundred francs pension, old cartridge cases, heroes' flotsam! ... –
Heroes? – They would have a good laugh at that! ... – No, thanks:
sailors!

Sailors! – That is not you, young *sailor boys,* for whom the
women always prepare dainty dishes. ... Ah, the old ones had
prouder appetites! Shrugging their shoulders they find you small.
At thirteen years old these pirates were eating Englishmen! You are
only *army navvies.* ... Ah, they don't make these *genuine old
originals* any more! Everything passes ... everything! The sea ... it

De leur temps, elle était plus salée et sauvage.
Mais, à present, rien n'a plus de pucelage ...
La mer ... La mer n'est plus qu'une fille à soldats! ...

– Vous, matelots, rêvez, en faisant vos cent pas
Comme dans les grands quarts ... Paisible rêverie
De carcasse qui geint, de mât craqué qui crie ...
– Aux pompes! ...
            – Non: fini! – Les beaux jours sont passés ...
– *Adieu mon beau navire aux trois mâts pavoisés!*
....

Tel qu'une vieille coque, au sec et dégréée,
Où vient encor parfois clapoter la marée:
Âme-de-mer en peine est le vieux matelot
Attendant, échoué ... – quoi: la mort?

                         – Non, le flot.

is no longer the *sea*! In their time it was saltier and wilder. But nothing is virgin any longer now. ... The sea. ... The sea is no more than a camp follower! ...

Dream, sailors, doing your hundred steps as in the long watches. ... A peaceful dream of groaning hulls, of masts cracked and shrieking. ... – To the pumps! ... – No; ended! – The good old days are past. ... – *Farewell, my fine three-master decked with flags!*

Like an old unrigged hulk high and dry, where still sometimes the tide comes lapping: the old sailor is a sea-soul in torment stranded and waiting ... – for what: death? – No, the tide.

Vénerie

Ô VÉNUS, dans ta Vénerie,
Limier et piqueur à la fois,
Valet-de-chiens et d'écurie,
J'ai vu l'Hallali, les Abois! ...

Que Diane aussi me sourie! ...
A cors, à cris, à pleine voix
Je fais le pied, je fais le bois;
Car on dit que: *bête varie* ...

– Un pied de biche: Le voici,
Cordon de sonnette sur rue,
– Bois de cerf: de la porte aussi;
– Et puis un pied: un pied-de-grue! ...

Venery *

O VENUS, in your venery, staghound and huntsman at the same time, kennel-boy and stable-boy, I have seen the mort and seen the bay! ...

Let Diana too smile upon me! ... With horns, with shouts, at the top of my voice, I go on foot, I beat the wood; for they say that *beasts differ.*

A hind's track: here it is, a bell-pull on the street, – a stag's antlers: the wooden door too; and then a foot: myself kicking my heels!

---

* This poem depends on a series of puns impossible to express in English, but playing for the most part on the idea of hunting a wild beast and hunting a woman. The third stanza is especially difficult: *pied-de-biche* can mean either *a hind's track* or *the handle of a bell-pull.* *Pied-de-grue* means *standing about and waiting*, and there is also a pun on *grue* in its slang sense of *prostitute.* In the fourth stanza there seems to be a play on the words *laie: a wild sow* and *Laïs: Lais, courtezan.* The ambiguity existing in the word *vénerie* suggesting at the same time *hunting* and various derivatives of *Venus* is also present in English.

Ô Fauve après qui j'aboyais,
– Je suis fourbu, qu'on me relaie! –
Ô Bête, es-tu donc une laie?
....
Bien moins sauvage te croyais!

Cantique du pardon de Sainte-Anne

MÈRE taillée à coups de hache,
Tout cœur de chêne dur et bon;
Sous l'or de ta robe se cache
L'âme en pièce d'un franc-Breton!

– Vieille verte à face usée
Comme la pierre du torrent,
Par des larmes d'amour creusée,
Séchée avec des pleurs de sang ...

– Toi, dont la mamelle tarie
S'est refait, pour avoir porté
La Virginité de Marie,
Une mâle virginité!

– Servante-maîtresse altière,
Très-haute devant le Très-Haut,
Au pauvre monde, pas fière,
Dame pleine de comme-il-faut!

O wild beast after whom I bayed, – I am foundered, let them re-place me! – O beast, are you a wild sow? – I thought you much less savage!

Canticle of the Pardon of Saint Ann

MOTHER hewn with blows of axes, all good hard heart of oak; under your dress's gold is hidden a free Breton's soul like wine in the wood!

Green old woman with a face worn like a stone in a stream, hol-lowed by tears of love, dried up by tears of blood. ...

You, whose withered breast was made whole again, because it bore Mary's virginity, a virile virginity!

Lofty Servant and Mistress, Most High before the Most High, not proud to poor folk, Lady full of courtesy!

– Bâton des aveugles! Béquille
Des vieilles! Bras des nouveaux-nés!
Mère de madame ta fille!
Parente des abandonnés!

– Ô Fleur de la pucelle neuve!
Fruit de l'épouse au sein grossi!
Reposoir de la femme veuve ...
Et du veuf Dame-de-merci!

– Arche de Joachim! Aïeule!
Médaille de cuivre effacé!
Gui sacré! Trèfle-quatre-feuille!
Mont d'Horeb! Souche de Jessé!

– Ô toi qui recouvrais la cendre,
Qui filais comme on fait chez nous,
Quand le soir venait à descendre,
Tenant l'ENFANT sur tes genoux;

Toi qui fus là, seule pour faire
Son maillot neuf à Bethléem,
Et là, pour coudre son suaire
Douloureux, à Jérusalem! ...

Stick for the blind! Crutch for old women! Arm for the new-
born! Mother of Madame your daughter! Parent of the forlorn!
   O Flower of the new maiden! Fruit of the wife with the swollen
breast! Resting-place for woman widowed ... and Lady of Mercy
for the widower!
   Ark of Joachim! Ancestress! Medal of worn brass! Holy mistle-
toe! Four-leafed clover! Mount Horeb! Stem of Jesse!
   O you who covered the ash, who spun as we do here, when evening came falling, holding the CHILD on your knees;
   You who alone were there to make his new vest at Bethlehem,
and there to sew his grievous shroud at Jerusalem!

Des croix profondes sont tes rides,
Tes cheveux sont blancs comme fils ...
– Préserve des regards arides
Le berceau de nos petit-fils!

Fais venir et conserve en joie
Ceux à naitre et ceux qui sont nés.
Et verse, sans que Dieu te voie,
L'eau de tes yeux sur les damnés!

Reprends dans leur chemise blanche
Les petits qui sont en langueur ...
Rappelle à l'éternel Dimanche
Les vieux qui traînent en longueur.

– Dragon-gardien de la Vierge,
Garde la crèche sous ton œil.
Que, près de toi, Joseph-concierge
Garde la propreté du seuil!

Prends pitié de la fille-mère,
Du petit au bord du chemin ...
Si quelqu'un leur jette la pierre,
Que la pierre se change en pain!

Your wrinkles are deep crosses, your hair is white as thread. ...
Keep the cradles of our grandsons from blighting glances!

Cause to come and keep in joy those to be born and those born
already. And pour the water from your eyes on the damned without
God seeing you!

In their white shirts take up the sickly children. ... Recall to the
eternal Sabbath the old dragging out their days.

Guardian dragon of the Virgin, keep the crib under your eye.
Near you let Joseph the concierge keep the threshold clean!

Have pity on the unmarried mother, on the child beside the road.
... If someone throws a stone at them, let the stone be changed to
bread!

– Dame bonne en mer et sur terre,
Montre-nous le ciel et le port,
Dans la tempête ou dans la guerre ...
Ô Fanal de la bonne mort!

Humble: à tes pieds n'a point d'étoile,
Humble ... et brave pour protéger!
Dans la nue apparaît ton voile,
Pâle auréole du danger.

– Aux perdus dont la vie est grise,
(– Sauf respect – perdus de boisson)
Montre le clocher de l'église
Et le chemin de la maison.

Prête ta douce et chaste flamme
Aux chrétiens qui sont ici ...
Ton remède de bonne femme
Pour les bêtes-à-corne aussi!

Montre à nos femmes et servantes
L'ouvrage et la fécondité ...
– Le bonjour aux âmes parentes
Qui sont bien dans l'éternité!

Lady kind on sea and land, show us heaven and harbour in storm or in war. ... O Beacon of righteous death!

Humble: there is no star at your feet, humble and courageous to shield! In the clouds appears your veil, the pale halo of danger.

To those who are lost, whose life is drunken (save your respect, lost through drink), show the belfry of the church and the road home.

Lend your chaste and gentle flame to the Christians here. ... Your wise-woman's cure for the horned beasts too!

Show our women and serving-girls work and fertility. ... Good day to the souls of our kinsmen who are already in eternity!

Nous mettrons un cordon de cire,
De cire-vierge jaune, autour
De ta chapelle; et ferons dire
Ta messe basse au point du jour.

– Préserve notre cheminée
Des sorts et du monde malin ...
A Pâques te sera donnée
Une quenouille avec du lin.

Si nos corps sont puants sur terre,
Ta grâce est un bain de santé;
Répands sur nous, au cimetière,
Ta bonne odeur-de-sainteté.

– A l'an prochain! – Voici ton cierge:
(C'est deux livres qu'il a coûté)
... Respects à Madame la Vierge,
Sans oublier la Trinité.

Paria

Qu'ils se payent des républiques,
Hommes libres! – carcan au cou –
Qu'ils peuplent leurs nids domestiques! ...
– Moi je suis le maigre coucou.

We shall put a band of wax, of yellow virgin wax, around your chapel, and cause your low Mass to be said at dawn.

Keep our hearth from spells and from the world of evil. ... At Easter we shall give you a distaff with some flax.

If on earth our bodies stink, your grace is a bath of health; in the graveyard spread on us your fine perfume of holiness.

To next year! – Here is your candle: (it cost two pounds). ... Our respects to Madame the Virgin without forgetting the Trinity.

Pariah

Let them have their republics, free men! – with a yoke on their necks – let them people their homely nests! ... I am the lean cuckoo.

– Moi, – cœur eunuque, dératé
De ce qui mouille et ce qui vibre …
Que me chante leur Liberté,
A moi? toujours seul. Toujours libre.

– Ma Patrie … elle est par le monde;
Et, puisque la planète est ronde,
Je ne crains pas d'en voir le bout …
Ma patrie est où je la plante:
Terre ou mer, elle est sous la plante
De mes pieds – quand je suis debout.

– Quand je suis couché: ma patrie
C'est la couche seule et meurtrie
Où je vais forcer dans mes bras
Ma moitié, comme moi sans âme;
Et ma moitié: c'est une femme …
Une femme que je n'ai pas.

– L'idéal à moi: c'est un songe
Creux; mon horizon – l'imprévu –
Et le mal du pays me ronge …
Du pays que je n'ai pas vu.

I – a eunuch heart deprived of all ecstasy and excitement. …
What does their freedom mean to me? Always alone. Always free.

My country … is throughout the world; and, since the planet is
round, I am not afraid of seeing its end. … My country is where I
place it: on land or sea it is beneath the sole of my feet – when I am
standing up.

When I am lying down, my country is the lonely bruised bed
where I shall force into my arms my other half, soulless like myself;
and my other half is a woman. … A woman I do not possess.

My ideal is a hollow dream; my horizon – the unforeseen – and
homesickness consumes me. … For a home I have never seen.

Que les moutons suivent leur route,
De Carcassonne à Tombouctou ...
– Moi, ma route me suit. Sans doute
Elle me suivra n'importe où.

Mon pavillon sur moi frissonne,
Il a le ciel pour couronne:
C'est la brise dans mes cheveux ...
Et dans n'importe quelle langue;
Je puis subir une harangue;
Je puis me taire si je veux.

Ma pensée est un souffle aride:
C'est l'air. L'air est à moi partout.
Et ma parole est l'écho vide
Qui ne dit rien – et c'est tout.

Mon passé: c'est ce que j'oublie.
La seule chose qui me lie,
C'est ma main dans mon autre main.
Mon souvenir – Rien – C'est ma trace
Mon présent, c'est tout ce qui passe
Mon avenir – Demain ... demain.

Let the sheep follow their road from Carcassonne to Timbuctoo.
... My road follows me. Doubtless it will follow me anywhere.
Above me flutters my ensign with the sky for a crown: it is the
breeze in my hair. ... And in any language I can put up with a
speech or be silent if I want.

My thought is an arid breath: it is the air. Everywhere the air belongs to me. And my speech is the empty echo which says nothing –
and that is all.

My past is what I forget. The only thing that binds me is my hand
in my other hand. My memory – nothing – it is my track. My present is everything that passes by. My future – to-morrow ... to-
morrow.

Je ne connais pas mon semblable;
Moi, je suis ce que je me fais.
– *Le Moi humain est haïssable* ...
– Je ne m'aime ni ne me hais.

– Allons! la vie est une fille
Qui m'a pris à son bon plaisir ...
Le mien, c'est: la mettre en guenille,
La prostituer sans désir.

– Des dieux? ... – Par hasard j'ai pu naître;
Peut-être en est-il – par hasard ...
Ceux-là, s'ils veulent me connaître,
Me trouveront bien quelque part.

– Où que je meure: ma patrie
S'ouvrira bien, sans qu'on l'en prie,
Assez grande pour mon linceul ...
Un linceul encor: pour que faire? ...
Puisque ma patrie est en terre
Mon os ira bien là tout seul ...

I know no fellow; I am what I make myself. – *The human Ego is hateful.* ... I neither love nor hate myself.

Come! Life is a girl who took me for her pleasure. ... Mine is: to reduce her to rags and prostitute her without desire.

Gods? ... By chance I was born; perhaps there are some – by chance. ... They, if they want to know me, will easily find me somewhere or other.

Wherever I die, without being asked my country will open wide enough for my shroud. ... Why even a shroud? ... Since my country is the earth, my bones will easily go there by themselves. ...

ISIDORE DUCASSE, COMTE DE LAUTRÉAMONT

Debout sur le rocher ...

DEBOUT sur le rocher, pendant que l'ouragan fouettait mes cheveux et mon manteau, j'épiais dans l'extase cette force de la tempête, s'acharnant sur un navire, sous un ciel sans étoiles. Je suivis, dans une attitude triomphante, toutes les péripéties de ce drame, depuis l'instant où le vaisseau jeta ses ancres, jusqu'au moment où il s'engloutit, habit fatal qui entraîna, dans les boyaux de la mer, ceux qui s'en étaient revêtus comme d'un manteau. Mais l'instant s'approchait où j'allais, moi-même, me mêler comme acteur à ces scènes de la nature bouleversée. Quand la place où le vaisseau avait soutenu le combat montra clairement que celui-ci avait été passer le reste de ses jours au rez-de-chaussée de la mer, alors, ceux qui avaient été emportés avec les flots reparurent en partie à la surface. Ils se prirent à bras-le-corps, deux par deux, trois par trois; c'était le moyen de ne pas sauver leur vie; car

Standing on the rock ...

STANDING on the rock, while the storm whipped my hair and cloak, in ecstasy I watched the strength of the tempest falling upon a ship beneath a starless sky. In an attitude of triumph I followed all the ups and downs of this drama, from the moment when the vessel cast anchor to the moment when it was engulfed like a fatal garment dragging down into the entrails of the sea those who had worn it like a cloak. But the moment was approaching when I myself was going to mingle as a participant in these scenes of natural convulsion. When the place where the vessel had carried on its fight clearly showed that it had gone to pass the rest of its days on the ground floor of the sea, then those who had been carried away by the waves partly reappeared on the surface. They took each other round the waist, two by two, three by three; it was the way not to save their

leurs mouvements devenaient embarrassés, et ils coulaient bas comme des cruches percées. ... Quelle est cette armée de monstres marins qui fend les flots avec vitesse? Ils sont six; leurs nageoires sont vigoureuses, et s'ouvrent un passage, à travers les vagues soulevées. De tous ces êtres humains, qui remuent les quatre membres dans ce continent peu ferme, les requins ne font bientôt qu'une omelette sans œufs, et se la partagent d'après la loi du plus fort. Le sang se mêle aux eaux, et les eaux se mêlent au sang. Leurs yeux féroces éclairent suffisamment la scène du carnage. ... Mais quel est encore ce tumulte des eaux, là-bas, à l'horizon? On dirait une trombe qui s'approche. Quels coups de rame! J'aperçois ce que c'est. Une énorme femelle de requin vient prendre part au pâté de foie de canard, et manger du bouilli froid. Elle est furieuse, car elle arrive affamée. Une lutte s'engage entre elle et les requins pour se disputer les quelques membres palpitants qui flottent par-ci, par-là, sans rien dire, sur la surface de la crème rouge. A droite, à gauche, elle lance des coups de dent qui engendrent des blessures mortelles. Mais trois re-

lives; for their movements became hampered, and they sank down like jars with holes in them. ...

What is this army of sea monsters swiftly cleaving the waves? There are six of them; their fins are vigorous and open a passage through the swelling waves. Of all those human beings, moving their four limbs in that shifting continent, the sharks soon make no more than an omelette without eggs, and share it out according to the law of brute strength. Blood mingles with the waters, and the waters mingle with blood. Their fierce eyes light up the scene of slaughter well enough. ...

But what is this new disturbance of the water over there on the horizon? One would say an approaching water-spout. What oar strokes! I see what it is. A huge female shark comes to share in the duck's liver pâté and eat cold boiled beef. She is savage, for she arrives hungry. A struggle begins between her and the sharks over the few palpitating limbs floating here and there, without saying anything, on the surface of the red cream. To right and left she deals bites producing mortal wounds. But three living sharks still sur-

quins vivants l'entourent encore, et elle est obligée de
tourner en tous sens, pour déjouer leurs manœuvres.
Avec une émotion croissante, inconnue jusqu'alors, le
spectateur, placé sur le rivage, suit cette bataille navale
d'un nouveau genre. Il a les yeux fixés sur cette courageuse
femelle de requin, aux dents si fortes. Il hésite plus, il
épaule son fusil, et, avec son adresse habituelle, loge sa
deuxième balle dans l'ouïe d'un des requins, au moment
où il se montrait au-dessus d'une vague. Restent deux
requins qui n'en témoignent qu'un acharnement plus
grand. Du haut du rocher, l'homme à la salive saumâtre
se jette à la mer et nage vers le tapis agréablement coloré,
en tenant à la main ce couteau d'acier qui ne l'abandonne
jamais. Désormais, chaque requin a affaire à un ennemi.
Il s'avance vers son adversaire fatigué, et, prenant son
temps, lui enfonce dans le ventre sa lame aiguë. La citadelle mobile se débarrasse facilement du dernier adversaire. ... Se trouvent en présence le nageur et la femelle de
requin, sauvée par lui. Ils se regardèrent entre les yeux
pendant quelques minutes; et chacun s'étonna de trouver
tant de férocité dans les regards de l'autre. Ils tournent en

round her, and she is compelled to turn in all directions to baffle
their manoeuvres. With growing emotion, unknown till then, the
spectator, placed on the shore, follows this new type of naval battle.
He has his eyes fixed on this brave female shark with such strong
teeth. He hesitates no longer, he shoulders his gun and, with his
habitual skill, plants his second ball in the gills of one of the sharks
at the moment when it showed itself above a wave. There remain
two sharks who only make proof of greater ferocity. From the top
of the rock the man with salty saliva throws himself into the sea and
swims towards the pleasantly coloured carpet, holding in his hand
the steel knife that never leaves him. Henceforward each shark has
to do with an enemy. He advances towards his tired adversary and,
taking his time, plunges his sharp blade into its stomach. The moving fortress easily gets rid of the last opponent. ...
  The swimmer and the female shark saved by him find themselves
alone. They looked each other in the eyes for some minutes; and
each of them was astonished to find so much ferocity in the glances

rond en nageant, ne se perdent pas de vue, et se disent à part soi: «Je me suis trompé jusqu'ici; en voilà un qui est plus méchant.» Alors, d'un commun accord, entre deux eaux, ils glissèrent l'un vers l'autre, avec une admiration mutuelle, la femelle de requin écartant l'eau de ses nageoires, Maldoror battant l'onde avec ses bras; et retinrent leur souffle, dans une vénération profonde, chacun désireux de contempler, pour la première fois, son portrait vivant. Arrivés à trois mètres de distance, sans faire aucun effort, ils tombèrent brusquement l'un contre l'autre, comme deux aimants, et s'embrassèrent avec dignité et reconnaissance, dans une étreinte aussi tendre que celle d'un frère ou d'une sœur. Les désirs charnels suivirent de près cette démonstration d'amitié. Deux cuisses nerveuses se collèrent étroitement à la peau visqueuse du monstre, comme deux sangsues; et, les bras et les nageoires entrelacés autour du corps de l'objet aimé qu'ils entouraient avec amour, tandis que leurs gorges et leurs poitrines ne faisaient bientôt plus qu'une masse glauque aux exhalaisons de goémon; au milieu de la tempête qui continuait de sévir, à la lueur des éclairs,

of the other. They circle swimming, not losing one another from sight, and say to themselves: 'I was mistaken till now; there is one wickeder than I.' Then, by common agreement, in still water, they slipped towards one another, with mutual wonder, the female shark cleaving the water with her fins, Maldoror beating the waves with his arms; and held their breath in deep veneration, each wanting to gaze for the first time on his living image. Arrived at a distance of three metres, without making any effort, they suddenly fell one against the other like two magnets and clasped each other with dignity and gratitude in an embrace as tender as that of a brother or a sister. Carnal desires followed close on this demonstration of friendship. Two sinewy thighs clung closely to the monster's slimy skin like two leeches; and, arms and fins being twined round the body of the beloved object which they encircled lovingly, while their throats and bosoms soon made but one glaucous mass, giving off the odour of seaweed; in the middle of the storm which continued to rage, by the light of flashes of lightning, with the foaming

ayant pour lit d'hyménée la vague écumeuse, emportés par un courant sous-marin comme dans un berceau, et roulant sur eux-mêmes vers les profondeurs de l'abîme, ils se réunirent dans un accouplement long, chaste et hideux! ... Enfin, je venais de trouver quelqu'un qui me ressemblât! ... Désormais, je n'étais plus seul dans la vie! ... Elle avait les mêmes idées que moi! ... J'étais en face de mon premier amour!

(*Les Chants de Maldoror: Chant Deuxième, 13*)

ARTHUR RIMBAUD

Le Cœur volé

MON triste cœur bave à la poupe,
Mon cœur couvert de caporal:
Ils y lancent des jets de soupe,
Mon triste cœur bave à la poupe:
Sous les quolibets de la troupe
Qui pousse un rire général,
Mon triste cœur bave à la poupe,
Mon cœur couvert de caporal!

wave for marriage bed, carried by an underwater current as if in a cradle, and rolling over one another towards the depths of the abyss, they were joined in a long, chaste, and hideous union!

At last I had found someone who resembled myself! ... Henceforward I was no longer alone in life! ... She had the same ideas as myself! ... I was before my first love!

The Stolen Heart

MY sad heart slobbers at the stern, my heart covered with shag tobacco: they spirt soup over it, my sad heart slobbers at the stern: under the jokes of the crew, who utter a general laugh, my sad heart slobbers at the stern, my heart covered with shag tobacco!

Ithyphalliques et pioupiesques
Leurs quolibets l'ont dépravé!
Au gouvernail on voit des fresques
Ithyphalliques et pioupiesques.
Ô flots abracadabrantesques,
Prenez mon cœur, qu'il soit lavé!
Ithyphalliques et pioupiesques,
Leurs quolibets l'ont dépravé!

Quand ils auront tari leurs chiques,
Comment agir, ô cœur volé?
Ce seront des hoquets bachiques
Quand ils auront tari leurs chiques:
J'aurai des sursauts stomachiques,
Moi, si mon cœur est ravalé:
Quand ils auront tari leurs chiques
Comment agir, ô cœur volé?

Their ithyphallic, barrack-room jokes have corrupted it! On the tiller one sees ithyphallic, barrack-room drawings. O magical waves take my heart that it may be washed! Their ithyphallic, barrack-room jokes have corrupted it!

When they have chewed their quids dry, how shall I act, O stolen heart? There will be Bacchanalian hiccoughs when they have chewed their quids dry: I shall have tremors in my stomach myself, if my heart is degraded again: when they have chewed their quids dry, how shall I act, O stolen heart?

Les Premières Communions

I

VRAIMENT, c'est bête, ces églises des villages
Où quinze laids marmots encrassant les piliers
Écoutent, grasseyant les divins babillages,
Un noir grotesque dont fermentent les souliers:
Mais le soleil éveille, à travers des feuillages,
Les vieilles couleurs des vitraux irréguliers.

La pierre sent toujours la terre maternelle.
Vous verrez des monceaux de ces cailloux terreux
Dans la campagne en rut qui frémit solennelle,
Portant près des blés lourds, dans les sentiers ocreux,
Ces arbrisseaux brûlés où bleuit la prunelle,
Des nœuds de mûriers noirs et de rosiers fuireux.

Tous les cent ans on rend ces granges respectables
Par un badigeon d'eau bleue et de lait caillé:

First Communions

I

REALLY, it is idiotic, these village churches where fifteen ugly
brats, dirtying the pillars and pronouncing the divine prattle with a
thick burr, listen to a black grotesque with sweaty shoes: but the
sun through the leaves awakens the old colours of the uneven windows.

The stone still smells of the maternal earth. You will see piles of
these earthy stones in the rutting countryside, which quivers
solemnly and bears near the heavy corn, on the ochre paths, those
scorched shrubs on which the sloe is blue, clumps of blackberry
bushes and pale roses.

Every hundred years they make these barns respectable with a
wash of blue water and curdled milk: if grotesque mystifications are

Si des mysticités grotesques sont notables
Près de la Notre-Dame où du Saint empaillé,
Des mouches sentant bon l'auberge et les étables
Se gorgent de cire au plancher ensoleillé.

L'enfant se doit surtout à la maison, famille
Des soins naïfs, des bons travaux abrutissants;
Ils sortent, oubliant que la peau leur fourmille
Où le Prêtre du Christ plaqua ses doigts puissants.
On paie au Prêtre un toit ombré d'une charmille
Pour qu'il laisse au soleil tous ces fronts brunissants.

Le premier habit noir, le plus beau jour de tartes,
Sous le Napoléon ou le Petit Tambour
Quelque enluminure où les Josephs et les Marthes
Tirent la langue avec un excessif amour
Et que joindront, au jour de science, deux cartes:
Ces seuls doux souvenirs lui restent du grand Jour.

to the fore near the statue of Our Lady or the stuffed Saint, flies
smelling pleasantly of the inn or the stables cram themselves with
wax on the sunny ceiling.

The child is bound to his home above all, the family of naïve
cares, of good exhausting work; they emerge, forgetting that their
skin crawls where Christ's priest laid his powerful fingers. The
Priest is paid a roof shaded by a hornbeam to leave all these bronzed
foreheads in the sun.

The first black coat, the nicest day of cakes, beneath the
Napoleon or the Little Drummer some coloured print where
Josephs and Marys put out their tongues with excessive love, to be
joined by two cards on the day of the catechism: these sweet
memories of the great day alone remain to him.

Les filles vont toujours à l'église, contentes
De s'entendre appeler garces par les garçons
Qui font du genre après Messe ou vêpres chantantes.
Eux qui sont destinés au chic des garnisons,
Ils narguent au café les maisons importantes,
Blousés neuf, et gueulant d'effroyables chansons.

Cependant le Curé choisit pour les enfances
Des dessins; dans son clos, les vêpres dites, quand
L'air s'emplit du lointain nasillement des danses,
Il se sent, en dépit des célestes défenses,
Les doigts de pied ravis et le mollet marquant;
– La Nuit vient, noir pirate aux cieux d'or débarquant.

2

Le Prêtre a distingué parmi les catéchistes,
Congrégés des Faubourgs ou des Riches Quartiers,
Cette petite fille inconnue, aux yeux tristes,
Front jaune. Les parents semblent de doux portiers.
«Au grand Jour, le marquant parmi les Catéchistes,
Dieu fera sur ce front neiger ses bénitiers.»

The girls still go to church, glad to be called lasses by the boys showing off after Mass or sung vespers. They, destined for the fashionable life of garrison towns, snap their fingers in the café at important houses, with new blouses on and yelling frightful songs.

Meanwhile the Curé chooses drawings for the children; in his garden, vespers over, when the air is filled with the distant humming of dances, in spite of heavenly prohibitions, he feels his toes itching and calf beating time; – Night comes like a black pirate landing on the golden skies.

2

The Priest noticed among the catechists, who came from the suburbs or rich parts of the town, this unknown little girl with sad eyes and sallow brow. The parents seem to be peaceable door-keepers. 'On the great day, remarking it among the catechists, God will cause his fonts to drop snow upon this brow.'

3

La veille du grand Jour, l'enfant se fait malade.
Mieux qu'à l'Église haute aux funèbres rumeurs,
D'abord le frisson vient, – le lit n'étant pas fade –
Un frisson surhumain qui retourne: «Je meurs ...»

Et, comme un vol d'amour fait à ses sœurs stupides,
Elle compte, abattue et les mains sur son cœur,
Les Anges, les Jésus et ses Vierges nitides
Et, calmement, son âme a bu tout son vainqueur.

Adonaï! ... – Dans les terminaisons latines,
Des cieux moirés de vert baignent les Fronts vermeils,
Et, tachés du sang pur des célestes poitrines,
De grands linges neigeux tombent sur les soleils!

– Pour ses virginités présentes et futures
Elle mord aux fraîcheurs de ta Rémission,
Mais plus que les lys d'eau, plus que les confitures,
Tes pardons sont glacés, ô Reine de Sion!

3

On the eve of the great day the child becomes ill. Stronger than in
the tall church with its dreary noises, first comes a fit of shivering –
it is not that her bed is damp – a superhuman shivering that returns:
'I am dying. ...'

And, as if stealing love from her stupid sisters, dejectedly, her
hands on her heart, she counts the Angels, the Jesuses, and her
snowy Virgins and calmly her soul drank all its conqueror.

Adonai! ... – In the Latin endings skies watered with green bathe
crimson brows, and great snowy cloths spotted with the pure blood
of heavenly bosoms fall on the suns!

For her present and future virginities she gnaws at the coolness of
your forgiveness, but your pardons are icier, O Queen of Sion,
than water-lilies or preserves!

4

Puis la Vierge n'est plus que la vierge du livre.
Les mystiques élans se cassent quelquefois …
Et vient la pauvreté des images, que cuivre
L'ennui, l'enluminure atroce et les vieux bois;

Des curiosités vaguement impudiques
Épouvantent le rêve aux chastes bleuités
Qui s'est surpris autour des célestes tuniques,
Du linge dont Jésus voile ses nudités.

Elle veut, elle veut, pourtant, l'âme en détresse,
Le front dans l'oreiller creusé par les cris sourds,
Prolonger les éclairs suprêmes de tendresse,
Et bave … – L'ombre emplit les maisons et les cours.

Et l'enfant ne peut plus. Elle s'agite, cambre
Les reins et d'une main ouvre le rideau bleu
Pour amener un peu la fraîcheur de la chambre
Sous le drap, vers son ventre et sa poitrine en feu. …

4

Then the Virgin is no more than the virgin of the book. Mystical
soarings are sometimes broken. … And there comes the poverty of
images coppered by boredom, the frightful coloured print and old
wood-cuts;

Vaguely shameless curiosity frightens the chaste blue dream that
surprised itself round heavenly tunics, the cloth with which Jesus
veils his nakedness.

She wants, yet she wants, her soul in distress, her forehead in the
pillow hollowed by muffled cries, to prolong the last flashes of
tenderness, and dribbles. … – The shadow fills houses and courtyards.

And the child can stand it no longer. She moves, arches her loins,
and with one hand opens the blue curtain to bring a little of the
room's coolness beneath the sheet, towards her burning stomach
and chest. …

5

A son réveil, – minuit, – la fenêtre était blanche.
Devant le sommeil bleu des rideaux illunés,
La vision la prit des candeurs du dimanche;
Elle avait rêvé rouge. Elle saigna du nez,

Et, se sentant bien chaste et pleine de faiblesse,
Pour savourer en Dieu son amour revenant
Elle eut soif de la nuit où s'exalte et s'abaisse
Le cœur, sous l'œil des cieux doux, en les devinant;

De la nuit, Vierge-Mère impalpable, qui baigne
Tous les jeunes émois de ses silences gris;
Elle eut soif de la nuit forte où le cœur qui saigne
Écoule sans témoin sa révolte sans cris.

Et faisant la Victime et la petite épouse,
Son étoile la vit, une chandelle aux doigts,
Descendre dans la cour où séchait une blouse,
Spectre blanc, et lever les spectres noirs des toits.

5

At her awakening – midnight – the window was white. Before the blue slumber of curtains lit by the moon, the vision of Sunday purities took her; she had dreamed red. She bled from the nose,

And feeling herself chaste indeed and full of weakness to savour her love returning to God, she thirsted for the night where the heart is exalted or cast down beneath the eye of the gentle heavens, while guessing their secrets;

For the night, impalpable Virgin-Mother, bathing all young emotions in her grey silences; she thirsted for the strong night where the bleeding heart may utter its dumb revolt without a witness.

And playing the Victim and the little wife, her star saw her go down, a candle in her fingers, into the courtyard, where a blouse was drying like a white ghost, and raise the black ghosts of the roofs.

6

Elle passa sa nuit sainte dans des latrines.
Vers la chandelle, aux trous du toit coulait l'air blanc,
Et quelque vigne folle aux noirceurs purpurines,
En deçà d'une cour voisine s'écroulant.

La lucarne faisait un cœur de lueur vive
Dans la cour où les cieux bas plaquaient d'ors vermeils
Les vitres; les pavés puant l'eau de lessive
Souffraient l'ombre des murs bondés de noirs sommeils.

7

Qui dira ces langueurs et ces pitiés immondes,
Et ce qu'il lui viendra de haine, ô sales fous
Dont le travail divin déforme encor les mondes,
Quand la lèpre à la fin mangera ce corps doux?

6

She passed her holy night in a privy. From the holes in the roof the white air flowed towards the candle, and some wild vine with its purple blackness collapsing this side of a neighbouring courtyard.

The skylight made a heart of bright light in the courtyard where the low skies touched the panes with ruby gold; the paving stones stinking of washing water sulphured the shadow of walls crammed with dark sleep.

7

Who shall tell of these languors and of this impure pity, and of the hatred that will come to her, when in the end leprosy shall devour that gentle body, O filthy fools, whose divine work still disfigures the universe?

8

Et quand, ayant rentré tous ses nœuds d'hystéries,
Elle verra, sous les tristesses du bonheur,
L'amant rêver au blanc million des Maries,
Au matin de la nuit d'amour, avec douleur:

«Sais-tu que je t'ai fait mourir? J'ai pris ta bouche,
Ton cœur, tout ce qu'on a, tout ce que vous avez;
Et moi, je suis malade: Oh! je veux qu'on me couche
Parmi les Morts des eaux nocturnes abreuvés!

«J'étais bien jeune, et Christ a souillé mes haleines.
Il me bonda jusqu'à la gorge de dégoûts!
Tu baisais mes cheveux profonds comme les laines,
Et je me laissais faire ... Ah! va, c'est bon pour vous,

«Hommes! qui songez peu que la plus amoureuse
Est, sous sa conscience aux ignobles terreurs,
La plus prostituée et la plus douloureuse,
Et que tous nos élans vers vous sont des erreurs!

8

And when, having drawn all her coils of hysteria in, she will see with grief, on the morning of the night of love, beneath the melancholy of happiness, her lover dreaming of the white million of Marys:

'Do you know I made you die? I took your mouth, your heart all there is to be had, all you have; and I am sick: Oh! would I were laid among the dead whose thirst is quenched with the waters of night!

'I was very young, and Christ soiled my breath. He crammed me full to the throat with disgust! You kissed my hair deep as a fleece, and I let you do it ... ah! go, it is all right for you,

'Men! Who little think that beneath her consciousness, with its vile terrors, the most amorous woman is the most prostituted and sorrowful, and that all our movements towards you are mistakes!

«Car ma Communion première est bien passée.
Tes baisers, je ne puis jamais les avoir sus:
Et mon cœur et ma chair par ta chair embrassée
Fourmillent du baiser putride de Jésus!»

9

Alors l'âme pourrie et l'âme désolée
Sentiront ruisseler tes malédictions.
– Ils auront couché sur ta Haine inviolée,
Échappés, pour la mort, des justes passions,

Christ! ô Christ, éternel voleur des énergies,
Dieu qui pour deux mille ans vouas à ta paleur,
Cloués au sol, de honte et de céphalalgies,
Ou renversés, les fronts des femmes de douleur.

Les Chercheuses de poux

QUAND le front de l'enfant, plein de rouges tourmentes,
Implore l'essaim blanc des rêves indistincts,
Il vient près de son lit deux grandes sœurs charmantes
Avec de frêles doigts aux ongles argentins.

'For my first Communion is long past. I can never have known
your kisses: and my heart and flesh embraced by your flesh crawl
with the putrid kiss of Jesus!'

9

Then the corrupt soul and the desolate soul will feel your curses
flow. – They will have lain down on your inviolate Hatred, escaped
from their just passions for death,
  Christ! O Christ, perpetual thief of energy, God who for two
thousand years consecrated to your own pallor the brows of the
women of sorrow, nailed to the ground with shame and head-
aches or thrown back.

Women Hunting Lice

WHEN the child's brow full of red torments begs for the white
swarm of hazy dreams, two tall charming sisters with delicate fingers
and silvery nails come near his bed.

Elles assoient l'enfant devant une croisée
Grande ouverte où l'air bleu baigne un fouillis de fleurs,
Et dans ses lourds cheveux où tombe la rosée
Promènent leurs doigts fins, terribles et charmeurs.

Il écoute chanter leurs haleines craintives
Qui fleurent de longs miels végétaux et rosés,
Et qu'interrompt parfois un sifflement, salives
Reprises sur la lèvre ou désirs de baisers.

Il entend leurs cils noirs battant sous les silences
Parfumés; et leurs doigts électriques et doux
Font crépiter parmi ses grises indolences
Sous leurs ongles royaux la mort des petits poux.

Voilà que monte en lui le vin de la Paresse,
Soupir d'harmonica qui pourrait délirer;
L'enfant se sent, selon la lenteur des caresses,
Sourdre et mourir sans cesse un désir de pleurer.

They seat the child in front of a wide-open window, where the
blue air bathes a mass of flowers, and through his heavy hair, on
which the dew falls, they run their terrible, slender, magic fingers.
   He hears their timid breath singing, smelling of slow vegetable
honey made from roses, and interrupted sometimes by a hissing,
saliva drawn back on the lip or the desire of kisses.
   He listens to their dark lashes fluttering under the scented
silence; and in his grey indolence their gentle, electric fingers make
the death of the little lice crackle beneath their royal nails.
   Now swells in him the wine of idleness, a harmonica's sighing
that might end in delirium; according to the slowness of the caresses
the child feels a desire to weep endlessly rising and dying within
him.

*Qu'est-ce pour nous, mon cœur, que les nappes
de sang ...*

QU'EST-CE pour nous, mon cœur, que les nappes de
sang
Et de braise, et mille meurtres, et les longs cris
De rage, sanglots de tout enfer renversant
Tout ordre; et l'Aquilon encor sur les débris;

Et toute vengeance? Rien! ... – Mais si, toute encor,
Nous la voulons! Industriels, princes, senats:
Périssez! Puissance, justice, histoire: à bas!
Ça nous est dû. Le sang! le sang! la flamme d'or!

Tout à la guerre, à la vengeance, à la terreur,
Mon esprit! Tournons dans la morsure: Ah! passez,
Républiques de ce monde! Des empereurs,
Des regiménts, des colons, des peuples, assez!

Qui remuerait les tourbillons de feu furieux,
Que nous et ceux que nous nous imaginons frères?
A nous, romanesques amis: ça va nous plaire,
Jamais nous ne travaillerons, ô flots de feux!

What does it mean to us, my heart, the sheets of blood ...?

WHAT does it mean to us, my heart, the sheets of blood and ash,
and a thousand killings, and the long shrieks of frenzy, the sobs of
every hell overturning all order, and the north wind still above the
ruins,
    And each revenge? Nothing! – But yes, we still want it all! In-
dustrialists, princes, senates: perish! Down with power, justice, and
history! That is our due. Blood! blood! The golden flame!
    Everything for war, revenge, terror, my soul! Let us take to
biting: Ah! pass away, republics of this world! Enough of emperors,
regiments, colonists, and peoples!
    Who should move the fierce whirlwinds of fire but we and those
we imagine to be our brothers? Help us, romantic friends: this will
please us. Never shall we toil, O waves of fire!

Europe, Asie, Amérique, disparaissez.
Notre marche vengeresse a tout occupé,
Cités et campagnes! – Nous serons écrasés!
Les volcans sauteront! Et l'Océan frappé …

Oh! mes amis! – Mon cœur, c'est sûr, ils sont des frères:
Noirs inconnus, si nous allions! Allons! Allons!
Ô malheur! je me sens frémir, la vieille terre,
Sur moi de plus en plus à vous! la terre fond.

Ce n'est rien : j'y suis ; j'y suis toujours.

Chanson de la plus haute tour

OISIVE jeunesse
A tout asservie,
Par délicatessse
J'ai perdu ma vie.
Ah! Que le temps vienne
Où les cœurs s'éprennent.

Europe, Asia, America, disappear. Our avenging march has occupied everything, cities and country! – We shall be crushed! The volcanoes will explode! And the smitten ocean. …

Oh! my friends! – My heart, it is certain, they are brothers: dark strangers, if we should march! March! March! O misfortune! I feel myself shivering, the ancient earth, the earth falls on me as I belong more and more to you!

It is nothing: I am there; I am still there.

Song of the Highest Tower

IDLE youth enslaved by everything; I have destroyed my life through sensitivity. Ah! let the time come when hearts fall in love.

Je me suis dit: laisse,
Et qu'on ne te voie:
Et sans la promesse
De plus hautes joies.
Que rien ne t'arrête,
Auguste retraite.

J'ai tant fait patience
Qu'à jamais j'oublie;
Craintes et souffrances
Aux cieux sont parties.
Et la soif malsaine
Obscurcit mes veines.

Ainsi la Prairie
A l'oubli livrée,
Grandie, et fleurie
D'encens et d'ivraies
Au bourdon farouche
De cent sales mouches.

Ah! Mille veuvages
De la si pauvre âme
Qui n'a que l'image
De la Notre-Dame!
Est-ce que l'on prie
La Vierge Marie?

I said to myself: Let it go and be seen no more: without the promise of higher joys. Let nothing stop you, solemn withdrawal.

I have been so patient that I forget for evermore; fear and suffering have left for the skies. And unhealthy thirst darkens my veins.

Like the meadow given over to neglect, grown and flowering
with incense and darnel to the savage buzzing of a hundred dirty
flies.

Ah, the thousand widowhoods of the poor soul who only has the
image of Our Lady! Does one pray to the Virgin Mary?

Oisive jeunesse
A tout asservie,
Par délicatesse
J'ai perdu ma vie.
Ah! Que le temps vienne
Où les cœurs s'éprennent!

Aube

J'AI embrassé l'aube d'été.

Rien ne bougeait encore au front des palais. L'eau était morte. Les camps d'ombres ne quittaient pas la route du bois. J'ai marché, réveillant les haleines vives et tièdes, et les pierreries regardèrent, et les ailes se levèrent sans bruit.

La première entreprise fut, dans le sentier déjà empli de frais et blêmes éclats, une fleur qui me dit son nom.

Je ris au wasserfall blond qui s'échevela à travers les sapins: à la cime argentée je reconnus la déesse.

Alors je levai un à un les voiles. Dans l'allée, en agitant les bras. Par la plaine, où je l'ai dénoncée au coq. A la

Idle youth enslaved by everything; I have destroyed my life through sensitivity. Ah, let the time come when hearts fall in love!

Dawn

I HAVE clasped the summer dawn.

Nothing moved as yet on the brow of the palaces. The water was dead. The camps of shadows did not leave the road in the wood. I walked, awakening warm and living breaths, and the precious stones watched, and the wings rose noiselessly.

The first venture, on the path already filled with cool, pale radiance, was a flower who told me her name.

I laughed at the blond wasserfall dishevelling its hair through the pine trees: on the silver summit I recognized the goddess.

Then one by one I raised the veils. In the path shaking my arms. On the plain, where I denounced her to the cock. In the great city

grand'ville, elle fuyait parmi les clochers et les dômes, et, courant comme un mendiant sur les quais de marbre, je la chassais.

En haut de la route, près d'un bois de lauriers, je l'ai entourée avec ses voiles amassés, et j'ai senti un peu son immense corps. L'aube et l'enfant tombèrent au bas du bois.

Au réveil, il était midi.

Being Beauteous

Devant une neige, un Être de Beauté de haute taille. Des sifflements de mort et des cercles de musique sourde font monter, s'élargir et trembler comme un spectre ce corps adoré; des blessures écarlates et noires éclatent dans les chairs superbes. – Les couleurs propres de la vie se foncent, dansent, et se dégagent autour de la Vision, sur le chantier. – Et les frissons s'élèvent et grondent, et la saveur forcenée de ces effets se chargeant avec les sifflements mortels et les rauques musiques que le monde, loin

she fled among the belfries and the domes; and, running like a beggar on the marble quays, I pursued her.

At the top of the road, near a laurel wood, I enclosed her with her clustering veils, and I felt her vast body a little. The dawn and the child fell at the foot of the wood.

At the awakening it was noon.

Being Beauteous

In front of snow, a beauteous Being tall in stature. Hisses of death and rounds of subdued music make this sweet body rise, stretch, and tremble like a ghost; scarlet and black wounds burst forth in the magnificent flesh. The very colours of life deepen, dance, and stand out around the vision, on the stocks. And the shudders arise and mutter, and the frantic flavour of these effects being burdened with the mortal hisses and harsh music which the world, far behind

derrière nous, lance sur notre propre mère de beauté, – elle recule, elle se dresse. Oh! nos os sont revêtus d'un nouveau corps amoureux.

*

Ô la face cendrée, l'écusson de crin, les bras de cristal! le canon sur lequel je dois m'abattre à travers la mêlée des arbres et de l'air léger!

Mauvais Sang

J'AI de mes ancêtres gaulois l'œil bleu blanc, la cervelle étroite, et la maladresse dans la lutte. Je trouve mon habillement aussi barbare que le leur. Mais je ne beurre pas ma chevelure.

Les Gaulois étaient les écorcheurs de bêtes, les brûleurs d'herbes les plus ineptes de leur temps.

D'eux, j'ai: l'idôlatrie et l'amour du sacrilège; – oh! tous les vices, colère, luxure, – magnifique, la luxure; – surtout mensonge et paresse.

J'ai horreur de tous les métiers. Maîtres et ouvriers, tous paysans, ignobles. La main à plume vaut la main à

us, hurls upon our own beauteous mother, – she draws back, she starts up. Oh, our bones are dressed in a new and loving body.

O the ashen face, the horsehair shield, the crystal arms! The cannon on which I must pounce through the scuffling of the trees and the light air.

Bad Blood

I HAVE the blue white eye, the scanty brain and the clumsiness in battle of my Gaulish ancestors. I find my clothing as barbarous as theirs. But I do not butter my hair.

The Gauls were the most unskilful flayers of animals and burners of grass of their time.

From them I have: idolatry and the love of sacrilege; – Oh! all the vices: anger, lust – magnificent lust – above all deceit and idleness.

I hate all trades. Masters and workmen are all peasants, all disgusting. The hand on the pen is the same as the hand on the

charrue. – Quel siècle à mains! – Je n'aurai jamais ma main. Après, la domesticité mène trop loin. L'honnêteté de la mendicité me navre. Les criminels dégoûtent comme des châtrés: moi, je suis intact, et ça m'est égal.

Mais! qui a fait ma langue perfide tellement, qu'elle ait guidé et sauvegardé jusqu'ici ma paresse? Sans me servir pour vivre même de mon corps, et plus oisif que le crapaud, j'ai vécu partout. Pas une famille d'Europe que je ne connaisse. – J'entends des familles comme la mienne, qui tiennent tout de la déclaration des Droits de l'Homme. – J'ai connu chaque fils de famille!

*

Si j'avais des antécédents à un point quelconque de l'histoire de France!

Mais non, rien.

Il m'est bien évident que j'ai toujours été race inférieure. Je ne puis comprendre la révolte. Ma race ne se souleva jamais que pour piller: tels les loups à la bête qu'ils n'ont pas tuée.

plough. – What a century for hands! – I shall never be lucky. Afterwards, domesticity leads too far. The honesty of beggars revolts me. Criminals are as disgusting as eunuchs: I myself am intact, and it is all the same to me.

But! Who made my tongue so treacherous that up till now it has guided and safeguarded my laziness? Without using even my body to live and more idle than the toad, I have lived everywhere. Not a family in Europe that I do not know. – I mean families like my own who have their very existence from the Declaration of the Rights of Man. – I have known every mother's son!

*

If I had antecedents at some point or other of French history! But no, nothing.

It is quite clear to me that I have always been an inferior race. I cannot understand revolt. My race never rose except to plunder: like wolves on the beast they have not killed.

Je me rappelle l'histoire de la France, fille aînée de l'Église. J'aurais fait, manant, le voyage de terre sainte; j'ai dans la tête des routes dans les plaines souabes, des vues de Byzance, des remparts de Solyme; le culte de Marie, l'attendrissement sur le Crucifié s'éveillent en moi parmi mille féeries profanes. – Je suis assis, lépreux, sur les pots cassés et les orties, au pied d'un mur rongé par le soleil. – Plus tard, reître, j'aurais bivaqué sous les nuits d'Allemagne.

Ah! encore: je danse le sabbat dans une rouge clairière, avec des vieilles et des enfants.

Je ne me souviens pas plus loin que cette terre-ci et le christianisme. Je n'en finirais pas de me revoir dans ce passé. Mais toujours seul; sans famille; même, quelle langue parlais-je? Je ne me vois jamais dans les conseils du Christ; ni dans les conseils des Seigneurs, – représentants du Christ.

Qu'étais-je au siècle dernier: je ne me retrouve qu'aujourd'hui. Plus de vagabonds, plus de guerres vagues. La race inférieure a tout couvert – le peuple, comme on dit, la raison; la nation et la science.

I remember the history of France, eldest daughter of the church. As a peasant I would have journeyed to the holy land; in my head I have roads in Swabian plains, views of Byzantium, ramparts of Jerusalem; the cult of Mary, pity for the Crucified awaken within me among a thousand profane fairy-tales. – I am seated as a leper on broken sherds and nettles at the foot of a wall eaten by the sun. – Later I would have bivouacked like a trooper beneath German nights.

Ah! once again: I am dancing the sabbath in a red clearing with old women and children.

I do not remember myself further back than this earth and Christianity. I could never see myself often enough in that past. But always alone without a family; what language did I speak even? I never see myself in Christ's councils; nor in the councils of the Lords – the representatives of Christ.

What was I last century: I only rediscover myself to-day. No more tramps, no more vague wars. The inferior race has covered everything – the people, as they say, reason; the nation and science.

Oh! la science! On a tout repris. Pour le corps et pour l'âme, – le viatique, – on a la médecine et la philosophie, – les remèdes de bonnes femmes et les chansons populaires arrangées. Et les divertissements des princes et les jeux qu'ils interdisaient! Géographie, cosmographie, mécanique, chimie! ...

La science, la nouvelle noblesse! Le progrès. Le monde marche! Pourquoi ne tournerait-il pas?

C'est la vision des nombres. Nous allons à *l'Esprit*. C'est très certain, c'est oracle, ce que je dis. Je comprends, et ne sachant m'expliquer sans paroles païennes, je voudrais me taire.

*

Le sang païen revient! L'Esprit est proche, pourquoi Christ ne m'aide-t-il pas, en donnant à mon âme noblesse et liberté? Hélas, l'Évangile a passé! l'Évangile! l'Évangile.

J'attends Dieu avec gourmandise. Je suis de race inférieure de toute éternité.

Oh, science! We have begun everything again. For body and soul – the viaticum – we have medicine and philosophy – old wives' cures and arrangements of popular songs. And the pastimes of princes and the games they forbade! Geography, cosmography, mechanics, chemistry! ...

Science, the new nobility! Progress. The world goes forward! Why should it not turn back? This is the vision of numbers. We are going towards the *Spirit*. What I say is quite certain, oracular. I understand and, not knowing how to make myself clear without pagan words, I should like to be silent.

*

The pagan blood returns! The Spirit is near, why does not Christ help me by giving my soul nobility and freedom? Alas, the Gospel has passed away! The Gospel! The Gospel.

I await God greedily. I have belonged to an inferior race from all eternity.

Me voici sur la plage armoricaine. Que les villes s'allument dans le soir. Ma journée est faite; je quitte l'Europe. L'air marin brûlera mes poumons; les climats perdus me tanneront. Nager, broyer l'herbe, chasser, fumer surtout; boire des liqueurs fortes comme du métal bouillant, — comme faisaient ces chers ancêtres autour des feux.

Je reviendrai, avec des membres de fer, la peau sombre, l'œil furieux: sur mon masque, on me jugera d'une race forte. J'aurai de l'or: je serai oisif et brutal. Les femmes soignent ces féroces infirmes retour des pays chauds. Je serai mêlé aux affaires politiques. Sauvé.

Maintenant je suis maudit, j'ai horreur de la patrie. Le meilleur, c'est un sommeil bien ivre, sur la grève.

*

On ne part pas. — Reprenons les chemins d'ici, chargé de mon vice, le vice qui a poussé ses racines de souffrance à mon côté, dès l'âge de raison – qui monte au ciel, me bat, me renverse, me traîne.

Here I am on the Armorican shore. Let the towns light up in the evening. My day is done; I am leaving Europe. The sea air will burn my lungs; remote climes will tan me. To swim, crush the grass, hunt, smoke above all; drink liquors strong as boiling metal – as my dear ancestors did around the fire.

I shall return with iron limbs, dark skin, fierce eye: by my mask I shall be judged to belong to a strong race. I shall have gold: I shall be lazy and brutal. Women look after these fierce invalids come back from hot countries. I shall be mixed up in politics. Saved.

Now I am accursed, I detest my country. The best is a drunken sleep on the beach.

*

There are no departures. – Let us take the roads of this land once again, loaded with my vice, the vice that has spread its roots of suffering in my side since the age of reason – that climbs to heaven, beats me, overthrows me, drags me.

268

La dernière innocence et la dernière timidité. C'est dit. Ne pas porter au monde mes dégoûts et mes trahisons.

Allons! La marche, le fardeau, le désert, l'ennui et la colère.

A qui me louer? Quelle bête faut-il adorer? Quelle sainte image attaque-t-on? Quels cœurs briserai-je? Quel mensonge dois-je tenir? – Dans quel sang marcher?

Plutôt, se garder de la justice. – La vie dure, l'abrutissement simple, – soulever, le poing desséché, le couvercle du cercueil, s'asseoir, s'étouffer. Ainsi point de vieillesse, ni de dangers: la terreur n'est pas française.

– Ah! je suis tellement délaissé que j'offre à n'importe quelle divine image des élans vers la perfection.

Ô mon abnégation, ô ma charité merveilleuse! ici-bas, pourtant!

De profundis Domine, suis-je bête!

*

Final innocence and final timidity. That is it. Not to carry my disgust and treason to the world.

Let us go! The journey, the burden, the desert, vexation, and wrath.

To whom shall I hire myself? What beast must I worship? What holy image do we attack? What hearts shall I break? What lie must I sustain? – Walk in what blood?

Preferably abstain from justice. – A hard life, pure exhaustion – to raise the coffin lid with a withered fist, to sit down and suffocate. So no old age and danger: terror is not French.

– Ah! I am so forsaken that I offer my aspirations towards perfection to any divine image.

O my abnegation, O my wonderful charity! Even down here on earth!

From the depths, Lord, I am a fool!

*

269

Encore tout enfant, j'admirais le forçat intraitable sur qui se referme toujours le bagne; je visitais les auberges et les garnis qu'il aurait sacrés par son séjour; je voyais *avec son idée* le ciel bleu et le travail fleuri de la campagne; je flairais sa fatalité dans les villes. Il avait plus de force qu'un saint, plus de bon sens qu'un voyageur – et lui, lui seul! pour témoin de sa gloire et de sa raison.

Sur les routes, par des nuits d'hiver, sans gîte, sans habits, sans pain, une voix étreignait mon cœur gelé: «Faiblesse ou force: te voilà, c'est la force. Tu ne sais ni où tu vas ni pourquoi tu vas, entre partout, réponds à tout. On ne te tuera pas plus que si tu étais cadavre.» Au matin j'avais le regard si perdu et la contenance si morte, que ceux que j'ai rencontrés *ne m'ont peut-être pas vu.*

Dans les villes la boue m'apparaissait soudainement rouge et noire, comme une glace quand la lampe circule dans la chambre voisine, comme un trésor dans la forêt! Bonne chance, criai-je, et je voyais une mer de flammes et de fumée au ciel; et, à gauche, à droite, toutes les richesses flambant comme un milliard de tonnerres.

While still quite a child I admired the ungovernable convict, on whom the prison always closes once again; I visited the inns and lodging-houses he had consecrated by his stay; *with his mind* I saw the blue sky and the flowery toil of the countryside; I scented his destiny in the towns. He had more strength than a saint, more common-sense than a traveller – and himself, himself alone! for witness of his fame and right reason.

On the roads on winter nights, without lodging, without clothes, without bread, a voice gripped my frozen heart: 'Weakness or strength: there you are, that is strength. You do not know where you are going or why you are going, enter everywhere, answer everything. You will no more be killed than if you were a corpse.' In the morning I had such a doomed look and such a dead face, that those I met *perhaps did not see me.*

In the towns the mud suddenly seemed red and black to me, like a looking-glass when a lamp is carried round the neighbouring room, like a hoard of treasure in the forest! Good luck, I shouted, and saw an ocean of flame and smoke in the sky; and, to left and right, all the wealth blazing like a thousand million lightnings.

Mais l'orgie et la camaraderie des femmes m'étaient interdites. Pas même un compagnon. Je me voyais devant une foule exaspérée, en face du peloton d'exécution, pleurant du malheur qu'ils n'aient pu comprendre, et pardonnant! – Comme Jeanne d'Arc! – «Prêtres, professeurs, maîtres, vous vous trompez en me livrant à la justice. Je n'ai jamais été de ce peuple-ci; je n'ai jamais été chrétien; je suis de la race qui chantait dans le supplice; je ne comprends pas les lois; je n'ai pas le sens moral, je suis une brute: vous vous trompez ...»

Oui, j'ai les yeux fermés à votre lumière. Je suis une bête, un nègre. Mais je puis être sauvé. Vous êtes de faux nègres, vous maniaques, féroces, avares. Marchand, tu es nègre; magistrat, tu es nègre; général, tu es nègre; empereur, vieille démangeaison, tu es nègre: tu as bu d'une liqueur non taxée, de la fabrique de Satan. – Ce peuple est inspiré par la fièvre et le cancer. Infirmes et vieillards sont tellement respectables qu'ils demandent à être bouillis. – Le plus malin est de quitter ce continent, où la folie rôde pour pourvoir d'otages ces misérables. J'entre au vrai royaume des enfants de Cham.

But orgies and the company of women were forbidden me. Not even a companion. I saw myself in front of an enraged crowd, before a firing squad, weeping because it was bad luck they could not understand me, and pardoning! – Like Joan of Arc! – 'Priests, professors, masters, you are mistaken in handing me over to justice. I was never one of this people; I was never Christian; I belong to the race that sung while under torture; I do not understand the laws; I have no moral sense, I am a brute: you are mistaken. ...'

Yes, I have my eyes closed to your light. I am a beast, a black. But I can be saved. You are false blacks, you are maniacal, fierce, avaricious. Merchant, you are a black; magistrate, you are a black; general, you are a black; emperor, old scab, you are a black; you have drunk an untaxed spirit from Satan's factory. – This people is inspired by fever and cancer. Invalids and old men are so respectable that they ask to be boiled. – The cleverest thing is to leave this continent, where madness prowls to provide these wretches with hostages. I am entering into the real kingdom of the children of Ham.

Connais-je encore la nature? me connais-je? – *Plus de mots*. J'ensevelis les morts dans mon ventre. Cris, tambour, danse, danse, danse, danse! Je ne vois même pas l'heure où, les blancs débarquant, je tomberai au néant.

Faim, soif, cris, danse, danse, danse, danse!

*

Les blancs débarquent. Le canon! Il faut se soumettre au baptême, s'habiller, travailler.

J'ai reçu au cœur le coup de la grâce. Ah! je ne l'avais pas prévu!

Je n'ai point fait le mal. Les jours vont m'être légers, le repentir me sera épargné. Je n'aurai pas eu les tourments de l'âme presque morte au bien, où remonte la lumière sévère comme les cierges funéraires. Le sort du fils de famille, cercueil prématuré couvert de limpides larmes. Sans doute la débauche est bête, le vice est bête; il faut jeter la pourriture à l'écart. Mais l'horloge ne sera pas arrivée à ne plus sonner que l'heure de la pure douleur! Vais-je être enlevé comme un enfant, pour jouer au paradis dans l'oubli de tout le malheur!

Do I know nature yet? Do I know myself? – *No more words*. I bury the dead in my belly. Shrieks, drums, dance, dance, dance, dance! I do not even see the hour when, as the whites land, I shall fall in to nothingness.

Hunger, thirst, shrieks, dance, dance, dance, dance!

*

The whites are landing. The cannon! We must submit to baptism, to wearing clothes, to working.

I have received the stroke of grace in my heart. Ah, I had not foreseen it!

I have done no evil. My days will be light, repentance will be spared me. I shall not have had the pangs of the soul nearly dead to goodness, where the light rises up as stern as funeral candles. The fate of the boy born with a silver spoon in his mouth, a premature coffin covered with limpid tears. No doubt, debauch is stupid, vice is stupid; we must throw decay aside. But the clock will not yet have come to only striking the hour of pure grief! Am I to be carried off like a child, to play in paradise forgetting all misfortune!

Vite! est-il d'autres vies? – Le sommeil dans la richesse est impossible. La richesse a toujours été bien publique. L'amour divin seul octroie les clefs de la science. Je vois que la nature n'est qu'un spectacle de bonté. Adieu chimères, idéals, erreurs.

Le chant raisonnable des anges s'élève du navire sauveur: c'est l'amour divin. – Deux amours! je puis mourir de l'amour terrestre, mourir de dévouement. J'ai laissé des âmes dont la peine s'accroîtra de mon départ! Vous me choisissez parmi les naufragés; ceux qui restent sont-ils pas mes amis?

Sauvez-les!

La raison m'est née. Le monde est bon. Je bénirai la vie. J'aimerai mes frères. Ce ne sont plus des promesses d'enfance. Ni l'espoir d'échapper à la vieillesse et à la mort. Dieu fait ma force, et je loue Dieu.

*

Quick! Are there other lives? – Sleep amid wealth is impossible. Wealth has always been quite public. Divine love alone grants the keys of knowledge. I see that nature is only a spectacle of goodness. Farewell fancies, ideals, mistakes.

The reasonable song of angels arises from the rescuing ship: it is divine love. – Two loves! I can die of earthly love and die of devotion. I have left behind souls whose pain will be increased by my departure! You choose me out among the shipwrecked; are not those who remain my friends?

Save them!

Reason is born in me. The world is good. I shall bless life. I shall love my brothers. These are no childish promises. Nor the hope of escaping old age and death. God is my strength, and I praise God.

*

L'ennui n'est plus mon amour. Les rages, les débauches, la folie, dont je sais tous les élans et les désastres, – tout mon fardeau est déposé. Apprécions sans vertige l'étendue de mon innocence.

Je ne serais plus capable de demander le réconfort d'une bastonnade. Je ne me crois pas embarqué pour une noce avec Jésus-Christ pour beau-père.

Je ne suis pas prisonnier de ma raison. J'ai dit: Dieu. Je veux la liberté dans le salut: comment la poursuivre? Les goûts frivoles m'ont quitté. Plus besoin de dévouement ni d'amour divin. Je ne regrette pas le siècle des cœurs sensibles. Chacun a sa raison, mépris et charité: je retiens ma place au sommet de cette angélique échelle de bon sens.

Quant au bonheur établi, domestique ou non ... non, je ne peux pas. Je suis trop dissipé, trop faible. La vie fleurit par le travail, vieille vérité: moi, ma vie n'est pas assez pesante, elle s'envole et flotte loin au-dessus de l'action, ce cher point du monde.

Boredom is no more my love. The rages, the debauches, the madness of all whose aspirations and disasters I know – all my burden is unloaded. Let us appreciate without vertigo the extent of my innocence.

I would no longer be capable of asking for the comfort of a beating. I do not believe that I have started out for a wedding with Jesus Christ for father-in-law.

I am not the prisoner of my reason. I have said: God. I want freedom in salvation: how am I to reach it? Frivolous tastes have left me. No more need of devotion or divine love. I do not regret the century of tender hearts. Everyone has his reason, his scorn, and his charity: I keep my place at the top of this angelic ladder of common sense.

As to established happiness, domestic or not ... no, I cannot. I am too dissipated, too weak. Life flowers through work, that is an old truth: as to me, my life is not heavy enough, it flies away and floats far above action, that precious part of the world.

Comme je deviens vieille fille, à manquer du courage d'aimer la mort!

Si Dieu m'accordait le calme céleste, áerien, la prière, – comme les anciens saints. – Les saints! des forts! les anachorètes, des artistes comme il n'en faut plus!

Farce continuelle! Mon innocence me ferait pleurer. La vie est la farce à mener par tous.

*

Assez! voici la punition. – *En marche!*

Ah! les poumons brûlent, les tempes grondent! la nuit roule dans mes yeux, par ce soleil! le cœur ... les membres. ...

Où va-t-on? au combat? Je suis faible! les autres avancent. Les outils, les armes ... le temps! ...

Feu! feu sur moi! Là! ou je me rends. – Lâches! – Je me tue! Je me jette aux pieds des chevaux!

Ah! ...

– Je m'y habituerai.

Ce serait la vie française, le sentier de l'honneur!

What an old spinster I am becoming, lacking the courage to love death!

If God granted me heavenly, airy tranquillity, prayer – like the old saints. – The saints! Strong men! The hermits, artists such as we no longer need!

What a continual farce! My innocence would make me weep. Life is a farce to be played by everyone.

*

Enough! Here is the punishment. – *Forward!*

Ah! My lungs are burning, my temples throbbing! Night rolls over my eyes, in this sun! My heart ... my limbs. ...

Where are we going? To battle? I am weak! The others are advancing. Tools, arms ... the weather! ...

Fire! Fire on me! There! Or I surrender. – Cowards! – I am killing myself! I throw myself at the horses' feet!

Ah! ...

– I shall get used to it.

This might be French life, the path of honour!

Matin

N'eus-je pas *une fois* une jeunesse aimable, heroïque, fabuleuse, à écrire sur des feuilles d'or, – trop de chance! Par quel crime, par quelle erreur, ai-je mérité ma faiblesse actuelle? Vous qui prétendez que des bêtes poussent des sanglots de chagrin, que des malades désespèrent, que des morts rêvent mal, tâchez de raconter ma chute et mon sommeil. Moi, je ne puis pas plus m'expliquer que le mendiant avec ses continuels *Pater* et *Ave Maria*. *Je ne sais plus parler!*

Pourtant, aujourd'hui, je crois avoir fini la relation de mon enfer. C'était bien l'enfer; l'ancien, celui dont le fils de l'homme ouvrit les portes.

Du même désert, à la même nuit, toujours mes yeux las se réveillent à l'étoile d'argent, toujours, sans que s'émeuvent les Rois de la vie, les trois mages, le cœur, l'âme, l'esprit. Quand irons-nous, par delà les grèves et les monts, saluer la naissance du travail nouveau, la sagesse nouvelle, la fuite des tyrans et des démons, la fin de la superstition, adorer – les premiers! — Noël sur la terre?

Morning

Did I not *once* have a pleasant, heroic, legendary youth to be written on leaves of gold – I was too lucky! Through what crime, what mistake have I deserved my present weakness? You who claim that beasts utter sobs of anger, that sick men despair, that the dead dream bad dreams, try to narrate my fall and my sleep. I can no more make myself clear than the beggar with his continual *Paters* and *Ave Marias*. *I no longer know how to speak!*

Yet to-day I think I have finished the account of my hell. It was really hell; the old one whose gates were opened by the son of man.

From the same desert, on the same night, my tired eyes always awaken to the silver star, always without the Kings of life, the three Wise Men from the east, the heart, soul and mind, being stirred. When shall we go, beyond the shores and mountains, to hail the birth of new labour, new wisdom, the flight of tyrants and demons, the end of superstition, to worship – for the first time! – Christmas on earth?

Le chant des cieux, la marche des peuples! Esclaves, ne maudissons pas la vie.

Adieu

L'AUTOMNE déjà! – Mais pourquoi regretter un éternel soleil, si nous sommes engagés à la découverte de la clarté divine, – loin des gens qui meurent sur les saisons.

L'automne. Notre barque élevée dans les brumes immobiles tourne vers le port de la misère, la cité énorme au ciel taché de feu et de boue. Ah! les haillons pourris, le pain trempé de pluie, l'ivresse, les mille amours qui m'ont crucifié! Elle ne finira donc point cette goule reine de millions d'âmes et de corps morts *et qui seront jugés*! Je me revois la peau rongée par la boue et la peste, des vers plein les cheveux et les aisselles et encore de plus gros vers dans le cœur, étendu parmi les inconnus sans âge, sans sentiment. ... J'aurais pu y mourir. ... L'affreuse évocation! J'exècre la misère.

Et je redoute l'hiver parce que c'est la saison du confort!

The song of the heavens, the advance of the peoples! Slaves, let us not blaspheme life.

Good-bye

AUTUMN already! – But why regret an everlasting sun, if we are engaged on the discovery of divine light – far from people dying by the seasons.

Autumn. Our ship raised in motionless mists turns towards the port of wretchedness, the vast city with its sky blotted with fire and mud. Ah! the rotten rags, the rain-soaked bread, the drunkenness, the thousand loves that crucified me! This ghoul, queen of millions of souls and bodies dead *and to be judged*, shall have no end then? Again I see my skin eaten by mud and plague, my hair and armpits full of worms, and larger worms still in my heart, see myself stretched out among strangers without age or feeling. ... I could have died there. ... What a frightful evocation! I hate misery.

And I fear the winter because it is the season of comfort!

– Quelquefois je vois au ciel des plages sans fin couvertes de blanches nations en joie. Un grand vaisseau d'or, au-dessus de moi, agite ses pavillons multicolores sous les brises du matin. J'ai créé toutes les fêtes, tous les triomphes, tous les drames. J'ai essayé d'inventer de nouvelles fleurs, de nouveaux astres, de nouvelles chairs, de nouvelles langues. J'ai cru acquérir des pouvoirs surnaturels. Eh bien! je dois enterrer mon imagination et mes souvenirs! Une belle gloire d'artiste et de conteur emportée!

Moi! moi qui me suis dit mage ou ange, dispensé de toute morale, je suis rendu au sol, avec un devoir à chercher, et la réalité rugueuse à étreindre! Paysan!

Suis-je trompé? la charité serait-elle sœur de la mort, pour moi?

Enfin, je demanderai pardon pour m'être nourri de mensonge. Et allons.

Mais pas une main amie! et où puiser le secours?

*

– Sometimes I see in the sky endless shores covered with white, joyful peoples. Above me a great gold ship waves its multi-coloured flags in the morning breezes. I created every feast, every triumph, every drama. I tried to invent new flowers, new stars, new flesh, new tongues. I thought to acquire supernatural powers. Well! I must bury my imagination and my memories! The fair fame of artist and story-teller is carried away!

I! I, who called myself a mage or an angel, excused all morality, I am returned to earth with a duty to discover and rough reality to grip! Peasant!

Am I deceived? Might charity be the sister of death for me?

Lastly, I shall ask pardon for having fed upon lies. And let us go forward.

But not a friendly hand! And where to find help?

*

Oui, l'heure nouvelle est au moins très-sévère.

Car je puis dire que la victoire m'est acquise: les grince-
ments de dents, les sifflements de feu, les soupirs empestés
se modèrent. Tous les souvenirs immondes s'effacent.
Mes derniers regrets détalent, – des jalousies pour les
mendiants, les brigands, les amis de la mort, les arriérés
de toutes sortes. – Damnés, si je me vengeais!

Il faut être absolument moderne.

Point de cantiques: tenir le pas gagné. Dure nuit! le
sang séché fume sur ma face, et je n'ai rien derrière moi,
que cet horrible arbrisseau! ... Le combat spirituel est
aussi brutal que la bataille d'hommes; mais la vision de la
justice est le plaisir de Dieu seul.

Cependant c'est la veille. Recevons tous les influx de
vigueur et de tendresse réelle. Et à l'aurore, armés d'une
ardente patience, nous entrerons aux splendides villes.

Que parlais-je de main amie! Un bel avantage, c'est que
je puis rire des vieilles amours mensongères, et frapper de
honte ces couples menteurs, – j'ai vu l'enfer des femmes
là-bas; – et il me sera loisible de *posséder la vérité dans une
âme et un corps*.

Yes, at least the new time is very stern.

For I can say that victory is mine: the grinding of teeth, the hissing of fire, the stinking breath become less. All unclean memories
are blotted out. My last regrets take themselves off – envy for beggars, brigands, friends of death, every kind of backwardness. –
Damned, if I took my revenge!

We must be absolutely modern.

No canticles: keep the foothold we have won. A bitter night!
The dried blood smokes on my face, and I have nothing behind me,
but this horrible bush! ... Spiritual battle is as brutal as that of men;
but the vision of justice is God's pleasure alone.

Meanwhile it is the evening. Let us accept every influx of vigour
and real tenderness. And at dawn, armed with burning patience, we
shall enter the glorious towns.

Why did I speak of a friendly hand! It is a great advantage that I
can laugh at old, deceitful loves and strike those lying couples with
shame – I saw the women's hell down there below – and it will be
lawful for me to *possess truth in a soul and body*.

ÉMILE VERHAEREN

Les Paysans

CES hommes de labour, que Greuze affadissait
Dans les molles couleurs de paysanneries,
Si proprets dans leur mise et si roses, que c'est
Motif gai de les voir, parmi les sucreries
D'un salon Louis-Quinze animer des pastels,
Les voici noirs, grossiers, bestiaux – ils sont tels.

Entre eux, ils sont parqués par villages; en somme,
Les gens des bourgs voisins sont déjà l'étranger,
L'intrus qu'on doit haïr, l'ennemi fatal, l'homme
Qu'il faut tromper, qu'il faut leurrer, qu'il faut gruger.
La patrie? Allons donc! Qui d'entre eux croit en elle?
Elle leur prend des gars pour les armer soldats,
Elle ne leur est point la terre maternelle,
La terre fécondée au travail de leurs bras.
La patrie! on l'ignore au fond de leur campagne.
Ce qu'ils voient vaguement dans un coin de cerveau,
C'est le roi, l'homme en or, fait comme Charlemagne,

The Peasants

THESE men of toil whom Greuze painted insipidly in the soft colours of peasant scenes, so neat in their dress and so pink that it makes a gay design to see them enliven the pastels amid the chocolate-box decorations of a Louis Quinze drawing-room – here they are – dark, coarse, bestial – they are like that.

Among themselves they are penned in villages: in short, the people from the neighbouring market towns are already foreigners, intruders who must be hated, destined enemies, men who must be deceived, ensnared, gobbled up.

The country? Come now! Which of them believes in it? It takes their lads to arm them as soldiers; for them it is not mother earth, land made fertile by the work of their hands. The country! In the depth of their fields they know nothing of it. What they hazily see in a corner of their brains is the king, the man in gold, like Charle-

Assis dans le velours frangé de son manteau;
C'est tout un apparat de glaives, de couronnes,
Écussonnant les murs de palais lambrissés,
Que gardent des soldats avec sabre à dragonnes.
Ils ne savent que ça du pouvoir. – C'est assez.
Au reste, leur esprit, balourd en toute chose,
Marcherait en sabots à travers droit, devoir,
Justice et liberté – l'instinct les ankylose;
Un almanach crasseux, voilà tout leur savoir;
Et s'ils ont entendu rugir, au loin, les villes,
Les révolutions les ont tant effrayés,
Que, dans la lutte humaine, ils restent les serviles,
De peur, s'ils se cabraient, d'être un jour les broyés.

Le Moulin

LE moulin tourne au fond du soir, très lentement,
Sur un ciel de tristesse et de mélancolie;
Il tourne et tourne, et sa voile, couleur de lie,
Est triste et faible et lourde et lasse, infiniment.

magne, seated in the fringed velvet of his robe; all the pageantry of
swords and crowns hanging in escutcheons on the walls of panelled
palaces guarded by soldiers with tasselled sabres. That is all they
know of the state. – It is enough. In other respects their mind, thick-
witted in everything, would walk in clogs through right, duty,
justice, and liberty – instinct paralyses them; all their knowledge is
a dirty almanack; and, if they have heard the towns roaring far off,
the revolutions have frightened them so much that they remain
slaves in the human struggle for fear of being crushed one day if
they rebelled.

The Mill

VERY slowly the mill turns in the depth of the evening against a
sorrowful, melancholy sky; it turns and turns, and its purple sail
is infinitely sad and weak, heavy and tired.

Depuis l'aube, ses bras, comme des bras de plainte,
Se sont tendus et sont tombés; et les voici
Qui retombent encor, là-bas, dans l'air noirci
Et le silence entier de la nature éteinte.

Un jour souffrant d'hiver sur les hameaux s'endort,
Les nuages sont las de leurs voyages sombres,
Et le long des taillis qui ramassent leurs ombres,
Les ornières s'en vont vers un horizon mort.

Autour d'un vieil étang, quelques huttes de hêtre
Très misérablement sont assises en rond;
Une lampe de cuivre éclaire leur plafond
Et glisse une lueur aux coins de leur fenêtre.

Et dans la plaine immense, au bord du flot dormeur,
Ces torpides maisons, sous le ciel bas, regardent,
Avec les yeux fendus de leurs vitres hagardes,
Le vieux moulin qui tourne et, las, qui tourne et meurt.

Since dawn its arms, like arms of entreaty, have been held out
and have fallen; and here they are falling again down there in the
blackened air and the total silence of lifeless nature.

A sick winter's day sleeps above the hamlets, the clouds are tired
of their dark journeys, and along the copses that gather their
shadows the dirt tracks go towards a dead horizon.

Around an old pond some beech-wood huts are wretchedly
placed in a circle; a copper lamp lights up their ceilings and slips a
gleam to the corners of their windows.

And in the vast plain, beside the sleeping wave, these torpid
houses beneath the low sky gaze with the split eyes of their sunken
window-panes at the old mill turning, turning, alas! and dying.

La Bêche

Le gel durcit les eaux; le vent blêmit les nues.

A l'orient du pré, dans le sol rêche
Est là qui monte et grelotte, la bêche
Lamentable et nue.

— Fais une croix sur le sol jaune
Avec ta longue main,
Toi qui t'en vas, par le chemin —

La chaumière d'humidité verdâtre
Et ses deux tilleuls foudroyés
Et des cendres dans l'âtre
Et sur le mur encor le piédestal de plâtre,
Mais la Vierge tombée à terre.

— Fais une croix vers les chaumières
Avec ta longue main de paix et de lumière —

Des crapauds morts dans les ornières infinies
Et des poissons dans les roseaux

The Spade

The frost hardens the waters; the wind makes the clouds pale.

To the east of the field in the harsh soil is the bare, mournful spade rising and shivering.

Make a cross with your long hand on the yellow earth, you who depart by the road.

The cottage is green with damp and its two lime-trees are blasted and there are ashes in the hearth and the plaster pedestal is still on the wall, but the Virgin has fallen to the ground.

Make a cross towards the cottages with your long hand of peace and light.

There are dead toads in the infinite furrows and fish in the reeds,

Et puis un cri toujours plus pauvre et lent d'oiseau,
Infiniment, là-bas, un cri à l'agonie.

– Fais une croix avec ta main
Pitoyable, sur le chemin –

Dans la lucarne vide de l'étable
L'araignée a tissé l'étoile de poussière;
Et la ferme sur la rivière,
Par à travers ses chaumes lamentables,
Comme des bras aux mains coupées,
Croise ses poutres d'outre en outre.

– Fais une croix sur le demain,
Définitive, avec ta main –

Un double rang d'arbres et de troncs nus sont abbatus,
Au long des routes en déroutes,
Les villages – plus même de cloches pour y sonner
Le hoquetant *dies irae*
Désespéré, vers l'écho vide et ses bouches cassées.

– Fais une croix aux quatre coins des horizons.

and then there is a bird's cry, ever weaker and slower, infinitely, a
death cry over there.
 Make a cross on the road with your piteous hand.
 The spider has spun the star of dust in the empty skylight of the
stable; and the farm on the stream crosses its beams through and
through its doleful thatch like arms with the hands cut off.
 Make a cross over to-morrow, a final cross with your hand.
 A double row of trees and bare trunks are cut down along ruined
roads, the villages – not even any more bells to sound the despairing, hiccoughing *dies irae* to the empty echo and its broken mouths.
 Make a cross to the four corners of the horizon.

Car c'est la fin des champs et c'est la fin des soirs;
Le deuil au fond des cieux tourne, comme des meules,
Ses soleils noirs;
Et des larves éclosent seules
Aux flancs pourris des femmes qui sont mortes.

A l'orient du pré, dans le sol rêche,
Sur le cadavre épars des vieux labours,
Domine là, et pour toujours,
Plaque de fer clair, latte de bois froid,
La bêche.

Vers le futur

Ô RACE humaine aux destins d'or vouée,
As-tu senti de quel travail formidable et battant,
Soudainement, depuis cent ans,
Ta force immense est secouée?

L'acharnement à mieux chercher, à mieux savoir,
Fouille comme à nouveau l'ample forêt des êtres,
Et malgré la broussaille où tel pas s'enchevêtre
L'homme conquiert sa loi des droits et des devoirs.

For it is the end of the fields and the end of the evenings; sorrow
turns its black suns like millstones in the depth of the skies; and
only maggots bring forth in the rotten sides of women who are
dead.
    To the east of the field in the harsh soil, over the scattered corpse
of old ploughlands, plate of bright steel, rod of cold wood, the
spade lords it for ever.

Towards the future

O HUMAN race vowed to golden destinies, have you felt by what
powerfully driving labour your vast strength has suddenly been
shaken for the last hundred years?
    The fury to discover more, to know more, ransacks, as if anew,
the wide forest of being, and, in spite of the briars where certain
footsteps are entangled, man conquers his law of rights and duties.

Dans le ferment, dans l'atôme, dans la poussière,
La vie énorme est recherchée et apparaît.
Tout est capté dans une infinité de rets
Que serre ou que distend l'immortelle matière.

Héros, savant, artiste, apôtre, aventurier,
Chacun troue à son tour le mur noir des mystères
Et grâce à ces labeurs groupés ou solitaires,
L'être nouveau se sent l'univers tout entier.

Et c'est vous, vous les villes,
Debout
De loin en loin, là-bas, de l'un à l'autre bout
Des plaines et des domaines,
Qui concentrez en vous assez d'humanité,
Assez de force rouge et de neuve clarté,
Pour enflammer de fièvre et de rage fécondes
Les cervelles patientes ou violentes
De ceux
Qui découvrent la règle et résument en eux
Le monde.

In the leaven, in the atom, in the dust vast life is sought and appears. Everything is snared in an infinity of nets that immortal matter compresses or distends.

Hero, scholar, artist, apostle, explorer, each one in his turn pierces the dark wall of mystery and, thanks to this collective or solitary toil, the new being feels itself the whole universe.

And it is you, you the towns, standing at intervals from one end to the other of the plains and estates, who concentrate within yourselves enough humanity, enough red strength and new light to enflame with fertile rage and fever the patient or violent brains of those who discover the rule and resume the world in themselves.

L'esprit de la campagne était l'esprit de Dieu;
Il eut la peur de la recherche et des révoltes,
Il chut; et le voici qui meurt, sous les essieux
Et sous les chars en feu des nouvelles récoltes.

La ruine s'installe et souffle aux quatre coins
D'où s'acharnent les vents, sur la plaine finie,
Tandis que la cité lui soutire de loin
Ce qui lui reste encor d'ardeur dans l'agonie.

L'usine rouge éclate où seuls brillaient les champs;
La fumée à flots noirs rase les toits d'église;
L'esprit de l'homme avance et le soleil couchant
N'est plus l'hostie en or divin qui fertilise.

Renaîtront-ils, les champs, un jour, exorcisés
De leurs erreurs, de leurs affres, de leur folie;
Jardins pour les efforts et les labeurs lassés,
Coupes de clarté vierge et de santé remplies?

Referont-ils, avec l'ancien et bon soleil,
Avec le vent, la pluie et les bêtes serviles,
En des heures de sursaut libre et de réveil,
Un monde enfin sauvé de l'emprise des villes?

The spirit of the countryside was the spirit of God; it was afraid
of discovery and revolts, it fell; and now it is dying beneath the
axle-trees and the fiery chariots of the new harvests.

Ruin sits down and blows to the four corners whence the winds
rage, over the desolate plain, while from afar the city draws away
from it what still remains of passion in its agony.

The red factory flares where the fields alone shone; the black
waves of smoke shave the church roofs; man's spirit marches on,
and the setting sun is no more the fertilizing Host in divine gold.

Will the fields one day be born again exorcized of their mistakes,
their terrors, their stupidity; gardens for tired effort and labour,
cups filled with virgin light and health?

Will they create again with the old kind sun, with the wind, the
rain, and menial animals, at hours of free uprising and awakening, a
world saved at last from the grip of the towns?

Ou bien deviendront-ils les derniers paradis
Purgés des dieux et affranchis de leurs présages,
Où s'en viendront rêver, à l'aube et aux midis,
Avant de s'endormir dans les soirs clairs, les sages?

En attendant, la vie ample se satisfait
D'être une joie humaine, effrénée et féconde;
Les droits et les devoirs? Rêves divers que fait,
Devant chaque espoir neuf, la jeunesse du monde!

JULES LAFORGUE

Locution de Pierrot

JE ne suis qu'un viveur lunaire
Qui fait des ronds dans les bassins,
Et cela, sans autre dessein
Que devenir un légendaire.

Retroussant d'un air de défi
Mes manches de mandarin pâle,
J'arrondis ma bouche et – j'exhale
Des conseils doux de Crucifix.

Or else will they become the last paradises, purged of the gods
and freed from their omens, where sages will come to dream at dawn
or noon before falling asleep in the clear evenings?

Meanwhile, abundant life is satisfied to be immoderate, fertile
human joy; rights and duties? The various dreams that the world's
youth creates before each new hope!

Pierrot's Speech

I AM only a lunar reveller making circles in ponds, and that without
any other design than to become legendary.

Tucking up my pale mandarin's sleeves with an air of defiance,
I round my mouth into a circle and ... I breathe forth gentle
Christian advice.

Ah! oui, devenir légendaire,
Au seuil des siècles charlatans!
Mais où sont les Lunes d'antan?
Et que Dieu n'est-il à refaire?

Esthétique

LA Femme mûre ou jeune fille,
J'en ai frôlé toutes les sortes,
Des faciles, des difficiles.
Voici, l'avis que j'en rapporte:

C'est des fleurs diversement mises,
Aux airs fiers ou seuls selon l'heure,
Nul cri sur elles n'a de prise;
Nous jouissons, Elle demeure.

Rien ne les tient, rien ne les fâche,
Elles veulent qu'on les trouve belles,
Qu'on le leur râle et leur rabâche,
Et qu'on les use comme telles;

Ah, yes, to become legendary on the threshold of charlatan centuries! But where are the moons of yesteryear? And why is God not to be remade?

Aesthetic

RIPE woman or young girl, I have had a brush with every kind, easy ones, difficult ones. Here is the opinion I bring back:

They are flowers variously dressed, with proud or lonely airs according to the hour; no cry has any power over them; we enjoy, She remains.

Nothing holds them, nothing angers them, they want us to find them beautiful, to croak it at them and keep on saying it and use them as such;

Sans souci de serments, de bagues,
Suçons le peu qu'elles nous donnent,
Notre respect peut être vague,
Leurs yeux sont hauts et monotones.

Cueillons sans espoirs et sans drames,
La chair vieillit après les roses;
Oh! parcourons le plus de gammes!
Car il n'ỳ a pas autre chose.

La Mélancolie de Pierrot

LE premier jour, je bois leurs yeux ennuyés ...
Je baiserais leurs pieds,
A mort. Ah! qu'elles daignent
Prendre mon cœur qui saigne!
Puis on cause. ... — et ça devient de la Pitié,
Et enfin je leur offre mon amitié.

C'est de pitié, que je m'offre en frère, en guide;
Elles, me croient timide,
Et clignent d'un œil doux:
«Un mot, je suis à vous!»

Without worrying about oaths and rings, let us suck the little
that they give us; our respect can be vague, their eyes are haughty
and monotonous.

Without hope or scenes let us pluck; after roses the flesh grows
old; Oh let us run through as many scales as possible! For there is
nothing else.

Pierrot's Melancholy

THE first day I drink their bored eyes. ... I would kiss their feet to
death. Ah, let them consent to take my bleeding heart! Then we
chat ... and it becomes pity, and at last I offer them my friendship.

It is from pity that I offer myself as brother and guide; they think
me timid and wink a gentle eye: 'A word and I am yours!' (I believe

(Je te crois.) Alors, moi, d'étaler les rides
De ce cœur, et de sourire dans le vide ...

Et soudain j'abandonne la garnison,
      Feignant de trahisons!
      (Je l'ai échappé belle!)
      Au moins, m'écrira-t-elle?
Point, et je la pleure toute la saison ...
– Ah! j'en ai assez de ces combinaisons!

Qui m'apprivoisera le cœur! belle cure ...
      Suis si vrai de nature!
      Ai la douceur des sœurs!
      Oh viens! suis pas noceur,
Serait-ce donc une si grosse aventure
Sous le soleil? dans toute cette verdure ...

L'Hiver qui vient

Blocus sentimental! Messageries du Levant! ...
Oh! tombée de la pluie! Oh! tombée de la nuit,
Oh! le vent! ...

you.) Then I begin to show the wrinkles of this heart and to smile
into the void. ...

    And suddenly I surrender the town, alleging treason! (I have
had a narrow escape!) At least she will write to me? No, and I
weep for her all that season. ... Ah, I have enough of these arrangements!

    Who will tame my heart! A fine cure. ... I am so true by nature!
I am as gentle as the nuns! Oh come! I am no rake, would it be such
a big adventure under the sun? In all this greenery. ...

Winter Coming On

Sentimental blockade! Levantine shipping companies! ... Oh
the falling of the rain! Oh the falling of the night! Oh the wind! ...

La Toussaint, la Noël, et la Nouvelle Année,
Oh, dans les bruines, toutes mes cheminées! ...
D'usines. ...

On ne peut plus s'asseoir, tous les bancs sont mouillés;
Crois-moi, c'est bien fini jusqu'à l'année prochaine,
Tous les bancs sont mouillés, tant les bois sont rouillés,
Et tant les cors ont fait ton ton, ont fait ton taine! ...

Ah! nuées accourues des côtes de la Manche,
Vous nous avez gâté notre dernier dimanche.

Il bruine;
Dans la forêt mouillée, les toiles d'araignées
Ploient sous les gouttes d'eau, et c'est leur ruine.
Soleils plénipotentiaires des travaux en blonds Pactoles
Des spectacles agricoles,
Où êtes-vous ensevelis?
Ce soir un soleil fichu gît au haut du coteau,
Gît sur le flanc, dans les genêts, sur son manteau.
Un soleil blanc comme un crachat d'estaminet
Sur une litière de jaunes genêts,
De jaunes genêts d'automne.

All Saints' Day, Christmas, and the New Year; Oh all my chimneys –
factory chimneys – in the drizzle! ...
  We can't sit down any more, all the benches are wet; believe me,
it is ended till next year; all the benches are wet, the woods have
rusted so, and the horns have blown so often: Ta-ta-, ta-ra! ...
  Ah, Clouds come from the Channel coast, you have spoiled our
last Sunday for us.
  It is drizzling; in the damp forest the spiders' webs bend beneath
the water-drops, and that is their ruin. Suns who have full power
over the labours in the fair rivers of gold of agricultural shows,
where are you buried? This evening an illshapen sun lies on the top
of the hill, lies on its side on its cloak in the broom. A sun white as
a gob of bar-room spit on a litter of yellow broom, of yellow

Et les cors lui sonnent!
Qu'il revienne ...
Qu'il revienne à lui!
Taïaut! Taïaut! et hallali!
Ô triste antienne, as-tu fini! ...
Et font les fous! ...
Et il gît là, comme une glande arrachée dans un cou,
Et il frissonne, sans personne! ...

Allons, allons, et hallali!
C'est l'Hiver bien connu qui s'amène;
Oh! les tournants des grandes routes,
Et sans petit Chaperon Rouge qui chemine! ...
Oh! leurs ornières des chars de l'autre mois,
Montant en don quichottesques rails
Vers les patrouilles des nuées en déroute
Que le vent malmène vers les transatlantiques bercails!...
Accélérons, accélérons, c'est la saison bien connue, cette
        fois.
Et le vent, cette nuit, il en a fait de belles!
Ô dégâts, ô nids, ô modestes jardinets!
Mon cœur et mon sommeil: ô échos des cognées! ...

autumn broom. And the horns call to him! Come back. ... Come
back to yourself! Tally-ho! tally-ho! And forward away! O mournful anthem, have you finished! ... And they play the fool! ... And
he lies there like a gland torn out of a neck, shivering with nobody
there! ...

    Forward, forward, and away! It is familiar winter coming on; O
the turnings of the high roads without Little Red Riding-Hood
walking there! ... O their ruts of last month's carts climbing like
quixotic rails towards the cloud patrols retreating, harried by the
wind to transatlantic folds! ... Hurry, hurry, this time it's the
familiar season. And the wind to-night has done some fine work!
O damage! O nests, O modest gardens! My heart and my slumber:
O echoes of axes! ...

Tous ces rameaux avaient encor leurs feuilles vertes,
Les sous-bois ne sont plus qu'un fumier de feuilles
      mortes;
Feuilles, folioles, qu'un bon vent vous emporte
Vers les étangs par ribambelles,
Ou pour le feu du garde-chasse,
Ou les sommiers des ambulances
Pour les soldats loin de la France.

C'est la saison, c'est la saison, la rouille envahit les masses,
La rouille ronge en leurs spleens kilométriques
Les fils télégraphiques des grandes routes où nul ne passe.

Les cors, les cors, les cors – mélancoliques! ...
Mélancoliques! ...
S'en vont, changeant de ton,
Changeant de ton et de musique,
Ton ton, ton taine, ton ton! ...
Les cors, les cors, les cors! ...
S'en sont allés au vent du Nord.

Je ne puis quitter ce ton: que d'échos! ...
C'est la saison, c'est la saison, adieu vendanges! ...
Voici venir les pluies d'une patience d'ange,

All those boughs still had their green leaves; the undergrowth is
nothing more than a compost heap of dead ones; leaves and clusters
of little leaves, may a good wind carry you away in long trails towards the ponds, either for the gamekeeper's fire or else for the mat-
tresses of ambulances for the soldiers far from France.

It's the season, it's the season; rust attacks the sledge-hammers,
rust gnaws the telegraph wires in their kilometric spleen on the
high roads where no one passes by.

The horns, the horns, the melancholy, melancholy horns continue changing tune, changing tune and music: Ta-ta, ta-ra, ta-ta!
... The horns, the horns, the horns have passed away on the North
wind.

I cannot leave this tune: what echoes! ... It's the season, it's the
season, farewell vintages! ... Here are the rains coming angelically

Adieu vendanges, et adieu tous les paniers,
Tous les paniers Watteau des bourrées sous les marron-
    niers,
C'est la toux dans les dortoirs du lycée qui rentre,
C'est la tisane sans le foyer,
La phtisie pulmonaire attristant le quartier,
Et toute la misère des grands centres.

Mais, lainages, caoutchoucs, pharmacie, rêve,
Rideaux écartés du haut des balcons des grèves
Devant l'océan de toitures des faubourgs,
Lampes, estampes, thé, petits-fours,
Serez-vous pas mes seules amours! ...
(Oh! et puis, est-ce que tu connais, outre les pianos,
Le sobre et vespéral mystère hebdomadaire
Des statistiques sanitaires
Dans les journaux?)

Non, non! c'est la saison et la planète falote!
Que l'autan, que l'autan
Effiloche les savates que le Temps se tricote!
C'est la saison, oh déchirements! c'est la saison!
Tous les ans, tous les ans,
J'essaierai en chœur d'en donner la note.

---

patient, farewell vintages, and all the baskets – all the Watteau
hoop-petticoats in dances beneath the chestnut trees; it's the
coughing in the dormitories of the returning lycée, it's the infusions
without a fire, pulmonary phthisis afflicting the district and all the
misery of big towns.

But, woollens, rubbers, chemist's shop, dreaming, curtains
drawn back from balconies standing like shores before the suburban
ocean of roofs, lamps, prints, tea, biscuits, will you not be my only
loves! ... (Oh and then do you know, apart from the pianos, the
weekly sober, vesperal mystery of health statistics in the papers?)

No, no! It's the season and the idiot planet! Let the storm, the
storm unravel the slippers that Time knits herself! It's the season, Oh
laceration! It's the season! Every year, every year I shall try to give
its tune in chorus.

Dimanches

BREF, j'allais me donner d'un «Je vous aime»
Quand je m'avisai non sans peine
Que d'abord je ne me possédais pas bien moi-même.

(Mon Moi, c'est Galathée aveuglant Pygmalion!
Impossible de modifier cette situation.)

Ainsi donc, pauvre, pâle et piètre individu
Qui ne croit à son Moi qu'à ses moments perdus,
Je vis s'effacer ma fiancée
Emportée par le cours des choses,
Telle l'épine voit s'effeuiller,
Sous prétexte de soir sa meilleure rose.

Or, cette nuit anniversaire, toutes les Walkyries du vent
Sont revenus beugler par les fentes de ma porte:
Vae soli!
Mais, ah! qu'importe?
Il fallait m'en étourdir avant!
Trop tard! ma petite folie est morte!
Qu'importe *Vae soli!*
Je ne retrouverai plus ma petite folie.

Sundays

IN short, I was going to give myself with an 'I love you', when I realized not without anguish that, in the first place, I did not really possess myself.

(My self is Galathea blinding Pygmalion! It is impossible to change this situation.)

So then, a poor, pale and wretched creature, only believing in his self at forgotten moments, I saw my fiancée disappear, carried away by the course of things, as the briar sees its loveliest rose shed its petals under pretext of its being evening.

Now, on this anniversary night, all the Valkyries of the wind have returned to bellow through the cracks of my door: *Woe to the lonely!* But, ah! What does it matter? They should have deafened me with it before! Too late! My little folly is dead! What does *Woe to the lonely* matter! I shall not find my little folly again.

Le grand vent bâillonné,
S'endimanche enfin le ciel du matin.
Et alors, eh! allez donc, carillonnez,
Toutes cloches des bons dimanches!
Et passez layettes et collerettes et robes blanches
Dans un frou-frou de lavandes et de thym
Vers l'encens et les brioches!
Tout pour la famille, quoi! *Vae soli!* C'est certain.

La jeune demoiselle à l'ivoirin paroissien
Modestement rentre au logis.
On le voit, son petit corps bien reblanchi
Sait qu'il appartient
A un tout autre passé que le mien!

Mon corps, ô ma sœur, a bien mal à sa belle âme ...
Oh! voilà que ton piano
Me recommence, si natal maintenant!
Et ton cœur qui s'ignore s'y ânonne
En ritournelles de bastringues à tout venant,
Et ta pauvre chair s'y fait mal! ...
A moi, Walkyries!
Walkyries des hypocondries et des tueries!

With the vast wind gagged, the morning sky at last puts on its
Sunday clothes. And then, come, ring out, all you bells of fine Sun-
days! And put on baby linen and collarettes and white frocks in a
rustling of lavender and thyme towards incense and rolls! Everything for the family, eh! *Woe to the lonely!* Certainly.

The young lady with the ivory prayer-book modestly comes
back to her home. It is apparent that her little body, made all white
once again, knows that it belongs to quite another past than mine!

My body, O my sister, has quite a pain in its beautiful soul. ... O
how your piano renews me – so like a birth now! And your heart,
ignorant of itself, stammers to every comer in the burdens of dance-
halls, and your poor flesh hurts itself! ... Help, Valkyries! Valkyries
of hypochondria and slaughter!

Ah! que je te les tordrais avec plaisir,
Ce corps bijou, ce cœur à ténor,
Et te dirais leur fait, et puis encore
La manière de s'en servir
De s'en servir à deux.
Si tu voulais seulement m'approfondir ensuite un peu!

Non, non! C'est sucer la chair d'un cœur élu,
Adorer d'incurables organes
S'entrevoir avant que les tissus se fanent
En monomanes, en reclus!

Et ce n'est pas sa chair qui me serait tout.
Et je ne serais pas qu'un grand cœur pour elle,
Mais quoi s'en aller faire les fous
Dans des histoires fraternelles!
L'âme et la chair, la chair et l'âme,
C'est l'esprit édénique et fier
D'être un peu l'Homme avec la Femme.

En attendant, oh! garde-toi des coups de tête,
Oh! file ton rouet et prie et reste honnête.

Ah! How gladly I would wring them for you, that darling body,
that tenor heart, and would tell you their business, and then again
the way to use them, to use them both of us together. If you would
only look into me a little afterwards!

No, no! That would be to suck the flesh of a dedicated heart, to
adore incurable organs, to get a glimpse of one another before the
tissues wither into monomaniacs, into hermits!

And it is not her flesh that would be everything to me. And I
would be something more than a great heart for her, but how can
one go playing the fool with this talk of brotherly love! The soul
and the flesh, the flesh and the soul, it is the proud spirit of Eden to
play the Man a bit with a Woman.

Meanwhile, Oh keep yourself from rash actions, Oh spin your
wheel and pray and remain honest.

– Allons, dernier des poètes,
Toujours enfermé tu te rendras malade!
Vois, il fait beau temps, tout le monde est dehors,
Va donc acheter deux sous d'ellébore,
Ça te fera une petite promenade.

RAYMOND DE LA TAILHÈDE

Ombres

QUAND nous sommes allés vers le soleil levant
Les matins étaient blancs comme des tourterelles;
Des brouillards s'étendaient dans la pourpre du vent
Sur des rivages de roses surnaturelles,
Quand nous sommes allés vers le soleil levant.

Mais, de l'Égypte jusqu'aux îles Baléares,
Quand le ciel fut rempli des clartés de Vénus,
Nous avons oublié les légendes barbares,
Nous avons vu grandir des astres inconnus
Sur la Sicile et les quatre îles Baléares.

Come, meanest of poets, you will make yourself ill, if you are always shut up! See, the weather is fine, everyone is out of doors; then
go and buy a pennyworth of hellebore. That will make a little walk
for you.

Shadows

WHEN we went towards the rising sun, the mornings were as white
as doves; on shores of supernatural roses mists lay in the purple of
the wind, when we went towards the rising sun.
But, from Egypt to the Balearic islands, when the sky was filled
with the light of Venus, we forgot the barbarous legends and saw
unknown stars grow above Sicily and the four Balearic islands.

Et c'est la basilique immense de la Nuit,
Les étoiles dans le silence; une par une
Elles ont apparu sur la mer qui reluit,
Toujours plus pâles à travers le clair de lune
Les planètes et les étoiles de la Nuit.

Sur la plaine des mers fauves et virginales
Nous avons regardé des choses d'autrefois;
Notre âme a traversé des fêtes triomphales;
Les dieux retentissaient avec de grandes voix
Sur la forêt des mers fauves et virginales.

Dans le tourment de sa pensée il regardait
L'épanouissement de ce rêve nocturne;
Les larmes de la vie entière qu'il perdait
Montèrent de son cœur ardent et taciturne
Que dans l'effroi de sa pensée il regardait.

Alors me reposant entre ses mains si douces
Je lui dis: Pour calmer ton esprit soucieux,
Ô mon ami, toi qui jamais ne me repousses,
La douceur de ma voix adoucira tes yeux,
La douceur de mes yeux rendra tes larmes douces.

And there is the vast Basilica of the night, the stars in the silence:
one by one, they appeared above the shining sea, ever more pale
through the light of the moon, the planets and the stars of the
night.

On the plain of the tawny, virginal seas we gazed at things of
former times; our soul passed through triumphal feasts; the gods
resounded with great voices over the forest of the tawny, virginal
seas.

In his thought's torment he watched the blossoming of this night
dream; the tears of the whole life he was losing rose from his silent
passionate heart, watching it in the terror of thought.

Then resting between his gentle hands I said to him: 'To calm
your troubled mind, my friend, you who never turn me away, my
voice's sweetness will sweeten your eyes, my eyes' sweetness will
make your tears sweet.'

Mais la Nuit et la Mer s'éloignaient lentement;
La lumière montait au-dessus des royaumes,
Et nous n'avons plus vu les dieux en ce moment,
Ni les étoiles, créatrices de fantômes,
Car la Nuit et la Mer s'éloignaient lentement.

EMMANUEL SIGNORET

Les Alcyons
à M. Camille Mauclair

J'ai peur des souvenirs ...
F. VIELÉ-GRIFFIN

I

Ô PRÊTRESSE élevant sous le laurier verdâtre
Une eau d'antiques pleurs dans le creux de tes mains,
Tes yeux sacrés feront resplendir mes chemins,
Tes mains couronneront de cèdre un jeune pâtre!

But the night and the sea slowly went away; light rose above the
kingdoms, and at that time we saw the gods no more, nor the stars,
the creators of ghosts, for the night and the sea slowly went away.

The Halcyons

I fear memories. ...
F. VIELÉ-GRIFFIN

I

O PRIESTESS raising water of ancient tears in the hollow of your
hands beneath the green bay-tree, your sacred eyes will make my
paths resplendent, your hands will crown a young herdsman with
cedar!

Mes cheveux s'étendront sur les vents: mes bras nus
S'en viendront secouer les colonnes du temple!...
Pour que s'élance aux cieux et renaisse plus ample
L'éclat des lampes d'or de l'antique Vénus.

2

Sur les prés scintillaient les larmes d'une race,
Mais le soleil dorait l'urne des lys séchés,
Les parfums des bouleaux rendaient ta gorge lasse
Et près des flots bénis, nous nous sommes couchés!

Ma barque emportera sous la lune marine
Ma ténébreuse sœur plus belle que les mers,
Les flots la jetteront souvent sur ma poitrine,
Ses deux lèvres boiront mes vieux sommeils amers!

3

Car ses beaux bras d'enfant ont une étreinte telle,
Ses mains ont soulevé tant de mes vains remords
Que tous mes souvenirs tomberont devant elle
De mon cœur, en silence, ainsi que des fruits morts.

My hair will float on the wind: my bare arms will come to shake
the pillars of the temple!... So that the brilliance of the golden lamps
of ancient Venus may dart to heaven and be born more abundantly
again.

2

On the meadows there sparkled a people's tears, but the sun gilded
the urn of withered lilies, the scent of the birches made your throat
tired, and we lay down near the blessed waves!

Beneath the sea moon my ship shall carry away my shadowy
sister lovelier than the sea, the waves will often throw her on my
breast, both her lips will drink up my old bitter slumbers!

3

For her lovely childish arms have such a grip, her hands have raised
so much of my vain remorse that all my memories will fall down
before her, silently, like dead fruit from my heart.

Elle m'a réservé de si grave délices
Qu'un chant de vagues sonne à mon luth en courroux;
Ses cheveux sont des lys d'orage aux noirs calices,
Les roses du rivage ont baisé ses genoux!

4

Et je la bercerai de tels chants sur la vague
Que les chênes sur la plage tressailleront:
Les vents des mers soulèveront sa tempe vague,
Les astres printaniers parfumeront son front.

Que le chant des oiseaux de mer a d'amertume!
Vas-tu sécher encore mes pleurs de tes cheveux?
Quand tes mains ont flotté sur mon luth dans la brume
A mes tempes chantait tout le sang des aïeux!

Les Oliviers

L'AILE en fureur, l'hiver sur les monts vole et vente;
Du sang glacé des fleurs se paissent les janviers:
Votre pleine verdure étincelle vivante,
Vous, oliviers que j'aime, oliviers, oliviers!

She has kept for me such serious delights that a song of the waves sounds in my angry lute; her hair is storm lilies with black calices; the roses of the shore have kissed her knees!

4

And I shall rock her to such songs on the wave that the oaks on the shore will tremble: the sea winds will stir her misty temples, the Spring stars will perfume her brow.

What bitterness there is in the song of sea-birds! Will you dry my tears again with your hair? When your hands floated on my lute in the mist all the blood of my ancestors sung in my temples.

The Olives

ITS wing in a frenzy, winter flies and gusts upon the hills; the Januaries are fed on the frozen blood of flowers: your entire verdure sparkles with life, you, olives that I love, olives, olives!

Votre être fortuné, c'est Pallas qui l'enfante;
Sa mamelle est d'argent, jadis vous y buviez;
Vos fruits broyés trempaient de flamme et d'épouvante
Les muscles des lutteurs par les dieux enviés.

Les siècles garderont ma voix, et d'âge en âge
Mon front resplendira sous un triple feuillage;
Car à mes beaux lauriers, à mes myrtes nouveaux,

Vous dont le sang nourrit un peuple ardent de lampes,
Sacrés oliviers d'or, vous joignez vos rameaux
Pour courber la couronne immortelle à mes tempes.

La Souffrance des Eaux: Élégie 2

Au cimetière de Tivoli.

La colonnade en marbre éclate sur le ciel:
Sur les cyprès fleuris puisant un sombre miel
Erre un troupeau léger d'abeilles rougissantes,
La source à la clarté joint ses ondes naissantes,

It is Pallas that brings forth your happy being; her breast is of silver; formerly you drank at it; your crushed fruits soaked with flame and terror the muscles of wrestlers envied by the gods.

The centuries will preserve my voice, and from age to age my brow will shine beneath a triple row of leaves; for to my lovely bays, to my green myrtles,

You whose blood feeds a burning tribe of lamps, sacred golden olives, you join your branches to bend the immortal crown to my temples.

The Suffering of the Waters: Elegy 2

At the Tivoli cemetery

THE marble colonnade shines against the sky: a light band of reddish bees wanders on the flowering cypresses collecting dark honey: the spring, where many a ghost sits quenching its thirst on living

Où maint spectre s'assied d'eau vivante abreuvé.
Quand l'astre couronné de lys sera levé,
Diane aux voiles blancs, l'œil clos sous sa couronne,
Que la brise du fleuve en grondant t'environne!
Nous mettrons aux bergers des flambeaux dans les mains,
Nous leur dirons: «Versez, par torrents, aux chemins
La lumière opulente! Assez d'âmes sont mortes! ...
De la maison sans joie allez! brisez les portes!
L'œil de l'homme a du ciel les charmantes couleurs,
Les membres parfumés des enfants sont des fleurs
Où, du pollen des dieux, l'homme vrai fructifie!
Des sépulcres brisés jaillit l'aube de vie!»

Le Vaisseau

LE vaisseau parfumé de couronnes de roses
Et dont le flanc de cèdre au soleil resplendit
Sur la vague a glissé loin des plages moroses
Et sur la terre et sur la mer il est midi.

water, joins its new-born waves to the light. When the star gar-
landed with lilies is risen, Diana of the white veils, her eye shut beneath her garland, let the murmuring breeze of the stream enclose
you! We shall put torches in the hands of the shepherds, we shall
say to them: 'Pour forth rich light in torrents on the paths! Enough
souls are dead! ... Go! Break down the doors of the joyless house!
Man's eye has the charming colours of the sky, the perfumed limbs
of children are flowers where, with the gods' pollen, the real man
bears fruit! From tombs broken open gushes the dawn of life!'

The Ship

THE ship perfumed with garlands of roses, whose cedar side shines
in the sun, has slipped over the waves far from dreary shores, and it
is noon above land and sea.

Sur les forêts d'ormeaux brillants et sur les sables
Il est midi! le vaisseau craque et tremble aux vents
Et l'homme tend ses bras aux cieux impérissables
Et la terre est vivante et les cieux sont vivants!

On tend la voile d'or, son ombre est rayonnante;
Au loin les chênes noirs et les verts citronniers
Décroissent sur la rive et la vague tonnante
Découpe, à son fracas, le chant des nautonniers:

«Adieux lacs blanchissants, chênes, torrents, vallées,
Antres pleins de ruisseaux et fermés de rochers!
Nous montons sur les mers par les brouillards voilées
Car la terre est sans fruits, car les dieux sont cachés.

«Tu partis d'Orient, lumière; le grand âge
Tant tu bus d'océans, tant tu gravis de monts,
Ô lumière! a flétri ton éclatant visage;
Nous ne te voyons plus, lumière, et nous t'aimons.

Above the forests of shining elms and above the sands it is noon!
The ship creaks and trembles in the winds, and man holds out his
arms to the immortal skies, and the land is alive, and the skies are
alive!

They spread the golden sail; its shadow is radiant; far away the
dark oaks and the green lemon-trees dwindle on the shore, and the
thunderous wave interrupts the sailors' song with its din:

'Farewell, white lakes, oaks, torrents, valleys, caves full of
streams and closed by rocks! We ride on seas veiled by mists, for
the land is barren and the gods are hidden.

'You left the East, O light; you have drunk so many oceans,
climbed so many mountains, that great age has soiled your bright
face; we see you no more, O light, and we love you.

«En ancres nous avons courbé le fer des coutres,
Le vieux vent des sillons dans la voile a soufflé,
Nous avons emportés les sources dans des outres,
Du blé de neuf moissons le vaisseau s'est enflé.

«Là-bas l'autre soleil se forme aux cieux fertiles,
Entre nos bras nerveux nous le ramènerons,
Sur les îles des mers nous sèmerons des villes
Au tonnerre des luths et des fougueux clairons!»

La proue est un massif de roses; sur la poupe
Ces hommes qui portaient dans leurs cœurs le destin
Mangèrent, le soleil se coucha dans leur coupe,
Le sommeil les raidit sculptés sur le festin.

Seul le pilote veille et Diane éclatante
Dont le beau char d'argent fend les nocturnes airs
Guide, étendant sur eux sa torche palpitante,
L'équipage endormi qui flotte sur les mers.

'We bent the iron of coulters into anchors; the old wind of the
furrows blew in the sail; we carried away the springs in goat-skins;
the ship is swollen with the corn of nine harvests.
'Over there the other sun appears in fertile skies; we shall bring
it back in our sinewy arms; we shall scatter towns on the islands of
the sea to the thunder of lutes and fiery trumpets!'
The prow is a pile of roses; on the poop the men, who carried
fate in their hearts, eat; the sun sank in their cup and sleep turned
them to stone carved above the board.
Only the pilot watches and bright Diana, whose lovely silver car
cleaves the night air, holding over them her quivering torch, guides
the sleeping crew, floating upon the sea.

INDEX OF FIRST LINES

A Saint-Blaise, à la Zuecca   111
Ainsi, toujours poussés vers de nouveaux rivages   10
Alors il était nuit, et Jésus marchait seul   41
Ami, poète, esprit, tu fuis notre nuit noire   84
Au pays parfumé que le soleil caresse   146

Beau chevalier qui partez pour la guerre   126
Belle épousée   108
Bizarre déité, brune comme les nuits   151
Blocus sentimental! Messageries du Levant   291
Booz s'était couché, de fatigue accablé   69
Bref, j'allais me donner d'un «Je vous jaime»   296

C'est plutôt le sabbat du second Faust que l'autre   211
Ces hommes de labour, que Greuze affadissait   280
Ces nymphes, je veux les perpétuer   190
Courage, ô faible enfant, de qui ma solitude   30
Cueillons, cueillons la rose au matin de la vie   16

Dans ce fossé cessons de vivre   1
Dans l'interminable ennui de la plaine   218
Dans le vieux parc solitaire et glacé   215
De la musique avant toute chose   224
Debout sur le rocher   243
Demain, dès l'aube, à l'heure où blanchit la campagne   59
Depuis que Maria m'a quitté   205
Devant une neige, un Être de Beauté de haute taille   263
Dis-moi, ton cœur, parfois, s'envole-t-il, Agathe   159

Elle a passé, la jeune fille   95
Elle était belle, si la Nuit   131
Enfer! – Enfer et paradis!   93

Fourmillante cité, cité pleine de rêves   164

Hier, j'ai trouvé ma pipe 207
Homme, libre penseur! te crois-tu seul pensant 107
Hyperbole! de ma mémoire 198

Il faut être toujours ivre 180
Il pleure dans mon cœur 217

J'ai de mes ancêtres gaulois l'œil bleu blanc 264
J'ai embrassé l'aube d'été 262
J'ai peur d'un baiser 221
J'aime le son du Cor, le soir, au fond des bois 18
J'avais capturé de mon séant 91
J'étais seul, l'autre soir, au Théâtre Français 127
Je ne suis qu'un viveur lunaire 288
Je pense à toi, Myrtho, divine enchanteresse 97
Je suis comme le roi d'un pays pluvieux 161
Je suis le ténébreux, – le veuf, – l'inconsolé 96
Je t'adore à l'égal de la voûte nocturne 152
Je t'apporte l'enfant d'une nuit d'Idumée! 189
Je vis dans la nuée un clairon monstrueux 74

L'aile en fureur, l'hiver sur les monts vole et vente 303
L'aube d'un jour sinistre a blanchi les hauteurs 183
La chair est triste, hélas! et j'ai lu tous les livres 188
La colonnade en marbre éclate sur le ciel 304
La connais-tu, Dafné, cette ancienne romance 100
La femme mûre ou jeune fille 289
La moisson débordant le plateau diapré 185
La mort et la beauté sont deux choses profondes 88
La nature est un temple où de vivants piliers 155
La Treizième revient. . . . C'est encore la première 101
La très-chère était nue, et, connaissant mon cœur 162
L'automne déjà! 277
Le désert est muet, la tente est solitaire 23
Le dieu Kneph en tremblant ébranlait l'univers 98
L'été, lorsque le jour a fui, de fleurs converte 54
Le gel durcit les eaux; le vent blêmit les nues 283
Le maçon Abraham Knupfer chante 89
Le moulin tourne au fond du soir, très lentement 281
Le noir roc courroucé que la bise le roule 204
Le premier jour, je bois leurs yeux ennuyés 290
Le temple enseveli divulgue par la bouche 202

Le temple est en ruine au haut du promontoire   181
Le vaisseau parfumé de couronnes de roses   305
Le vierge, le vivace et le bel aujourd'hui   197
Les plaines de la mer, immobiles et nues   141
Lorsque le grand Byron allait quitter Ravenne   112

Maintenant que Paris, ses pavés et ses marbres   60
Mère taillée à coups de hache   235
Midi, roi des étés, épandu sur la plaine   139
Mon cœur, comme un oiseau, voltigeait tout joyeux   156
Mon triste cœur bave à la poupe   247

N'eus-je pas *une fois* une jeunesse aimable   276
Non. Il fut gallican, ce siècle, et janséniste   223

Ô prêtresse élevant sous le laurier verdâtre   301
Ô race humaine aux destins d'or vouée   285
Ô toison, moutonnant jusque sur l'encolure   153
Ô Vénus, dans ta Vénerie   234
Oisive jeunesse   260
On me demande, par les rues   109
On parlera de sa gloire   3
Oui, c'est au vieux Gallus qu'appartient l'héritage   182
Oui, l'œuvre sort plus belle   137

Parsifal a vaincu les Filles   226
Pour l'enfant, amoureux de cartes et d'estampes   167
Puisque j'ai mis ma lèvre à ta coupe encor pleine   53

Quand l'aigle a dépassé les neiges éternelles   186
Quand le front de l'enfant, plein de rouges tourmentes   257
Quand l'ombre menaça de la fatale loi   196
Quand le Seigneur, levant au ciel ses maigres bras   102
Quand nous sommes allés vers le soleil levant   299
Qu'est-ce pour nous, mon cœur, que les nappes de sang   259
Qu'ils se payent des républiques   239
Que tu me plais dans cette robe   132

Ramenez-moi, disais-je, au fortuné rivage   14

Sagesse d'un Louis Racine, je t'envie — 222
Si l'orgueil prend ton cœur quand le peuple me nomme — 49
Sourires, fleurs, baisers, essences — 209
Sous les noirs acajous, les lianes en fleur — 142
Souvenir, souvenir, que me veux-tu — 214
Souvent, pour s'amuser, les hommes d'équipage — 149
Sur les tuiles où se hasarde — 134

Te souvient-il, ô mon âme, ô ma vie — 7
Tournez, tournez, bons chevaux de bois — 219
Tous deux ils regardaient, de la haute terrasse — 184
Tout à coup et comme par jeu — 201
Toute l'âme résumée — 203
Tu demandes pourquoi j'ai tant de rage au cœur — 99

Une chambre qui ressemble à une rêverie — 175
Une nuit claire, un vent glacé. La neige est rouge — 144

Voici le soir charmant, ami du criminel — 147
Voici venir les temps où vibrant sur sa tige — 150
Vos marins de quinquets à l'Opéra ... comique — 227
Votre âme est un paysage choisi — 215
Vraiment, c'est bête, ces églises des villages — 249

Waterloo! Waterloo! Waterloo! morne plaine! — 55

Yeux, lacs avec ma simple ivresse de renaître — 187